The History of U.S. Higher Education

The first volume in the **Core Concepts in Higher Education** series, *The History of U.S. Higher Education* rebuilds a constructive relationship between the field of higher education and the disciplinary field of history. Written primarily for students in higher education graduate and PhD programs, this book explores critical methodological issues in the history of American higher education, including often-overlooked issues such as race, class, gender, and sexuality.

Chapters include: **Reflective exercises** that combine theory and practice, **Research Method Tips**, and **Further Reading Suggestions**. The text allows students to understand the processes that historians use when conducting their own research and addresses the following questions:

- What do historians choose to include in their work?
- What do historians choose to leave out of their work and why?
- How do historians answer their research questions when sources are not available?
- How do historians evaluate their sources?
- What motivates historians to pursue particular research questions?
- How do historians frame and organize their work?

Leading historians and those at the forefront of new research explain how historical literature is discovered and written, and provide readers with the methodological approaches to conduct historical higher education research of their own. The contributors guide readers as they develop a rich appreciation for the craft of history and the importance of understanding higher education's past.

Marybeth Gasman is an Associate Professor of Higher Education in the Graduate School of Education at the University of Pennsylvania.

Core Concepts in Higher Education
Marybeth Gasman and Edward P. St. John, Series Editors

The History of U.S. Higher Education
Methods for Understanding the Past
Marybeth Gasman, editor

The History of U.S. Higher Education

Methods for Understanding the Past

Edited by
Marybeth Gasman

 Routledge
Taylor & Francis Group

NEW YORK AND LONDON

First published 2010
by Routledge
270 Madison Avenue, New York, NY 10016

Simultaneously published in the UK
by Routledge
2 Park Square, Milton Park, Abingdon, Oxon OX14 4RN

Routledge is an imprint of the Taylor & Francis Group, an informa business

© 2010 Taylor & Francis

Typeset in Minion by
RefineCatch Limited, Bungay, Suffolk
Printed and bound in the United States of America on acid-free paper by
Edwards Brothers, Inc.

Library of Congress Cataloging-in-Publication Data
The history of U.S. higher education : methods for understanding the past /
  Marybeth Gasman, editor.
    p. cm.—(Core concepts in the history of higher education vol. 1)
  Includes bibliographical references and index.
  1. Education, Higher—United States—History.   2. Education, Higher—Study
  and teaching (Graduate)—United States.   3. Universities and colleges—United
  States—Graduate work—History.   I. Gasman, Marybeth.
  LA228.5.H57 2010
  378.7309—dc22   2009046038

ISBN10: 0–415–87364–9 (hbk)
ISBN10: 0–415–87365–7 (pbk)
ISBN10: 0–203–85244–3 (ebk)

ISBN13: 978–0–415–87364–2 (hbk)
ISBN13: 978–0–415–87365–9 (pbk)
ISBN13: 978–0–203–85244–6 (ebk)

This book is dedicated to those who bring laughter and joy to my life

CONTENTS

SERIES EDITOR INTRODUCTION

The History of U.S. Higher Education represents a breakthrough in texts written for higher education as a field of study. It illustrates a third generation of scholarship on the history of higher education. The first period started with histories of higher education written by historians, perhaps best symbolized by Frederick Rudolph's *The American College and University: A History*. The second period witnessed an expanding number of histories, with excellent works by historians from within the field of higher education, symbolized by the *ASHE Reader on the History of Higher Education*, which provides a collection of important published works, including both new and time-proven histories. The third phase, ushered in by this collection of thoughtful essays by leaders within this specialization, provokes us all to think critically about our field, with both historical and future perspectives.

A part of what is new about Marybeth Gasman's editorial leadership is that the contributing authors in *The History of U.S. Higher Education* provide engaging, inclusive, and reflective insights into the social-critical issues that have been overlooked in the original histories; at the same time, they pay respect to those who created the foundations for contemporary historical scholarship in the field. The book symbolizes the maturation of both higher education and history, two fields that seek to diversify experiences by using divergent lenses and methods to gain new insights into how the contemporary institutions known as colleges and universities came into being, how they evolved, and how they responded, and frequently failed to respond, to the new challenges that emerged in the nation's and the world's history. *The History of U.S. Higher Education* provides a text that empowers students to engage in historical scholarship that addresses new, compelling and overlooked issues.

The History of U.S. Higher Education, therefore, is an ideal first text for Routledge's new series *Core Issues in Higher Education*. The dual goals of this series are to: (1) provide texts for the core courses in the field, that (2) move thought, action, and scholarship forward by valuing, reconstructing, and building on the foundations of the field. Moving forward involves both thinking critically about the field to discover what has been left out and what needs to be learned and providing frameworks and constructs for addressing challenges facing higher education. Why focus on building on, and even reconstructing, the foundations of the field? So that scholars and practitioners educated in higher education programs are better prepared to provide authentic leadership for colleges and universities, academic communities that study these institutions, and the communities served by colleges and universities.

When I was asked by Sarah Burrows of Routlege to consider being a series editor for a new text series, Marybeth Gasman was the first person I thought of as an author or editor who could do a book on history that empowered students and faculty to engage in the difficult task of discovering the voices that have too frequently been left out of the histories of our field, a process the moves the specialization forward and engages more people in doing this difficult work well. The ASHE reader series provides collections of works previously published, providing foundations for the core courses, but a series that informs scholars and practitioners in these specialized areas about critical issues facing our community and frameworks for addressing them was also needed. As co-editors of the new series on *Core Issues in Higher Education*, Marybeth and I will work with other scholars in moving our field—the combination of research, teaching and practice that makes our work so very special—forward into a third generation of scholarship.

Edward P. St. John

LIST OF FIGURES AND TABLES

Figures

Tables

ACKNOWLEDGMENTS

At the request of Edward St. John, a dear colleague from the University of Michigan, I agreed to edit a book on "doing history" despite having a ridiculously full plate. It's hard to say no to Ed! Fortunately, this volume has been a joy to edit. I have had the opportunity to work with some wonderful seasoned and new scholars that met deadlines, produced innovative and engaging work, and agreed to pursue this venture with me. Perhaps what I liked the most is that I feel warmly about each of the authors in this volume and they have all made or are about to make wonderful contributions to the fields of higher education and history of education. I am grateful to each of the authors for taking this work so seriously.

As with any book project, there are multiple people one wants to thank. In this case, I am grateful to Sarah Burrows, my editor at Routledge, for her guidance on the project. I am also indebted to Julie Vultaggio, who copy-edited each chapter, and who served as my research assistant while I worked on this book. Julie is wicked smart and incredibly attentive to detail (who could ask for more?). I am also thankful to my other research assistants who supported all of my work during the writing and editing of this book—Valerie Lundy Wagner, Jessica Kim, Tafaya Ransom, and Darryl Peterkin. Having their support and honest feedback makes me a much better scholar.

I also thank my dear colleagues at Penn. I truly believe that we have the most innovative, supportive, and engaging higher education faculty in the country. What a team of terrific individuals! Lastly, I'd like to thank my family and friends who are always supportive of my research endeavors and provide ample laughs along the way—in particular, Edward Epstein, Chloe Epstein, Noah Drezner, and Nelson Bowman.

INTRODUCTION

Although most higher education programs include a course on the history of American higher education, these programs place little emphasis on exploring historical issues or using historical methods to examine higher education problems. Why? Because most history of higher education courses are taught by higher education scholars with little background in history. Rather than learning how the history of higher education has been constructed by historians and about important concepts and movements that developed over time, students are taught about names, dates and events in less than exciting ways (note: this was my experience early on in graduate school until I discovered my mentor John Thelin—he brought history alive for me). Moreover, with the exception of survey texts, higher education faculty members do not have the tools to teach the history of higher education in a comprehensive manner. Thus, students who choose to pursue historical research usually have to fend for themselves, searching for methods texts and proceeding with uncertainty about exactly how to "do" historical research.

Ironically, most history departments have few classes on how to "do history"—instead, the historical methods classes are focused on theory or ways of thinking about history. There's nothing wrong with learning how to think about history, but students want to know how to "do it" as well as how to think about it. I can't count the number of students who have told me, in history and history of higher education alike, that their advisors just told them to "do it"—go into an archive, get the materials, and write it up. The problem is that students don't necessarily know how to find the archive, to determine what is valuable in terms of archival material, whether that archival material is enough or if other data sources are needed, or how to capture the essence of the material.

The purpose of this new edited volume is to explore, explain, and examine ways of doing history in the area of American higher education. By "doing history" I mean both subject-specific and methodological ways of approaching the craft of history. Of note, this volume also focuses on themes that are often ignored, such as race, class, gender, and sexuality. I asked each of the authors to think methodologically, but to also think

1

about the ways their work touches upon issues of diversity as this is particularly important to me.

I think the beauty of this volume is the personal nature of each chapter. The chapters
are reflective, combining engaging and provocative writing with deep methodological
and contextual discussions. I hope that reading about the intellectual successes and
struggles of colleagues in the field will motivate and guide young and old scholars alike.
I hope this book will attract new individuals to the profession and help non-historians
to develop a rich appreciation for the craft of history and the importance of having a
critical understanding of higher education's past.

This volume also encourages students to understand the thought processes that historians use in their writing and research. What do these scholars choose to include in an
article or book? What do they leave out? Why? When the most obvious sources are not
available, how do historians answer their research questions? How do they evaluate their
sources? What motivates historians to pursue particular research questions? And, how
do historians frame and organize their work?

ORGANIZATION OF THE VOLUME

This edited volume is organized into three sections: methodological approaches, new
historical lenses, and critical examinations of special issues. In the first section, the
authors explore various methodological approaches—some "tried and true" and others
new. In Section II of the book, the authors focus on new lenses through which to view
historical problems. And, in Section III, the authors are concerned with the various
topics and populations that are often overlooked or misunderstood in historical
research.

Section I begins with Darryl Peterkin's chapter entitled " 'Within These Walls': Reading and Writing Institutional Histories." Herein, Peterkin provides those who venture
into the land of institutional histories with useful instructions on how to pursue such
tasks. In addition, he discusses the perceptions of institutional history within the field
of history and the difficulty of writing a rigorous, engaging history. In my own work,
I have pursued two institutional histories. The first was a history of the United Negro
College Fund (UNCF) entitled *Envisioning Black Colleges*. I pursued this topic of my
own accord and, as such, it is a critical history of the UNCF; I delved deeply into the
major players in the organization—both Black and White—and made no apologies
for being tough on some of these players. I remember sending a copy of the book to
UNCF president Michael Lomax and fearing his displeasure over my depiction of the
organization. To my surprise, he loved it and made it required reading for staff members. Currently, I am working on a history of the Morehouse School of Medicine, which
Louis W. Sullivan, the former Secretary of Health and Human Services, and President
Emeritus of the Morehouse School of Medicine, commissioned me to write. Writing
this kind of institutional history is a bit tricky in that almost all of the players are alive
and the most significant figure in the history of the institution asked me to write the
book. It has been a good relationship, but I have had to gently approach many subjects.
What do you do when the archival documents say something happened one way, but the
past president remembers it another? How do you write a balanced portrayal of an
institutional president when he is paying you to write a book about that institution?
I have learned many lessons from this endeavor on writing institutional history—

including how to bring the life out of an institution—a lesson that Peterkin points to in his robust chapter.

In Chapter Two, Katherine Chaddock guides the reader through the craft of oral history. Of note, she defines oral history, differentiating it from journalism. Chaddock also discusses her triumphs and troubles in the pursuit of just the right oral history interview, detailing family reactions (anger) and interference in this pursuit (mistresses who refuse to talk). She demonstrates the vividness that oral histories can add to an historical project and urges the reader to probe deeply in order to get the full story. Like Chaddock, I have conducted hundreds of oral history interviews. In fact, some of my best research stories are a result of crazy, unbelievable, and touching things that have happened in the midst of doing an oral history interview (e.g., being introduced to someone's *entire* family, enduring dirty jokes, watching someone consume six bottles of beer and a bag of peanuts as I interviewed him, and being led down a long hallway into a dark room only to meet the interviewee's 98-year-old, bed-ridden spouse). Also, like Chaddock, I had to learn how to "warm people up." I realized that the first thirty minutes of the interview might not be used in a book or article, but the time invested would get me to the "good stuff"—the material that would add wonderful spirit and context to my work.

In "Autobiography and Biographical Research in Higher Education," Wayne Urban discusses the very personal and political nature of doing biographical research. I particularly like his discussion of his own motivations for studying the African American historian and Lincoln University President Horace Mann Bond. Like Bond, Urban held several administrative posts and found them tedious and a roadblock in his pursuit of research. He felt a connection with Bond even across racial lines. Much of what Urban says resonates with me in a deep way. Like Urban, I pursued biography. I did so to help me understand African American leadership at historically Black colleges and universities. And like Urban, I was White attempting to write a biography about a Black leader named Charles S. Johnson. I felt connected to this leader as he believed in building scholars and leaders—something about which I feel strongly. Also like Urban, I wondered if I had captured the essence of the man; I wondered if my race stood in the way of truly understanding his motives, experiences, and leadership. In hindsight, I am sure that an African American scholar may have depicted him differently than I did. What I like best about Urban's chapter is how he depicts the journey that is biography and that is research. He discovered biography, moved away, and returned to it.

Chapter Four, entitled " 'No Food, No Drinks, Pencil Only': Checklists for Conducting and Interpreting Archival Research," was written by a refreshing young scholar named Jordan Humphrey. As she is in the midst of conducting her dissertation research, I thought she would be perfect to write about the ins and outs of doing archival research. Her sense of humor is a bonus given the tedious nature of combing through archives for evidence. Jordan provides ample detail for the new historian, demystifying the research process. She explains how one should analyze an historical document and how vital a good relationship with an archivist can be. On this second point, I am reminded of my many visits to Fisk University to conduct archival research for my own dissertation. I was nervous and clumsy—being new at the craft and being way too conscious of my Whiteness at a Black college. I visited the archives at least six times before the archivist (who has since become a friend) trusted me with the "good" materials. She wanted to see if I was serious and, by the sixth visit, I had proven that I was. The energy that I put into visiting the archive over and over paid off not only in garnering wonderful resources for my dissertation and subsequent book, but also in the strong relationship that developed with the archivist. Jordan provides a road map for historians and anticipates many of the roadblocks and pitfalls that one typically encounters. For example, she describes her own experience showing up to an archive, excited and eager to look at the materials on the finding aid, only to find out that none of the materials were available or even existed. I had a similar experience when I visited the Ford Foundation in the late 1990s. I arrived knowing exactly what I wanted only to find out that most of the documents I needed were heavily censored and, in fact, blacked out with a *Sharpie*® marker.

In Chapter Five, Linda Eisenmann provides a beautiful, reflective guide to writing historiography. She has ample experience and traces the challenges to writing strong literature reviews. In explaining her process, which I think is ideal, she talks about her work on women. In many ways, including her ability to frame the literature in the history of higher education, Linda has defined research on women in this area. In defining the field, she has also opened herself up for critique from younger scholars. In this chapter, she discusses being open to critique as one builds the historiography. I have only ventured once into a true historiography—a piece on women at Black colleges entitled "Swept under the Rug." In order to build what became a massive undertaking, I looked to scholars like Eisenmann, as well as Ronald Butchart and Jana Nidiffer. Each of these scholars has contributed rich, useful historiographies in the history of education that serve as models to those who come after them.

John Thelin, in Chapter Six, introduces us to the concept of "horizontal history"—or histories that cut across institutions—and leads Section II of the book, which is dedicated to new historical lenses. Although he finds merit in studying colleges and universities, he urges the reader to break free from the obsession with these same institutions. Thelin finds merit in studying those institutions that work with many colleges and universities, such as the American Association of University Professors, the American Council of Education, foundations, and one familiar to me, the United Negro College Fund. I first became familiar with Thelin's ideas around "horizontal history" when he wrote the foreword to my *Envisioning Black Colleges* book. He pulled the phrase out of nowhere and labeled my research "horizontal history." He was right, as my depiction of the United Negro College Fund cut across many Black colleges, foundations, and civil rights organizations to provide the reader with an understanding of African American higher education.

In Chapter Seven, entitled "Photographs as Primary Sources," Michael Bieze helps the reader examine photographs as primary sources for understanding history. He is wonderfully enthusiastic about the topic and, as such, has a ferocious appetite for uncovering the use (and misuse) of photography in historical narrative and text. Bieze uses his own work on Booker T. Washington—work that I find to be wonderfully innovative—to demonstrate the ways that photography has been used to manipulate our understanding of history. Like Bieze, I am fascinated with images and how they are used to change our minds and make us think. When I was doing my research for *Envisioning Black Colleges* (emphasis on "envisioning"), I became enthralled by the "Mind is a Terrible Thing to Waste" fundraising campaign. The UNCF, with the help of the Ad Council, was a master at using photography and images to bring attention to the cause of historically Black colleges and universities. Bieze's work helped me immensely to understand the images and analyze them. His background in art history and the history of higher education combine to give him a unique vantage point from which readers will benefit.

Jane Robbins, in Chapter Eight, focuses on what she calls "cognitive history" or the quantification of history. We tend to think of history as a qualitative method, but as Robbins demonstrates it has elements of both qualitative and quantitative approaches. She shows, through examples from her own work, how a quantitative approach enables us to make meaningful historical comparisons. I was particularly interested in having Robbins write this chapter because I personally struggle and experience frustration when I have quantitative questions about my historical research, but am not sure how to approach them (despite having taken way too many statistics courses in graduate school).

William Tierney wrote Chapter Nine, which is entitled "Life History and Voice: On Standpoints and Reflexivity." At first glance, those of you who are historians of education might wonder why I would ask a non-historian to write a chapter for this book. Here's the answer. Any time I can get others to understand the value of historical approaches, especially those who use other methodological approaches or hail from other disciplinary perspectives, I'm game. Tierney, in this beautiful essay, shows how one can use traditionally historical methods to research contemporary issues and problems. He, in effect, makes historical research less scary to non-historians. Tierney, much like Wayne Urban, discusses his experiences doing research across racial and sexuality lines (border crossing), allowing the reader to peer into his mind and experience his thought processes while conducting research. Of note as well, Tierney urges us to listen while capturing one's life history, noting the times when he did not listen as carefully as he could and crediting those who taught him to listen.

In Section III of the book, I have included chapters that critically examine special issues that I think need more attention by historians of higher education. Jana Nidiffer's chapter entitled " 'Poor' Research: Historiographical Challenges When Socio-Economic Status is the Unit of Analysis" leads the section. Nidiffer offers a convincing and compelling argument detailing how issues of class are overlooked in the history of higher education. We, as historians, tend to privilege elite schools, elite leaders, wealthy philanthropists and the like, but rarely do we think about the non-elites. At times we touch upon issues of race and gender, but we rarely bring class into the mix or examine it on its own. Nidiffer's chapter is particularly personal to me as I grew up in a very poor home—the kind of home in which we regularly ate chipped beef on toast without the beef. Of course, I didn't know I was poor until someone told me in 8th grade (they discovered my free lunch card). I was happy and, as far as I knew, healthy with two parents and lots of siblings. Upon application to college, I realized that my choices were limited by my poverty. My parents, having no college education, let alone finishing secondary school, did not know how to fill out the financial aid forms and were scared by the tuition costs. I enrolled in college with no idea of how I would pay. Eventually, I learned that a positive relationship with the business office clerk and a summer job were my only ways of paying for what was left over after my Pell Grant and student loans ran out. I rarely read about my story or stories like it in history of higher education books; Nidiffer encourages historians to notice this omission and counter it with new research.

Sharon Lee, a dynamic young scholar whose work I use in my classes, wrote Chapter Eleven—a beautiful essay entitled "Where is Your 'Home'? Writing the History of Asian

Americans in Higher Education." Lee shares her sometimes tearful childhood as an Asian American and its impact on her scholarship. As I read, I felt privileged to share in her journey as a scholar. I met Lee a few years ago at a History of Education Society annual meeting and was captivated by her honesty, intellect, and willingness to push the research on Asian American higher education forward. I hope that future scholars will see Lee as a role model and that historians of higher education will use her work to add depth and diversity to their classes.

Like Sharon Lee, Christopher Tudico is a young scholar exploring his ethnicity through the pursuit of scholarship on Mexican Americans and their higher education experiences. In the interest of full disclosure, I am the chair of Chris's dissertation committee. His chapter, entitled "Beyond Black and White: Researching the History of Latinos in American Higher Education," acknowledges the importance of researching African American struggles and success, but also urges us to think about issues related to other racial and ethnic minorities. For too long, Tudico argues, Mexican Americans and Latinos in general have been overlooked by historians of education.

In Chapter Thirteen, Philo Hutcheson writes about historical policy—with a lively and sometimes biting sense of humor, I might add. Too often scholars do not see the connection between history and policy—Hutcheson makes this connection crystal clear by referring to his own work on the Truman Commission for Higher Education. Of particular value, he discusses presentism within the policy context and explains to the new historian why and how it is to be avoided. In addition, Hutcheson includes a riveting discussion of policy terms, showing how their meaning changes over time and the implication of the changing meanings.

The last chapter in Section III was contributed by Amy Wells and addresses the challenges of writing about the South. Hailing from Kentucky herself and employed as a faculty member at the University of Mississippi, I thought Wells would be the perfect historian to write this chapter. Wells studies issues of race and gender but does so within a southern context. She is not afraid to challenge the status quo of the South, but she is also willing to embrace that which she finds appealing and authentic. Wells's chapter is perhaps the most challenging for me in that I am just not southern. I lived in the South for six years and tried my best to adapt, but alas, I was, in other people's words, "too assertive," "a bit too forthright," and for heaven's sake, I "don't cook!" Wells brings a new spirit to studying the South and does so with immense grace and a feisty spirit.

This edited volume comes to a conclusion with a short piece by Jane Robbins entitled "A Note on Footnotes." The footnote or endnote is really the heart and soul of historical writing. Footnotes set us apart from other disciplines. They tell the story underneath the story. They keep us honest and show the rigor of our work. I know it is odd but I love crafting a footnote. Robbins loves them too and provides ample guidance.

It is my hope that readers of this edited volume will come away knowing how to "do history" and having multiple lenses through which to approach historical work. I also hope that readers will have a better appreciation for the craft of history and those who do it.

Section I
Methodological Approaches

1

"WITHIN THESE WALLS"

Reading and Writing Institutional Histories

Darryl L. Peterkin

All who teach and study within these walls were chosen because they are presumed to have pride in their heritage, pride in themselves, and pride in their capacity to achieve excellence in their chosen fields. Our abiding faith is that they know also the difference between the genuine pride that is grounded in achievement of excellence and that proud arrogance which is the ploy of the inferior performer.
> —*Convocation Address* of Dr. Broadus N. Butler, President of
> Dillard University, September 23, 1969

Historians who embark upon the journey of writing an institutional history are plunged head-first into the churning sea of ideas and beliefs, personalities and politics, passions and pragmatism, the competing ideals of conformity and rebellion, and a thousand other things that define the human condition. Like any explorer then, the institutional historian must possess the proper tools so that she might be successful in her voyage of discovery. Among these are an open and inquisitive mind, attention to detail, and patience enough to slog through mountains of the mundane—the proverbial haystack—in search of not just the needle, but the thread that holds the institutional narrative together.

This chapter will consider several important questions: (1) What are the elements of good institutional history? (2) What are the advantages and disadvantages of using narrative as a tool for historical analysis? (3) Is institutional history still valuable as a sub-specialty of the field? (4) What does institutional history say about the society that created it? This chapter will attempt to do so in three stages. First, it will discuss the university as a mythological place, not unlike Mount Olympus or Asgard, where ideals take form. Second, it will briefly survey histories written about four archetypical institutions of higher education—the large state university, an Ivy League university, an historically Black college, and a women's college—and make observations (far from exhaustive) about the strengths and weaknesses of these institutional narratives. Finally, this chapter will provide a few suggestions for approaching the craft of writing an institutional history.

INSTITUTIONS OF HIGHER LEARNING AS MYTH

The university is the ultimate physical expression of our aspirations for civilization; an expression of belief in a certain mythology. Institutions of higher learning are rarely brought into the world without difficulty. This is because they are the nexus of what is the best of humanity—creativity, learning, generating new ideas and patterns of thought, and testing and discarding old and outdated ones—with what is practical. How can this notion be packaged and sold, molded into a physical form that can be replicated?

The United States is a particularly fertile ground for this kind of thing because our aspirations vary so wildly and our genius for creation or reinvention is nearly limitless. All institutions of higher education, like all great religions, have their creation stories, their mythologies of existence. And these stories are powerful—in what they tell us and what they do not.

The women's college and the Historically Black College and University (HBCU) share some common elements in their origin stories. Both of these institutions are born out of cultures of repression—in this case gender and racial repression. Thus from the very beginning these schools had to define themselves against the dominant culture while making the argument for why their graduates should be full members of that culture.

The traditional small liberal arts college often enjoys the association with pastoral myth: it is a veritable Garden of Eden. Often situated in places far from the corrupting influence of urban areas, these colleges are places where intellect and morality can be nurtured and nourished.

The state university is that institution meant to embody the aspirations of the republic: that the citizenry will be educated, informed, and prepared to render service to the larger society. Most of the great exemplars of this segment of higher education came into existence in the middle of the nineteenth century, during an era of tremendous upheaval; the American nation itself teetered on the brink of extinction. Yet the legislation that made the creation of state universities possible was itself an act of faith—a belief that our founding principles had to be preserved, refined, and passed on to the rising generations.

THE INSTITUTIONAL HISTORY AS A CASE STUDY

The University of California-Berkeley is one of the great public universities founded in the wake of the Morrill Act, in 1868. California itself had not been in the Union for two full decades; yet it embodied the restless spirit of opportunity that had become synonymous with America. The new state university reflected this energetic sensibility, from its expansive campus setting to its ambitious building plans, the decision to admit women from the moment it opened its doors, the vigorous recruitment of prominent faculty and administrators from the nation's finest institutions of higher learning, and its epic battles with the state legislature over funding. The sheer expanse of the institutional narrative itself can be intimidating to the institutional historian. However, Patricia A. Pelfrey, in her *A Brief History of the University of California*, makes the task look deceptively easy.[1] The most notable thing about her book is that it is, in fact, brief—130 pages. One could call it the Strunk and White of institutional histories: concise and not a wasted word.

The immediate temptation is to critique this work as far too short to be useful.

Palfrey, however, demonstrates that she is in absolute command of her material. Her central narrative is one of continuous progress from a frontier college to a premier university boasting an international reputation. This basic framework leaves her with plenty of room to introduce the reader to a fascinating cast of characters and the complexities involved in sustaining an institution of higher learning. One gets a sense of the larger public vision of the University of California and the ever-present tension between and among the elites who created and guided the university.

But it is Palfrey's mastery of the history of the university that leaves the reader clamoring for more in-depth examinations of prominent individuals and singular events in the university's history. In her capable hands the full-bodied richness that is the University of California is rather like the grapes dangling above the unfortunate Tantalus. But unlike that tortured soul, readers of Palfrey's book would be well advised to think of it as an historical sketch that whets the appetite and points the way to more comprehensive—and possibly less focused and riveting—histories of one of the great public universities in the United States.

Joe M. Richardson's *A History of Fisk University, 1865–1946* is a chronicle of one of the most prominent of the nation's 103 Historically Black Colleges and Universities.[2] Richardson's portrait of Fisk, like Palfrey's of the University of California, gives the reader a sense of a nation in transition after a traumatic civil war that ended slavery and determined the course of American destiny. Whereas the University of California was built, in part, on the enthusiasm for the wealth California represented, Fisk was created by the American Missionary Association, which believed fervently in the potential of an entire race released from the shackles of slavery. Perhaps more so than other institutions of higher learning, HBCUs were dependent upon forceful personalities, be they early benefactors or presidents. The historian of an HBCU may, therefore, faces the challenge of separating the lives of these individuals from the development of the institution itself.

Richardson approaches the history of Fisk with this delicate balance between biography and institutional narrative in mind. The fifth chapter of his book, entitled "Head or Hand," is an excellent example of this. Here Richardson discusses the intellectual debate over the type of education that Blacks should receive: the vocational model put forward by Tuskegee's Booker T. Washington or a liberal arts education famously advocated by W. E. B. Du Bois. Fisk was firmly in the camp of the liberal arts; but it was not averse to offering programs of a more "applied" nature like sewing, nursing, and woodworking.[3] The extent of the philosophical differences between Washington and Du Bois has been greatly exaggerated by some scholars, but the issue was real enough to have an impact upon the type and amount of support that a Black college would receive from donors.[4] Presidents James G. Merrill (1890–1908) and George A. Gates (1909–1912) walked the uneasy line between what influential donors like the Slater Fund wanted to see in terms of industrial education and what Fisk trustees expected in terms of curricular development in the liberal arts.[5]

Of note to institutional historians, Richardson's last chapter, which focuses on the achievements of Fisk alumni, should have been an appendix rather than a stand-alone chapter. While it shows how Fisk has made positive contributions to American society, it is more informational than contextual, and does not advance the central narrative of the book.

Edward Potts Cheyney's *History of the University of Pennsylvania,* is one of those irresistible "older" institutional histories, a majestic tome full of high purpose and occasional literary flourish.[6] The brainchild of Founding Father Benjamin Franklin, the story of the University of Pennsylvania is tied inextricably to that of the Early Republic itself. One of Cheyney's tasks in this book is to explain the Founders' strong belief in education as a central pillar of the *novus ordo seclorum* (the new order of the ages) that they had forged in the fires of revolution. Cheyney ably weaves this thread throughout his 400-page narrative. Indeed, it is immediately obvious to the reader that the story of the University of Pennsylvania is the soul of this work.

This circumstance is, simultaneously, the source of its value as an institutional history and its problematic nature as a resource for institutional historians. Books of this type can often be considered primary sources themselves. If the modern historian is in search of ground-breaking analysis or an overarching theory of higher education, she will not find it, per se, in a work of this nature. That said, the sheer wealth of detail in Cheyney's history underscores the thoroughly encyclopedic knowledge that characterizes a bygone era of academe. The potential danger for the modern scholar is the temptation to treat Cheyney's work dismissively, rather than as a point of departure for an institutional history that is more reflective of current trends in scholarship. A marvelous recent example of this approach is James Axtell's *The Making of Princeton University: From Woodrow Wilson to the Present,*[7] the intellectual successor of Thomas Jefferson Wertenbaker's *Princeton, 1746–1896.*[8] At over 600 pages, Axtell's history of Princeton, in bulk at least, is reminiscent of Cheyney. However, he skillfully juxtaposes student culture, administrative transition, and town–gown tensions with the larger external upheavals of world war, the struggle for civil and women's rights, and the new world order after the end of the Cold War. In short, he shows how Princeton managed to evolve from the most exclusive of enclaves for White, male privilege into a world-class research university with a diverse student body and faculty, and led by a dynamic female president.

Polly Welts Kaufman's *The Search for Equity: Women at Brown University, 1891–1991*[9] examines the history of Brown University through the lens of a particular constituency: women. Unlike the other books discussed in this chapter, Kaufman's work is not a standard institutional history. Rather, it is a collection of essays around a central theme. The obvious strength of this approach is the use of different perspectives of analysis. Particularly intriguing in this regard is Lyde Cullen Sizer's essay *"A Place for A Good Woman": The Development of Women Faculty at Brown,* which traces the movement of female faculty from what can be described as "adjunct" or "special" categories to full-fledged members of the community of scholars at an Ivy League institution.[10]

Kaufman's volume constantly reminds the reader that a university is a complex and multifaceted enterprise that cannot always be easily defined or described, especially in relationship to the individuals or groups whose place in the larger society is in any way ambiguous or contested (as is similarly demonstrated in Richardson's history of Fisk). However, the inherent weakness of this approach to institutional history is that it assumes the reader already has a basic familiarity with the institution. Thus, it cannot be the source of "first contact" for potential scholars. Here again lies the worth of the older institutional history, which does not presume such prior knowledge and is capable of carrying the reader along in the stream of the narrative. That said, Kaufman's treatment of Brown's history is exceptionally valuable as an example of how to push the boundaries of established interpretations of institutional history.

THE "RULES" FOR RESEARCHING AND WRITING
INSTITUTIONAL HISTORY

In my courses on the history of higher education, I often told my students that a college or university is, in many ways, just like them: a living, breathing organism that consumes resources, grows, has dreams, makes friends and enemies, makes mistakes and, on very rare occasions, achieves greatness. This comparison often met with skeptical stares and more than a few giggles and remarks about the psychological stability of their professor. Yet anyone who takes a close look at the evidence—such as the evolution of Harvard from a small Puritan college hewn out of the wilderness of the Massachusetts Bay Colony in 1636 into the premier institution of higher learning in the world (I am a Yale graduate, so you have *no* idea how difficult it is for me to say this), to the rise of the great state universities after the passage of the Morrill Acts in the nineteenth century, and finally the emergence of the online colleges at the beginning of the twenty-first century—must concede that the analogy is at least superficially compelling.

One thing that appears to be beyond dispute, however, is the generally low opinion of institutional histories, the historical equivalent of the eccentric aunt who (1) knows everything about the entire family (and insists upon airing the dirty laundry at the most inappropriate times) and (2) is flamboyantly anachronistic in dress and manner. In fact, modern historians of higher education have an unfortunate and rather nasty habit of denigrating the work of earlier institutional historians as lacking scholarly rigor and focusing too much upon individual personalities over larger educational or sociocultural issues. I *know* this is the case because I was guilty of the same offense while researching my dissertation on the University of North Carolina at Chapel Hill.[11] The last thing I wanted to do after a long day in the archives was to dive into Kemp Plummer Battle's majestic two-volume *History of the University of North Carolina, 1789–1868 (1907–12).*[12]

While it may be true that these classic books do not possess the depth of analysis which characterize the current field (especially since the quantitative revolution of the 1970s), they are nonetheless extremely valuable sources of information. These older narratives can tell us a great deal about the milieu in which an institution of higher learning came into being, the powerful personalities who led them, and the complex interplay between town and gown. Thus, we have come to my first rule in writing institutional histories of higher education: RESPECT THE OLD GUYS.

Rather than seeing the venerable institutional history of the university you are researching as a literary jungle, you must hack your way through, consider it as a long-neglected gold mine that still has some nuggets of significant value—if you are willing to do the real work of prospecting. Allow me to illustrate with an example from the previously mentioned *History of the University of North Carolina* (UNC). One of the most prominent features of the university during its early years was its two literary societies: the Dialectic and Philanthropic Societies. The "Di and Phi" formed the center of the students' academic and social lives at UNC. It was in the societies' elaborate debating halls where students made life-long friendships, formed significant social connections, and honed the intellectual and elocution skills that they would need as members of the North Carolina elite. The societies had their own libraries, which were larger than that of the university itself. Such was the power of the "Di and Phi" that if a student was expelled from his society, he typically withdrew from the university as well.

Embedded within Battle's exhaustive discussion of the activities of the societies are lists of topics debated by the members. I overcame the desire to skip over these pages and read them more closely. To my amazement, I discovered that some of the topics dealt with potentially explosive issues like the morality of slavery, the value of war, and whether women should be educated. While it would have been a gross exaggeration for me to claim that these topics were evidence of a nascent liberal consciousness among the sons of the North Carolina planter elite, it seemed clear that the societies were aware of the subjects that could threaten the Southern social order. By having its members grapple rigorously with these issues in the comfortable environs of the debating halls, the societies quietly prepared new generations of defenders of the status quo.

Now that we have learned that the older institutional narratives are more valuable than at first glance, let us turn to the subjects of these books themselves and to the second rule of writing institutional histories: LET THERE BE LIFE (apologies to the Book of Genesis). The colleges and universities about which you will be writing are, of course, constructed of bricks, mortar, and wood; but the *people* who made them are—or were—flesh and blood. Historians are charged with the honorable and difficult task of taking the documents, artifacts, and ephemera that these individuals left behind (if any) and making their creators live again. As hard as this may be, the historian whose subjects are still alive and strutting across the stage confront a different challenge: these individuals are often aware of the impact that they have on their institutions and desire, naturally enough, to actively influence how they will be perceived in times to come. In this case the historian must find a way to maintain accuracy and integrity while allowing her subject, in the words of T. S. Eliot's reflective J. Alfred Prufrock, "[t]o swell a progress, start a scene or two." I wish her luck.

Fortunately for me, the actors in my institutional play were all long dead by the time I began my research. The particular disadvantage that I had was that "everything about them was already known." While this may be comforting to the intellectually lazy, the true historian—or anyone else who has common sense—knows that this is utter balderdash. Few of us even know the names of the people who live next door, let alone any significant details about their lives. How mysterious, then, must someone who lived next door *two centuries ago* be! The historian must be willing to peer beyond what is safe and obvious and be open to the unexpected. And if she is lucky, the unexpected is resting comfortably in an acid-free folder in the university archives. Allow me to illustrate this with another example from my work on the University of North Carolina.[13]

The Reverend Joseph Caldwell was 33 years old when he was appointed as the first president of the University of North Carolina in 1804. A 1791 graduate of the College of New Jersey (Princeton), Caldwell had taught mathematics at the university since 1799. He was a no-nonsense administrator with an uncanny reputation for appearing just when students were about to engage in mischief. In fact, the students nicknamed him "Old Bolus," after the Devil (Diabolus or Diablo), whom they believed had the power to appear and disappear without warning. Within a year of taking office, Caldwell faced one of the largest student rebellions in the Antebellum Period. The revolt, called the "Great Secession," centered on a dispute over the Monitor Act, a disciplinary measure passed by the trustees. The students signed a petition stating their objections to the policy and threatened to leave the university if the measure was not rescinded. Caldwell and the trustees of course refused, and 50 students—a huge percentage of the student body—"seceded" from the institution in September 1805.

Historians of higher education have seen the Great Secession as one of many examples of the inevitable tension between students, faculty, and administrators on college campuses. It is, in other words, an old tale often told. However, what is much less well known is how Caldwell, a young and ambitious man at the beginning of what would turn out to be his life's work, viewed this significant blow to his reputation and his leadership of the fledgling University of North Carolina. As it happened, the answer lay in a folder tucked in a rarely opened box in the UNC Archives.

The Great Secession was actually the second student uprising that Caldwell had experienced during his time at the university. The first, in 1799, was so violent that he found it necessary to barricade himself in his room with a gun. Understandably then, he had had enough of student rebels. As he was a respected Presbyterian minister and intellectual, Caldwell decided against resigning his post and instead poured his fury into an unpublished allegorical tale called, "An Attempt at a Most Foul and Unnatural Murder!" The story was about a "respectable matron" who had a "large family of children." Fearing that her ill-behaved offspring might become "the pests of society," she "fell upon the expedient of appointing some of them to inspect the conduct of the rest requiring them either to put a check upon it, or to make report to her of those who misbehaved." To insure faithful compliance to her wishes, she also required her inspectors to swear an oath of obedience. When the time came to appoint new inspectors, the children objected to the oath. The indulgent mother responded by replacing the oath with "a bare promise." The children soon found this concession equally unbearable and endeavored to free themselves of their maternal tyrant. Caldwell described the villainous intent of the children in the ensuing scene: "They suddenly and impetuously flew towards her in a body," he wrote, "grasped her by the throat . . . with unrelenting fury, and raised a promiscuous oritory [sic] that they would rather die than submit to such tyranny." The matron managed to escape her attackers, who then fled the house. Having survived a mortal threat, "the good old matron" resolved that she would never again allow "such unnatural children" into her home.

Anyone familiar with recent events at the university would recognize this manuscript as a thinly veiled account of the Great Secession. It was an intensely personal document, significantly different from Caldwell's other writings, in which he often adopted the persona of a detached, well-informed observer. By expressing his feelings about the incident in unambiguous terms, Caldwell shows us his humanity and the depth of his attachment to the institution he had been chosen to lead. He has become a man we can understand and one we hope will succeed. Though he was deeply offended by what the students had done to him and the university, Caldwell somehow left his bitterness on the page and spent the next thirty years rebuilding what had been lost. He put his tale in a drawer, and it lay unnoticed for almost two centuries.

The third rule of writing institutional history is WALK THE GROUND. In my opinion, an historian can neither write about nor understand an institution of higher learning without visiting *it*, not just its archives. The campus, as I have said elsewhere in this chapter, is alive. It has stories to tell. Get out of the archives and take the campus tour. A piece of local lore casually mentioned by the tour guide (or one of the guests) might provide useful information or context for your work. It might even reveal fascinating contractions in behavior or interpretation. Submitted for your approval, here is my tour of Washington and Lee University, or "Why Robert E. Lee Might Be Spinning in His Grave."

Washington and Lee University is situated on a beautiful campus in Lexington, Virginia, just next door to the Virginia Military Institute. Formerly known as Washington College, it was catapulted into renown after the Civil War when Confederate General Robert E. Lee was appointed its president in 1865. Lee held this position until his death on October 12, 1870, and was buried beneath the college chapel. In 1883 the chapel was enlarged to house the Lee family crypt in the lower level and, on the main floor, a haunting memorial sculpture by sculptor Edward Valentine entitled *Lee in Repose*.

In the nearly 140 years since Lee's presidency, the campus of Washington and Lee University has been a popular destination for visitors, Civil War enthusiasts, and the generally curious (I include myself in the latter category). The chapel itself now also houses the university museum. Having read a little about the history of the university (including the fact that Lee's beloved horse "Traveller" is interred in a plot outside the chapel), I was eager to take the campus tour and observe firsthand the enduring aura surrounding Robert E. Lee. The main chamber of the chapel, which houses the Lee statue, was the last stop on the tour.

It is impossible for me to describe the depth of the hush that fell over the crowd as we approached the famous statue, which was unnaturally white, bathed in a gentle light, and surrounded by Confederate flags. Our tour guide, a pleasant, bubbly, and well-spoken young White woman, breezed easily through her script. She then said something that caught even my jaded ear by surprise: Valentine carved his masterpiece out of a block of Vermont marble. When the tour guide finished her presentation and asked if there were any questions, I raised my hand. "Given that Robert E. Lee was such an icon of the South," I asked, "why did Edward Valentine decide to use Yankee marble to create his memorial sculpture?" The tour guide looked at me—to this day, I wonder if she noticed that I was the lone African American in her tour group—and without missing a beat replied, "There wasn't marble *white enough* [her emphasis] in the South for his statue, so he had to use some from Vermont."

I was so stunned by her answer that I do not recall if anyone else wanted to follow up on this or asked questions of their own. My guess is that the irony of her answer eluded my fellow visitors, who were eager to get to the museum gift shop and buy souvenirs emblazoned with the image of the late Confederate hero who, in marble at least, was the whitest man in the South.

Obviously, one can question the value of this story beyond its use as a cocktail party anecdote (which I have used religiously for nearly fifteen years). For the careful historian, there are clues to how historical memory is created and presented to the public. What, for example, is the role of art in the interpretation of historical events or figures? For the historian of higher education, this anecdote from Washington and Lee and the thousands like it from institutions around the country offer a window into how the university becomes part of the history of its surrounding community or region. Of course, the historian must treat such local lore critically and refrain from using it as a substitute for documentary evidence.

The fourth rule of writing institutional history is GET TO KNOW THE STAFF OF THE UNIVERSITY'S ARCHIVES. As it happens, one of the essays in this volume directly addresses how to use archival personnel and resources effectively, so I will keep my remarks general. Archives are one of the few places left in our world of instant gratification and constant communication where the old rules of human courtesy still apply. Letters of introduction are still requested and presented, and archive directors still interview potential researchers. The institutional researcher must plan her visit carefully, as time and research funds are usually in short supply. I would argue that part of this research plan should be taking the time to get to know at least some of the staff who work in the archive in which one will be conducting research, especially if the project will entail repeated visits to the archive, as was the case with me. Whenever possible—and when I was invited—I joined members of the archival staff on coffee breaks or at lunch. I sometimes bought the coffee; lunch was typically beyond my budget.

As I got to know them and they got to know me, the staff often brought me materials that I would not have otherwise discovered. I read them all, even if they were only tangentially related to my topic, and I usually found something useful. When I had returned home with my piles of photocopies and notes (I went to graduate school in the era before scanners and digital cameras), I paused long enough to write genuine thank you notes to the archival director and the members of the staff. There is no substitute for the handwritten letter. I would say that even if I were not an historian.

MASTERING THE MAGIC OF INSTITUTIONAL HISTORY

As should be immediately obvious to anyone who has ever attempted historical writing and research, the task is far from being as simple as it might appear at first glance. Colleges and universities are like people: they are born, they mature and thrive, and (at least some of them) eventually die. A great deal of mundane, miraculous, and mayhem occurs in between these two poles.

Institutions of higher learning are not in the least immune from the influence of powerful individuals, momentous social, cultural, and economic forces, or cataclysmic events of any kind. Indeed, in many cases, colleges and universities are born of these same forces. The institutional historian must reach into this swirling tangle of human and external factors and extract threads of truth—or at least weave those threads into a coherent tapestry of narrative and analysis. This is no simple parlor trick. The university is a mirror of the society (or subset of society) that created it, and the institutional historian must be able to gaze deeply enough into this looking glass to understand, without being mesmerized by what she sees.

The task before the institutional historian is often complicated by the sheer weight of the documentary evidence left behind by presidents, trustees, faculty, students, and God knows who else who had some sort of connection to the institution being studied. Universities and those associated with them are keenly aware of their place in the stream of history and work hard to preserve that legacy, be it real or imagined. If a picture is worth a thousand words, then a university archive is worth ten or a hundred times that many stories. The best institutional histories are able to combine compelling stories with sharp analysis of the institution's purpose and place in society. However, behind the anecdotes, lists of notable alumni and their achievements, charts of enrollment, retention, and graduation statistics, and endowment tables reside the simple yet elegant truth that institutions of higher learning, the "free and ordered spaces" praised so eloquently by the late Bart Giamatti, are the true embodiment of the American Dream.[14]

QUESTIONS FOR DISCUSSION

1. What are the principal social, cultural, and intellectual forces that contribute to the creation of institutions of higher learning? How are these forces affected by geographical region and historical moment?
2. Is it possible to avoid the "indispensable man" (or woman) paradigm in writing institutional history? How?
3. How useful is biography as a tool for writing institutional history? What are the strengths and weaknesses of this approach?
4. How might institutional histories benefit from the adoption of the techniques of prosopographical analysis?
5. What are the most challenging aspects of writing institutional history and how might they be used to teach the craft of history?

NOTES

1. Patricia A. Pelfrey, *A Brief History of the University of California*, 2nd Ed. (Berkeley: University of California Press, 2004).
2. Joe M. Richardson, *A History of Fisk University, 1865–1946.* (University, AL: The University of Alabama Press, 1980).
3. Ibid., 59–60.
4. See, for example, ibid., 56–70.
5. Ibid., 63–4.
6. Edward Potts Cheyney, *History of the University of Pennsylvania, 1740–1940.* (Philadelphia: University of Pennsylvania Press, 1940).
7. James L. Axtell, *The Making of Princeton University: From Woodrow Wilson to the Present.* (Princeton: Princeton University Press, 2006).
8. Thomas Jefferson Wertenbaker, *Princeton, 1746–1896.* (Princeton: Princeton University Press, 2006).
9. Polly Welts Kaufman, ed., *The Search for Equity: Women at Brown University, 1891–1991.* (Hanover, NH: Brown University Press, 1991).
10. Lyde Cullen Sizer, "'A Place for A Good Woman': The Development of Women Faculty at Brown," in Polly Welts Kaufman, ed., *The Search for Equity: Women at Brown University, 1891–1991.* (Hanover, NH: Brown University Press, 1991), 183–217.
11. Darryl L. Peterkin, "Lux, Libertas, and Learning: The First State University and the Transformation of North Carolina, 1789–1816." (Ph.D. diss., Princeton University, 1995).
12. Kemp Plummer Battle, *History of the University of North Carolina from Its Beginning to the Death of President Swain, 1789–1868.* (Raleigh: Edwards and Broughton, 1907–12. Repr. Spartanburg, SC: Reprint Company, 1974).
13. "'An Attempt at a Most Foul and Unnatural Murder!': The Fall and Rise of Joseph Caldwell at the University of North Carolina, 1805–1835." Paper presented at the annual meeting of the History of Education Society, New Haven, CT, October 2001.
14. A. Bartlett Giamatti, *A Free and Ordered Space: The Real World of the University.* (New York: W. W. Norton and Company, 1996).

2

ORAL HISTORY . . . AS SCHOLARSHIP

Katherine Chaddock

Most of the time I think of "oral history" as spoken description about the past captured in ways that help scholars achieve complete and accurate historical portrayals and analyses. But sometimes I begin to question myself on that point. If I find in *Vanity Fair* magazine, as I did recently, an anecdotal article subtitled, "An Oral History of the Bush White House,"[1] does that mean magazine journalists are poaching on territories that should be reserved for scholars digging for truths? With just a few interviewees among the hundreds who peopled the Bush White House, can we really get something that is thorough and accurate? What about all those interviews in *People, Playboy,* and *Ladies Home Journal?* In other words, how can I think of "oral history" as a method of scholarly historical research and analysis when it is also used to make news, provide titillating detail about noteworthy people and events, entertain with firsthand tidbits from insiders, and in general sell media products?

As a one-time journalist who later became a university professor and historical researcher, I am fascinated by the conundrum inherent in defining and delineating oral history. I like to think I have figured it out by referring back to the ancient adage I learned as an undergraduate journalism major: "When dog bites man, that's not news; when man bites dog, that's news." I have come up with this: "When man bites dog, that's news; when man explains the context, circumstance, physical setting, emotions, outcomes, feel, and taste of the biting incident—and is corroborated by additional information—that's oral history." Journalists seek a focused account that creates attention and interest. Oral historians seek a comprehensive account that contributes to meaningful exploration and discovery.

Therefore, scholarship supported by oral history can be distinguished from journalism that uses spoken words by its intent, scope, methods and use. For example, as a journalist, I long ago wrote a biographical article for *Working Woman* magazine about Inez Aimee, the first female vice president of the National Football League and the first female president of the United States Ski Team.[2] After two interviews with Ms. Aimee and one with a board of trustees member, I wrote an interesting account of my subject's climb to the top in men's domains, ideal for the magazine's female audience. Clearly, I was still very far from fully describing my subject; but that was okay, because my journalistic intent implied narrow scope, limited methods and a brief shelf life. Later, as a scholar, I wrote a biographical book about Black Mountain College founder John Andrew Rice.[3] Although the college had been closed for 40 years and Mr. Rice had been dead 25 years, my research included 58 interviews with living family members, friends, students, colleagues and lovers. I also was able to collect tapes and transcriptions from earlier scholars and review hundreds of boxes of archival materials. My intent, clearly different from the journalistic piece, was to produce a complete biography that could inform history and become a resource for other interested scholars for many years. I should also mention differences in outcome concerning these two cases of "oral history." While I became good friends with Inez Aimee after the article appeared, a number of Mr. Rice's family members refused to speak to me after the book appeared. The truth-revealing part of scholarly oral history can be perilous.

It is vitally important for scholars to approach oral history research methods in ways that cannot be confused with journalistic research, asking: Did I pursue every possible oral history that could contribute to answering my research questions, only stopping when information got so redundant as to be no longer useful? Did I probe for detail, jog memories with what I already knew, return for repeat interviews to help explain my emerging findings? Did I listen? Did I seek out other media for the spoken word beyond my interviews—e.g., interviews by others, transcribed memories? Did I collect all possible other secondary and archival materials to thoroughly complete and analyze the information I uncovered?

The difference between journalistic and scholarly approaches to oral history leads to two important corollaries that frame this chapter. First, because interviews are the backbone of oral histories, the talents and activities required of the oral historian are different from those required of other historical researchers and writers. Second, although interviews are important, they are not the only route to oral history; and they alone rarely suffice for telling the whole story.

STORIES AND STORY TELLERS

In his book, *Contemporary History*, Anthony Seldon maintains, "Interviews are almost always an inferior source of information to documents written at the time."[4] Concerns about faulty memories, overly fond recollections, and incomplete candor abound among researchers who prefer to work with documents and artifacts. However, in researching the history of higher education, I often find the oral contributions of those who were on the scene to be more reliable than other resources. Do faculty meeting minutes allow a glimpse at the power politics and horse trading that really result in decision making? Can 50-year-old yearbooks—or even letters to the parents—really explain what it was like for Jewish students to be snubbed by the Greek system? Furthermore, American institutions of higher education bulge with students worried about their grades and graduations and with faculty worried about their tenure and promotions. Those informants are likely to become much more candid later in life, and many remember important details 50 years later.

In conducting research for a book about the College of Charleston, the country's first municipal college, I started in the archives. When I uncovered letters written home to England by a faculty member in 1799, I was in research heaven. When I found a memoir by illustrious alumnus John C. Fremont about his experiences on campus in 1830 (mostly cutting classes to be with his girlfriend), I was thrilled.[5]

Then my research moved ahead in time to include finding and interviewing graduates well into their 80's who struggled to stay in college during the Depression. It advanced again and entailed speaking to individuals who left campus to fight in World War II and to African Americans who arrived on campus after a long struggle for access. Even after the exciting archival detective work on the front end of my research, oral history offered much more. It provided a way to "get" the story, not to only be "given" the story from the written record that had survived several hundred years. The detail, generally in the form of exemplary anecdotes of memorable experiences, was rarely blurred by fuzzy memories. For example, Otto German, one of the first African American students at the College of Charleston, described his experience on the basketball teams of 1970 though 1973:

> We used to travel in '57 Chevies up and down I-95 and I-26 playing in little matchbox gyms. We sometimes found ourselves in hostile environments at games out of state—in North Carolina or Virginia. Remus Harper and I were called everything. There were times when restaurants wouldn't serve us, so we'd all have to drive further to get a meal. Entering North Carolina, there were signs, "You Are Entering KKK Country."[6]

Margaret Welsh Lever recalled her freshman year, 1939, as typical of Depression era scrimping and saving:

> Nobody had a lot of money to spend. Dates were movies, dances. We had dates for church. Sororities did not have houses, but meeting rooms. We didn't do a lot, but we did play bridge in the rooms. . . . Our socializing was really very plain. It wasn't very big or exciting by today's standards. But we had a wonderful time. There were four movie theatres: The Garden, the Gloria, the Riviera, and the Majestic.[7]

These interviewees had impressive memories. To help their recall, I brought to the interviews pages I copied at the college library from the yearbooks of their class years— always including their own class photos. I also started by asking for some physical descriptions: Where did you live? What buildings were on campus? Where did you eat? Then I moved on to academic and social life. The real challenge was to go beyond this contextual information and dig for personal detail. It is easy, but not very illuminating, to allow an interviewee to go no further than recalling, "Some faculty weren't very helpful." Not very helpful? What does that mean? How not helpful? Can you give an example? Early African American student Kenneth Riley then explained of an instructor: "Lots of students stood in line at her desk after class. Other students were making appointments with her for guidance with the geometry problems, but she just told me and Mary Green, the other African American student in the class, to go find someone to help us."[8]

I term my job in the interviewing process: Stop, drop, and roll. Not that I am exactly on fire at most interviews, but the phrase serves as a reminder. First, I need to stop an interviewee's inability to recall by gently reminding her of her past. Then, I drop my interview questions into the general conversation that is underway about the past.

Those questions work as a checklist to remind me what I want to cover in a semi-structured interview, but they are not asked in a particular order. Many get answered conversationally before I ask them. Finally, I keep things rolling: First, with very interested body language that allows and encourages the interviewee simply to reminisce in various directions and then with probing for specific explanations, details, examples, and more.

Probing is hard work. It means second guessing what I will want to find and use at later stages. I wanted the story of campus desegregation; and getting it from student interviewees meant asking for specific instances of acceptance and/or of isolation. I wanted detail about the effects of the Depression; but I knew a large question like, "What was it like during the Depression?" would get me answers like, "Really tough." Instead I asked about part-time jobs, savings, tuition payments, and purchases. And if I got an answer like, "Everyone had a part time job," I was ready with, "Where? How often? How much earned?" Eventually, the strength of the written piece at the end of the research will not rest on *telling* the history, but on *showing* the history through examples, instances, and anecdotes.

Showing what happened, however, is never completely comprehensive. Historians make choices that start with the selection of a subject for investigation and continue with decisions about areas of emphasis regarding that subject. For example, in my history of the College of Charleston, I wanted to include students who left campus to fight in World War II and students who were on campus during Vietnam War protests, and I sought them out. But, I was less interested in students of the 1950's, and I did not seek them out.

Does this mean I didn't aim for a truly comprehensive history? Absolutely. "Major" events and eras were emphasized in my research questions at the expense of "all" events and eras. Ronald Grele, former director of the Columbia University Oral History Research Office, explained that oral histories "are constructed, for better or for worse, by the active intervention of the historian. They are a collective creation and inevitably carry within themselves a pre-existent historical ordering, selection and interpretation."[9] Those preexistent elements can come in very handy for knowing what to listen and probe for in an interview.

DIGGING DEEP: THE INTESTINAL FORTITUDE FACTOR

About halfway through my research on John Andrew Rice, I discovered that he appeared to have had, at about age 50, an extramarital affair with an 18-year-old student at Black Mountain College. That affair seemed to loom large in his divorce and in the decision of his colleagues to ask him to resign as president and then as a faculty member of the college he founded, which he did in 1940. Yet, although there was some indication of the affair in the written record, I couldn't get enough archival information to say for certain that it took place. Finally, through Mr. Rice's grandson, I discovered the name of the student involved, now in her 70's, and I managed to locate and contact her. To avoid scaring her off, I simply told her I was writing a biography and would like to interview her about her recollections of Mr. Rice. She refused. Back to square one.

Fortunately, I was soon to have my fourth interview with Frank Rice, John Andrew Rice's oldest son. He had never dropped any clue of the affair in our many hours of conversation about his father, so I assumed this would be a touchy subject for him. I approached it carefully, using the old journalism technique of putting the words in others' mouths: "Some former students seem to think. . . ." I was amazed when he responded,

"Oh, didn't I tell you about that?" He then described his parents visiting him at college and his angry mother telling him that she had caught his father and the young lady (now the older lady who refused to be interviewed) in the act. Frank had burst into tears at the time and had not spoken to either his mother or father for many months. I knew right away that I would want to use not only the information of the affair in the book, but also Frank's account of learning about it. However, it still seemed personal and touchy, so I asked in my most sympathetic way, "Frank, is there any way you could let me use this story in the book?" He let out a guffaw: "Hell, yes, use it. My father did it, not me!"[10]

Important information deserves the effort of tracking down sources, undertaking multiple interviews, broaching touchy subjects, and pursuing doggedly every possibility of getting the story right. Oral historians cannot succeed if they are frightened or discouraged by rejection. Not everyone wants to talk. In addition to a few of his former students, John Andrew Rice's second wife and the daughter of his second marriage both refused my interview requests, rebuking even my best line: "You know, it's not like he was Abraham Lincoln. This is going to be his one and only biography, so I need your help to make certain it's complete." When even that appeal didn't work, I admitted rejection and moved on.

A number of recent practitioners of oral history caution interviewers to understand their work not only as information gathering, but also as an interactive undertaking "where the focus is on process, on the dynamic unfolding of the subject's viewpoint."[11] This concept of the oral history process emphasizes allowing subjects to speak from their own points of view, to explain meanings in their own terms, and to weave stories that go beyond answering the question at hand. Such a process takes a great deal of listening, patience, and revisiting on the part of the oral historian; and it is a process that is more appropriate for some informants than others. If I had not spent many hours developing an interactive process with Frank Rice, I may never have been able to verify his father's affair with a student. On the other hand, with many other interviewees—generally those less central and more compartmentalized in the history I am researching—I can accomplish my aims by simply collecting data. An oral historian's intuition about level and extent of investment with each subject is essential.

CHECKING BACK AND CHECKING OUT

Interviewees may or may not be willing or able to tell the whole story or the accurate story. Everything bears checking out—internal criticism for veracity and completeness. When I am able to check more than one account of how, when, where, or why something happened, I am amazed at the inconsistencies. In listening to the tape of a 1967 interview of John Andrew Rice by author and historian Martin Duberman, I loved the part about bringing Josef Albers from the Bauhaus to teach at Black Mountain College in 1933. Noted architect Philip Johnson had advised Rice that Albers would be perfect for the job and should be brought out of Nazi Germany. Rice elaborated in his interview with Duberman: "Have you ever seen the look on the face of someone who has seen a truly great teacher in action with his students? That was what Johnson had when he spoke of Albers."[12] The quote had made its way into my first draft when I decided to interview Philip Johnson to see if he could add any interesting detail about his conversation with Rice. He was happy to talk and recalled the conversation well; but as for his euphoria upon seeing a "truly great teacher in action," he explained: "No, I never saw

Albers teach. But I knew him, knew his work, knew his personality, knew the feeling at the Bauhaus."[13] I was sad to delete the Rice quote, but glad I had checked.

Additionally, checking back with interviewees themselves is a good idea. Irving Seidman suggests series of three separate interviews with key informants.[14] Each time, rapport is built and memories are further jogged. Additionally, once you transcribe earlier interview information, you are likely to think of questions you wish you had asked. I never leave an interview without mentioning that I may make contact again for more information. And if I plan to quote someone's words attached to their name, I send that individual their quotes in writing (not in context, only their quotes); and I ask them to adjust or expand as preferred and to formally (with signature) agree to use.

Good questions that historical researchers typically ask themselves about their informants (whether in writing or orally) are:

- How well could this individual observe what he/she reports?
- How accurately could this individual recall what he/she reports?
- How does he/she define words and phrases used that might have various meanings?
- Do statements sound biased, agenda-laden, or improbable?
- Do statements contradict other evidence?
- Was questioning of the informant free of bias or misinterpretation?

Such questions are particularly useful when assertions from interviewees are so intriguing as to be "big news." These merit great effort in corroboration with other sources. Yet, some simply cannot be either verified or discredited with further digging. While researching a biography of educator, novelist, and concert pianist John Erskine, I was fortunate to be able to interview his nearly 90-year-old daughter, Anna Erskine Crouse, at her home in New York City. She was candid, open about even touchy subjects (yet another extramarital affair), and clear about the past. I previously had poured over thousands of archival documents at Columbia University where Erskine taught and at the Juilliard School where he was president. Therefore, I was stunned to hear from his daughter that she was convinced he took the job at Juilliard because his Columbia colleagues indicated he was no longer welcome there.

Nothing in the written record indicated such internal dissention, but it was information I wanted to be able to use if it were true. My probing for details with Mrs. Crouse left me with no certainty, although she was quite definite.[15]

Only one other primary source that I had not yet accessed remained for further checking: 100-year-old former Erskine student, friend, and then colleague, Jacques Barzun. Through friends of friends of friends, I was able to contact his family and ask that the question be put to him. A gracious note arrived from his wife, Marguerite Barzun: "Mr. Barzun is in hospital. . . . Jacques' recollection of Erskine's leaving Columbia is that he was not pushed out in any way. His interests were in music and creative work, rather than the administrative demands of running an English Department. At the time it seemed a good solution all around for him to move to Juilliard."[16] Definitive? No. After all, Erskine never actually rose to the point of "running the English Department" at Columbia, so maybe the information wasn't quite trustworthy. On the other hand, maybe Barzun saw Erskine as informally running the department, even though he never became department chair. Maybe Mrs. Crouse and Dr. Barzun defined "pushed out" quite differently. Conundrums like these call for careful disclosure—the kind that leaves room for doubt without inviting distrust.

The best way to provide such disclosure, necessary when interviewee conclusions or ideas cannot be verified as more than best guess or conjecture, is simply to present the idea as the opinion or recollection of another. This allows researchers to avoid stating affirmatively what may prove erroneous later. For example, in *The Last Campaign: Robert F. Kennedy and 82 Days That Inspired America*, Thurston Clarke deftly explained, without committing himself to the explanation, Robert Kennedy's popularity among American Indians: "Fred Dutton thought Indians liked Kennedy because. . . ." And, "The psychologist Robert Coles believed Kennedy appealed to poor people like Native Americans because. . . ." Clear conjectures from Kennedy friends made the point without committing to its veracity.[17]

OTHER VOICES, OTHER NARRATIVES

Clearly, the interviews conducted by the historical researcher contribute only part of the information necessary for achieving scholarship in the history of higher education. Secondary sources provide context and sometimes corroboration; and archival documents provide official records. Additional items that can be categorized in close proximity with oral histories are those that I refer to as "personal historical narratives." These can be used in very much the same way as interviews by the researcher, since they are truly voices—although voices captured by other individuals or by means other than interviews. They include: oral history interviews conducted by others, but preserved on transcripts or electronically; diary narratives by individuals who are no longer available for interview; and memoirs by the same.

Oral history collections are exceedingly popular among university archives, as well as among various libraries, museums, and other organizations. In recent decades, it appears that those interested in preserving history have started to take seriously the possibility of participant mortality. Anyone involved with an important time or event, from the Great Depression to Hurricane Katrina, is likely to be interviewed in order to provide a record that includes anecdotes, emotions, and detailed personal experiences that only individual participants can provide. University archives house both general oral history collections (usually interviews of long-time or particularly notable faculty and students) and specialized oral history collections. The latter focus on topical areas, such as World War II (Rutgers University), Native Americans (University of Illinois), jazz (Tulane University), September 11, 2001 (Columbia University), and Jewish heritage (College of Charleston).

The good news is the possibility that someone else interviewed an individual who is no longer available for an oral history by the immediate researcher. The bad news is the probability that the interviewer asked few or no questions relevant to the current research. The bad news may not be a problem if I am doing a biography that covers an individual's entire life. Anything I get is relevant. At the Library of Congress, audiotapes of John Erskine in the 1930's netted me nothing of real substance; but, they allowed me to hear his voice and describe the tone (very deep and patrician) and cadence (even and slow) with which he spoke. However, if I had been doing a more focused piece on Erskine's initiation of the Great Books movement, his patterns of speech would not have mattered to me, and I would have been disappointed that none of the substance touched on my subject. Some oral history collections have printed and/or online transcriptions of their interviews, which is wonderfully convenient. When only audio forms exist, the exercise of listening highlights in the extreme a tedious reality: Historical researchers spend most of their time finding things they can't use.

Two other important sources of personal historical narratives, diaries and memoirs, provide wonderful primary information but can be deceptive in terms of candor and veracity. Consider the writer. Even a diarist who locks her volume and keeps it in a secret place may not be completely candid and may write selectively. Generally, diaries provide the extremes of lived experiences—the great highs and the great lows. Few would fill their diaries with dreary happenings that occur day in and day out, even though the pattern of daily life generally contains a great deal of ho-hum material.

In a book about two centuries of student experiences at the University of South Carolina, my co-author and I wanted to be sure to include graduate students when possible. A 1910 diary by John Henry Hammond, grandson of a popular South Carolina governor, was the most extensive of our primary sources for describing law school at that time. But anyone assuming that the diary told the whole law student story would be convinced that this was a field that required very little attention to studying. Some of Hammond's entries included in our book:

> April 14: Caught ball a little. Went to a cheap show with Quitman Marshall. I am not studying as I should.

> April 15: Had a fine time in the game against the Juniors. They beat us 11 to 6. Most of the fellows were drunk before the end of the game.

> April 18: Took tea at Marshalls'. Carried Miss Janie to Shandon Dance. Had a fine time. Miss Janie is quite popular for a debutante. Miss Sue Flynn asked me to tea for Sunday and Miss Fitzsimmons for Friday.

> April 24: Called on Emma Beth. Took tea at Flynn's. Miss Sue is just the sweetest lady I ever met.

> April 28: Moot court and beer. Had a time. Nearly everybody drunk. Serenaded both colleges.

> April 29: Have something wrong with my kidneys.

> May 2: Presided over Southern Oratorical Contest. Carter won it, although he broke down on his delivery. Went home with Miss Marshall. Wrote to Mama. I have got to do more studying.

> May 3: Did little all day. Went to a reception at Miss Annie Lowry's. Had a fine time. Strong punch.[18]

Many more entries continued in the same vein! After graduation, the diarist became a well-regarded lawyer and a senator in the South Carolina legislature. Hopefully, his anecdotal diary entries left out much of the total law school experience! However, his work is instructive in terms of the selectivity of diary keepers, as well as the selectivity of a youthful diary keeper. Most individuals confronted with noting the events of the day do not aim for a full recording. Diaries are only artifacts. They are wonderful artifacts that can be used for many purposes, but they are still only what has survived. It is a lucky historian who finds comments in a diary that answer questions he or she would have asked in an interview.

Memoirs, recalled and written after some time has gone by, share some of the same problems as diaries and as oral histories produced from interviews with others. And they have additional problems of a known audience. A memoirist is writing to be read by someone specific—perhaps descendants, future historians, or a general audience in like circumstances. Therefore, a memoirist has an objective in mind—perhaps to inform, to entertain, to shock, to instruct, to retaliate, or to set the record straight. Published memoirs and autobiographies, in particular, deserve great skepticism; and the facts in them merit great attention to checking elsewhere for accuracy and truthfulness. By the time they have gone from the author to an agent and an editor, each with a different suite of motives in getting the volume into print, nothing is certain. Yet these can be useful sources if cross-checked; and when cross-checking consistently produces a different story, something important has been discovered about the memoir writer.

One last source that may be considered by some to be in the category of personal narratives outside typical oral history is the focus group. Some researchers maintain that a group of individuals in discussion produces a situation that is "more relaxed than a one-on-one interview."[19] In the hands of a skilled moderator, such a group can be given free rein to inspire and remind one another, with just gentle guidance toward initiating the dialogue, getting back on topic when drifting far astray, and including detail and examples as necessary. For historical recall, such groups may be helpful if their topic is circumscribed by like experiences. For example, a group of World War II veterans in a discussion of how they felt when they heard about the G.I. Bill might be very useful. It might bring out perceptions both of delight about getting a higher education and of skepticism about accepting "hand outs." But a group of World War II veterans discussing their varied experiences with higher education before they joined the military might not be as fruitful, since each experience would likely be in a different place and time. At the very least, any group discussion aimed at personal historical narrative should be kept smaller than is generally recommended for focus groups, with the ideal being three or four participants.

FINAL THOUGHTS

My final thought perhaps should have been my first thought, as it is about preparation for oral histories. However, it is easier to think about preparation after you have thought about the who, why, and how of oral histories. The logistics of preparation is the easy part, especially concerning interviews: (1) make sure your recording equipment is charged and working properly; (2) have plenty of pens and paper on hand; (3) decide what you will do if the informant does not agree to be taped; (4) bring a release form (or mention that you will send one later with printed quotes attached) for the interviewee to grant permission to be quoted by name, and/or capture this statement on tape; (5) bring a list of questions (but don't use it slavishly); (6) make certain the last question asks permission to re-contact for follow-up; and (7) remind yourself that you will inevitably need to probe for details and examples.

The more difficult item in the preparation category is the one about doing homework. The best oral histories captured as interviews happen *after* all other possible primary and secondary sources have been exhausted. The interviewer who thoroughly knows all that can be known through existing sources and *then* goes to live informants is able to ask relevant questions, check earlier information for accuracy, know when to probe for more depth and detail, and leave out questions that have been authoritatively answered elsewhere. Additionally, it is just not professional to put an informant in the position of covering ground that could have been covered by careful review of secondary or existing primary sources.

Preparation also means finding out as much as possible about the individuals who will be interviewed. Some of this information can be discovered in print or in conversations with others, while additional detail can be surfaced in the phone or email interaction that set up the interview. I learned this by experience. While working on a history of the Medical University of South Carolina, I was delighted to hear that Rosslee Green Douglas, the first African American student at that institution's College of Nursing, might be willing to be interviewed; so delighted, in fact, that I didn't ask her much about herself on the phone when I set up the interview. I couldn't wait to hear about her experiences as a very different, and perhaps rather isolated, student on campus in 1970, and I armed myself with a list of questions about interactions with other students, social life, study groups, and the like. I drove two and a half hours to her home in rural Walterboro, SC, got lost along the way, and finally arrived to find a much older lady than I had anticipated. In 1970, Mrs. Douglas was a well-trained and experienced nurse in her early 40's who sought the designation Bachelor of Science in Nursing as soon as it became available at the Medical University. She managed to accomplish that by taking only a limited number of courses and rarely interacting at all with faculty or her much younger fellow students. She had no real campus experience outside the time and place of her classes. Our interview was very brief. I consoled myself by listening to the Elvis Channel on satellite radio on my drive home. And by telling myself that at least I now knew the way to Walterboro.

Every historian has these stories. We make mistakes. Then we learn from them and make different mistakes. Or, we do everything right, and fate intervenes to squelch our best efforts. Potential interviewees refuse to help. Others fall ill or die before we get our chance. Computers crash. Flash drives flush down the toilet. Dogs (once a guinea pig in my case) eat our tapes. Contact information for key people just doesn't exist. The perfect cache of letters, noted by a helpful informant, no longer can be found. The photos that would have so well complemented our work disappear in a basement flood. The list goes on and on. And, fortunately, so does the historian's insatiable curiosity. So we regroup, cope, redo, adjust, and work with what we've got. Then we manage to turn out something that makes us glad for the effort and eager to start the next project.

QUESTIONS FOR DISCUSSION

1. This chapter emphasizes the differences between scholarly and journalistic approaches used in oral history *research*—getting the story. Are there also differences between scholarly and journalistic approaches used in oral history *writing*—telling the story? If so, what are those differences?

2. Some potential informants are very private people who are reluctant to be interviewed and included in your work. How can you decide when you should "push" them to agree to be interviewed and quoted vs. when you should respect their privacy and simply move on?

3. How might the personal background and characteristics of an interviewer become limiting factors in interactions with interviewees?
4. In reviewing memoirs and diaries as rich sources of research, it is easy to interpret them through what we know and feel in the present. What are some steps a researcher might take to better understand these sources (and their authors) from the perspective of the time and context in which they were written?

NOTES

1. Cullen Murphy and Todd S. Purdum, "Farewell to All That," *Vanity Fair*, February 2009, 88–101.
2. Katherine Chaddock, "Inez Aimee is Going for the Gold," *Working Woman*, July, 1982, 63–70.
3. Katherine Chaddock Reynolds, *Visions and Vanities: John Andrew Rice of Black Mountain College* (Baton Rouge: Louisiana State University Press, 1998).
4. Anthony Seldon, *Contemporary History* (Oxford, UK: Basil Blackwell, 1988), 3.
5. Katherine E. Chaddock and Carolyn B. Matalene, *College of Charleston Voices: Campus and Community Through the Centuries* (Charleston, SC and London, UK: History Press, 2006). See also, John C. Fremont, *Memoirs of My Life* (Chicago: Belford, Clarke & Co., 1887) and Caleb Cotton letters, 1799–1800, in South Carolina Historical Society, Charleston, SC.
6. Ibid., 147.
7. Ibid., 112.
8. Ibid., 148.
9. Ronald J. Grele, "Movement Without Aim," in *The Oral History Reader*, eds. R. Perks and A. Thomson (New York: Routledge, 1998), 42.
10. Frank A. Rice, interview with the author, November 5, 1995.
11. Kathryn Anderson and Dana C. Jack, "Learning to Listen," in *The Oral History Reader*, eds. R. Perks and A. Thomson (New York: Routledge, 1998), 169.
12. John Andrew Rice, interview with Martin Duberman, June 10, 1967, audiotape in Martin Duberman Papers, Personal Collection 1678, North Carolina State Division of Archives and History, Department of Cultural Resources, Raleigh.
13. Philip Johnson, interview with the author, January 16, 1996. See also, Reynolds, *Visions and Vanities*, 105–107.
14. Irving Seidman, *Interviewing as Qualitative Research: A Guide for Researchers in Education and the Social Sciences* (Thousand Oaks, CA: Sage Publishing, 2006).
15. Anna Erskine Crouse, interview with the author, March 26, 2008.
16. Marguerite Barzun letter to the author, February 27, 2008, in author's possession.
17. Thurston Clarke, *The Last Campaign: Robert Kennedy and 82 Days That Inspired America* (New York: Henry Holt and Co., 2008), 159–160.
18. Carolyn B. Matalene and Katherine C. Reynolds, *Carolina Voices: Two Hundred Years of Student Experiences* (Columbia, SC: University of South Carolina Press, 2001), 109–113.
19. Catherine Marshall and Gretchen B. Rossman, *Designing Qualitative Research* (Thousand Oaks, CA: Sage Publishing), 110.

3

AUTOBIOGRAPHY AND BIOGRAPHICAL RESEARCH IN HIGHER EDUCATION

Wayne Urban

Robert Hampel, Secretary-Treasurer of the History of Education Society, recently published an article in the *Chronicle of Higher Education* that deals with how to help doctoral students undertake a successful research project.[1] Hampel argues that traditional advice to students, such as find a topic that is related to other topics and fills a distinct niche in scholarship, is overrated. What it often yields is a study that is severely hampered, perhaps most importantly by the student's lack of any real personal commitment to the project. In place of this traditional approach, Hampel offers four alternatives: research that builds on current research, research that is autobiographical, research that arises from conversations, and research that responds to funding initiatives. Those of us in the scholarly vineyard of the history of higher education seldom have the opportunity to obtain funding for our work, let alone the work of our students, though in the following account of my work, funding does surface as important at key times. Hampel's other three alternatives offer more insight into the choices that I have made regarding biographical research projects. It is a combination of two of his particulars, however—that research is often autobiographical, and that research comes from other research—which I want to highlight in this chapter on biographical research in higher education.

THE ROAD TO HORACE MANN BOND

I choose the autobiographical suggestion to discuss first because it was the jumping-off point for the biography of Horace Mann Bond that I published in 1992.[2] Known best, perhaps, as the father of the noted civil rights activist, Julian Bond, Horace Bond was president of two Black colleges, one in Georgia and one in Pennsylvania, as well as the author of several books on Black education. In the Preface to my Bond biography, I noted two personal reasons why I had chosen to do the Bond biography: first, my dissatisfaction with what I called the social scientific orientation of educational history at that time and, second, my then recent, near decade long, experience as a department head. What bothered me about history of education at that time was its tendency to try and establish itself as a social science, a field in which knowledge was built on additively and systematically as if it were all adding up to support some grand synthesis or scheme or conclusion. The conclusion of traditional educational historians that the public school was a great institution in the generation and continuation of American democracy was then being challenged by the conclusion of revisionist historians, armed with significant amounts of social science evidence, that it was more likely a challenge, if not an obstacle, to democracy and social mobility. A biography, I thought then, and still do now I might add, would be a welcome counter to both of those additive and systematic orientations. Choosing to study a life, in all its complexity and ambiguity, would allow me to explore a form of work that I had not experienced in my own scholarly career to that point and that was being devalued by omission in my field.

The subject of that biography, I had decided, was to be an historian of education; that is, someone who did work like my own and with whom I would share an intellectual affinity that came from working in the same scholarly field. It would enable me to get some perspective on my own academic work and how it was progressing at the same time that it allowed me to contribute to my field.

My ultimate choice of Horace Mann Bond as a subject, a Black scholar and university administrator, meant one additional thing, namely that I would have to contend with the issue of being a White scholar doing a biography of a Black subject. My experience with that set of issues was discussed in an essay in Craig Kridel's edited volume on educational biography, published in 1998.[3] In that essay, I responded to criticism I had received for dedicating my Bond biography to my father, an immigrant's son and physician, and comparing the experiences of the two men of different racial backgrounds who were contemporaneous chronologically. Bond was born in 1904, my father in 1908. While my father died in 1953, Bond lived until 1972. I responded as best I could to the criticism, noting the reasons for both my dedication of the book to my father and for the explicit comparison between him and Horace Bond. I also responded to other criticisms of the book by some Black scholars that in a very profound way, I did not, and perhaps could not, really understand Horace Mann Bond.

My response to this line of criticism was what I had produced was a life of Bond written from my own perspective. I in no way thought that my perspective was the only perspective from which an account of Bond's life could be written and I welcomed further work on Bond's life, written from the perspective of an African American scholar, that might modify, criticize, supplement, or otherwise respond to my own views. Alas, as far as I know, that work has not ensued. Given that lack of work, my interpretation of Bond still awaits comparison to the work of a Black scholar who comes to the life from a different racial experience, and by now a different generational experience, than my own.

For the purposes of this essay, I want to return to the autobiographical aspect of my work on the Bond book. As mentioned earlier, I wrote it just after finishing a long stint as a department head. I became increasingly frustrated at that job, largely because I found that it competed with, actually began to take away from, the teaching and research that I considered at the center of my own academic work. While I could live with a half time release from my teaching duties, I became increasingly resentful of the time the job of department head took away from my research. I was proud that in the early years of my administrative work, I managed to publish my first monograph, *Why Teachers Organized*.[4] In the years after its publication, as I continued as a department head, I found it increasingly difficult to gain the sustained amounts of time to do research that I found necessary for my work.[5] By the late 1980s, when I had stepped down as a department head and was granted a fellowship that released me from all duties except my research for one calendar year, I was relieved and energized by the chance to do research and writing full time.

The significance of my personal encounter with university administration for the content of my Bond book may be seen when I note its major theme: that Horace Mann Bond was a trained social and institutional historian whose dissertation and early work marked him as one of great scholarly promise both as an historian and as a critical analyst of Black education.[6] Bond, however, confronted a reality in his academic career that steered him toward the rewards, both material and reputational, that went with success in administration in Black colleges and away from the rewards that would come with scholarly accomplishment. I argued in *Black Scholar* that Bond was concerned that responding to the positive incentives of administrative work severely hampered his scholarly development. In fact, I argued, it stunted him as a scholar.

This argument, though occasionally noticed, was more often ignored by reviewers of *Black Scholar*. One reviewer, however, made it the centerpiece of his review. David Stameshkin of Franklin and Marshall College devoted the clear majority of his review to the tension between administration and scholarship in Bond's academic work, and my reasons for highlighting the tension and its consequences for his career. Stameshkin noted, accurately, that I tried to give Bond credit for some significant administrative accomplishments in his leadership role as Dean at Dillard University and as President of Fort Valley (Georgia) State College. Stameshkin also noted, again correctly I think, that those accomplishments did not outweigh some substantial negatives that marred his accomplishments as the first Black President of Lincoln University, the historically Black college in Pennsylvania that Bond himself had attended as an undergraduate.[7] In a sense, I was just as pleased, or perhaps more pleased, that Stameshkin had read the book that I had written about Bond than I was that he largely approved of my thematic treatment of Bond in it. I had never met Professor Stameshkin nor was I familiar with anything he had written, other than another book review or two. But it struck me as more than coincidental that his insightful presentation and analysis of my argument in *Black Scholar* had more to do with something in his background than with my own scholarly acuity when I discovered that he was an historian who was working as a full time administrator at his institution when he wrote the review, and is still doing so.[8] Thus, my conclusion is that just as authors write a book often from an autobiographical perspective, as I did in my Bond biography, reviewers just as often review the book from their own particular autobiographical perspective. I do not wish to make too much of this conclusion, that is, to make it somehow an overarching epistemological postulate, but I do think it accounts for some of the reviews I received from Black reviewers and in particular the review I was given by David Stameshkin.

I want to make one final comment about *Black Scholar* and its analysis. Nothing I have said thus far should be interpreted to mean that I am convinced that meaning is completely subjective or impossible to communicate to others who are not predisposed to listen. My work as a biographer, like my other work as an historian, should be judged first by its adherence to scholarly standards. Such judgments will relate to use of relevant and sufficient secondary and primary sources to document analysis, care and commitment to the accuracy of what is concluded from those sources, and critical analysis of subject based on the sources and some genuine respect, if not regard, for one's subject. Negative judgments of my work, or any scholarly work, according to these criteria make discussions such as my own of the perspectives of authors and reviewers and the relationship of those perspectives to the autobiographies of authors and reviewers unimportant, and seriously misleading. Scholarly standards underlie, in fact, they out-rank, concerns about perspectives, at least for me as an historian and a biographer.

Having said that, let me return to the initial point that I made in this essay, agreeing with Robert Hampel that one's autobiography is a powerful tool to use in choosing a research topic. This insight, and its communication to students and other researchers, should lead to research projects, including dissertations, which animate their authors enough to sustain the effort needed to produce competent scholarship. Autobiographical interest is surely not the only way to sustain research to the point that it yields competent scholarship, but it seems to me to be a powerful way to do so and one that we should not ignore when considering our own work, as well as the work of our students. It also serves, at least for me, as a way to engage the emphasis on researcher perspective that is so important to our colleagues in educational research who utilize qualitative methods, as well as our colleagues in education and outside of it who subscribe to the relativist predilections or prescriptions of post-modernism. Again, to be completely clear, I am neither a relativist nor a committed skeptic about meaning; I am, however, one who admits, in fact even celebrates, a personal dimension to scholarship that should, if reinforced, allow fledgling scholars to sustain interest to the completion of dissertations. Setting this discussion in the context of biographical work, as I have done and will continue to do in the rest of this essay, highlights the individuality of both autobiography and perspective by putting them in the context of trying to understand the biography and perspective of one's subject.

FROM HORACE MANN BOND TO JAMES BRYANT CONANT

After publishing my Bond biography, I returned my attention to historical studies of teacher associations, namely the National Education Association (NEA) and its constituent organizations. This marked a return to a topic and orientation that had characterized my work before my Bond biography. This return to teacher associations was accomplished with support from the NEA, support that was given openly with no strictures about the interpretations of the association or any of its sub-groups. I was commissioned initially by the NEA Research Division to write a history of the Division on the occasion of its 75th anniversary. This support illustrates Hampel's notion that researchers often take on topics for which there is financial aid available. While working on the history of the research division, I also undertook research related to a history of the NEA itself in the twentieth century. The NEA work proved to be a productive move for me, resulting in publication of two books, one edited book, and several articles.[9]

Building on that work, that is using it as a jumping-off point for further, related work, I received a grant from the Spencer Foundation to study the Educational Policies Commission (EPC), an organization sponsored by the NEA to function as a quasi think tank on educational problems and policies. The EPC was to be both an intellectual pillar and the policy advocacy arm of the entire American educational profession, a purview undertaken by the NEA but best served by a prestigious group sponsored, but not controlled, by the association. EPC's influence was to come both from its ideas and from the reputations of the roster of educational leaders who comprised its membership. My EPC proposal was made with the idea in mind that I was studying a significant group in American educational history that lived a vibrant, though ultimately circumscribed life, beginning in 1936 and ending in 1968.

Support from Spencer for this project speaks to Hampel's ideas about doing research that others would sponsor, but I want to point out both that my EPC work was built on my earlier studies of NEA and that Spencer had to be convinced of the importance of the work in order to gain their financial support. I managed to produce several articles on the Educational Policies Commission (EPC), articles that illustrated the reasons for its rise and demise, as well as to discuss some of its notable publications. The makeup of the EPC illustrated something important that was present in my Bond work, though I have not talked about it yet, and something that I will refer to again later in this essay. That something is that anyone working in the history of education needs to understand, for most people inside and outside of education, the distinction between higher education and elementary and secondary education is much less important than the good of the entire educational enterprise. In fact, the distinction between K-12 and higher education often hides more than it reveals: that narrows and distorts the study of the educational enterprise rather than expanding its understanding.

Let me be more specific. Horace Mann Bond thought of himself as an educator who was intent on improving the educational prospects of African American children at all levels of the educational system, not just the college students who attended the institutions he served. The history of Black colleges, like the history of White colleges, featured institutions that, at their beginnings, and often well into maturity, served students at several levels of preparation, many of which were below what we now think of as higher education. In fact, Bond's major publication in the 1930s was a comprehensive account of Black education at all levels.[10] The members of the Educational Policies Commission, though chosen for their accomplishment in elementary education, secondary education, higher education, and outside of education, downplayed their position in the educational organizational hierarchy to try and think creatively about educational issues wherever they occurred. University presidents were a mainstay of the EPC membership over the years, but the university presidents who served on the EPC were there to address the welfare of the entire educational enterprise, not the well-being of their own institution, or other institutions of higher education. While there is much to say critically about the EPC, and I will say some of that below, the members usually rose above issues of self-interest to address larger problems in the educational universe.

To return to the EPC itself, I began my studies convinced that it was a fundamentally important institution in American education and in American educational history, and one which had been largely neglected by educational historians. To establish this importance, I set out to analyze the plethora of reports that the EPC produced in its thirty some years of existence and relate them to the educational circumstances that provoked their publication and the changes that they sought to achieve. The initial publications of the EPC were devoted to coping with the consequences of the Great Depression in education and sought both the financial well-being and the ideological invigoration of American public education in a time of great crisis. As World War II intervened, the EPC responded to larger questions of social and economic advancement brought to the fore by the end of the war. I looked particularly at three EPC publications, the first in 1945 in which it sought, unsuccessfully, a dramatic overhaul and extension of American secondary education to where it would take over the first two years of higher education from colleges and universities.[11] The second publication I studied was a 1950 report that advocated moral education in public schools in a Cold War climate of increasing concern over the moral health of children, especially in an ostensibly secular institution like the public school.[12] The third publication I considered was a 1960s account of an analysis of the educational problems of disadvantaged American children.[13] None of the reports I studied proved to be decisive in determining the fate of American education. Thus, looking only at the published reports of the EPC, at least the three reports discussed above, it is hard to avoid the conclusion that it failed to influence American educational practice in a distinctive way. Of course, the plethora of think tanks that have succeeded the EPC in our own time have in large part repeated that accomplishment, or rather lack of accomplishment. I doubt that any of them would want to be held to a standard of distinctively influencing educational practice or they, too, would be judged to have failed.

More important than the success or failure of the EPC in influencing educational practice was a theme that I was slowly developing during my years of work on the body. The thematic emphasis that I am talking about was initially encompassed in my desire to account for the demise of the EPC in 1968. As an historian of the National Education Association, I had an idea initially about an important aspect of what was behind that demise. The NEA was in the process of becoming a teachers' union in the late 1960s and early 1970s and sponsoring a body of educational thinkers and administrators from both elementary-secondary and higher education was not at the top of its priority list. Perhaps this can be seen as a pushing of EPC out of the NEA for eminently justifiable reasons, given the change in the NEA from a stance of being an advocate for the entire educational profession into that of being a vigorous advocate for teachers. But there was more than a push from the NEA involved. The EPC itself saw the changes happening in the NEA and tried to take steps to arrange for alternative support for itself, both before and after it was expelled from the teachers' union. Alas, no support from any foundation, or other funding agency, was forthcoming to replace the financial support given by the NEA. Thus the EPC ceased to exist in 1968, much to the dismay of its leadership and its members.[14]

As I was ending my formal study of the EPC, and coming to at least the initial conclusion about its demise offered in the preceding paragraph, I left Georgia State University after more than three decades on the faculty and moved to the University of Alabama in January of 2006. At Alabama, I took up a position working in an educational policy center and on the faculty of a higher education program. Neither of these emphases seemed particularly conducive to further effort in studying the NEA or the EPC. The end of funding from Spencer for my EPC project also contributed to the end of that effort.

At Alabama, I became enmeshed in a world devoted to the analysis of educational policy, in elementary, secondary, and higher education. I had a strong desire to show how history related to the policy world, and that, along with some distinctly local factors, quickly led to my next major project. As I settled in on the campus at Tuscaloosa, my colleagues and I in the Education Policy Center became aware of the pending 50th anniversary of the National Defense Education Act (NDEA), an important piece of federal educational legislation passed by Congress and signed into law by Dwight D. Eisenhower in September of 1958. Two things about NDEA appealed to a scholar in

Alabama. The first was that its two major sponsors, Lister Hill in the Senate and Carl Elliott in the House of Representatives, were both from Alabama. The second was that the University of Alabama used NDEA to advance itself significantly as an institution of higher education, both through the large numbers of NDEA loans to undergraduate students which added to undergraduate enrollment and the many NDEA fellowships to graduate students that basically built a graduate school in Tuscaloosa at an institution that previously, at best, had a few graduate programs. I wrote several papers on various parts of the NDEA story that eventually became chapters in a book on NDEA that will be published in 2010.[15]

My argument in this volume was twofold. First, I tried to establish that NDEA was more than the science and mathematics education measure that it is traditionally conceived to have been. I tried to show that the ten titles of NDEA contained much more than science and mathematics education improvements, and that as NDEA evolved over its first decade it encompassed more and more subject matter areas. My second claim in the NDEA book related to the argument that it would never have been passed without the successful launch of the Sputnik satellite by the Soviet Union in October of 1957. That launch, in the midst of a Cold War political anxiety over the rivalry between the USA and the Soviet Union, meant that Sputnik necessitated a response. Educational change, as often in the history of American education, facilitated the appearance of doing something to respond to Sputnik in a political climate in which this was absolutely necessary. The changes themselves, however, were largely unrelated to the actual event that provoked them. That is, no one could directly link Sputnik to American educational failures, though many tried to do so. NDEA, however, allowed the Eisenhower administration to respond to Sputnik, which created a near panic over national defense, in an educational arena largely detached from national defense. The administration was convinced that Sputnik was at best a temporary achievement for the Soviet Union, one that masked its clearly secondary position in terms of scientific and technological development to the U.S. Passage of NDEA allowed the administration to appear to do something, that is, to provide federal aid to science education, without essentially altering the defense picture, which it believed needed no alteration.

I began my study of NDEA by first looking closely at the educational and political factors that had been behind its advocacy by Lister Hill in the Senate, and by Carl Elliott in the House. Hill and Elliott, and most of their congressional colleagues who supported NDEA, had in mind an extension of educational opportunity to bring the fruits of education, particularly in secondary schools and in colleges and universities, to individuals capable of benefiting from it but in need of financial help and to educational institutions in states like Alabama where large groups of these needy individuals and poorer schools were concentrated. This is a gross oversimplification of a complex political environment, but it is not a substantial distortion of the views of either Alabama politician. Returning to the Eisenhower administration, I argued that NDEA allowed Elliot Richardson and other moderate Republicans to bypass the antipathy of their more conservative colleagues to any kind of federal involvement in education through cooperating with Hill, Elliott, and other Democrats in the Congress. It was interesting, in light of my current plan to return to a biography, that I centered these three chapters on the significant individuals in the Congress and in the administration who led the effort for the passage of NDEA. I was slowly being drawn back into the orbit of biography without consciously realizing what was happening.

In two additional chapters, I looked at the stance of two of the most directly involved interest groups in the passage of NDEA: educators and scientists. Education was represented in the federal government by the United States Office of Education (OE), a sub-cabinet agency housed in the recently created Department of Health, Education, and Welfare. OE had close relations with the NEA; many of its prominent staff members, including its Commissioner, were former officers or other leaders in the NEA or one of its constituent groups. I showed how the NEA, then arguably, and self-consciously, the best single representative of the American educational enterprise if there were one, never grasped the opportunity presented by NDEA for accomplishing its own larger goal of significant federal aid to American education. I located most of the responsibility for this missed opportunity in the actions of William G. Carr, Executive Secretary of NEA, and contrasted Carr's own hesitancy about NDEA with the actions of some of his staff—and more importantly, with the actions of NEA members in its annual Representative Assembly. I contrasted Carr's clumsiness, caused by his ideological devotion to a form of federal aid not represented in NDEA, with the adroitness of the scientists who were led by Eisenhower's Scientific Advisor, James R. Killian, and the members of the President's Science Advisory Committee. Here again, I focused on the individuals who led both groups, the educators and the scientists, one of whom was successful and one of whom was not. As I will show in the next section of this essay, Carr's maladroit behavior was an episode in a larger study of a loss of influence by professional educators in the middle of the twentieth century.

Of course, it is easy to contrast the influence of a relatively large, and diffuse, group of educators with that of scientists who were still benefiting from the positive image earned in weapons development during World War II and were also gaining positive press because of the scare caused by Sputnik. The influence of these scientists was represented in the federal government in agencies such as the National Science Foundation (NSF) as well as in bodies such as the President's Science Advisory Committee (PSAC). Founded by President Harry Truman in the early 1950s, the PSAC increased in its influence as it was taken directly into the White House operations under Dwight D. Eisenhower. The large discrepancy in influence between scientists and educators was real in the late 1950s, but as already suggested, educators would lose even more influence in the federal education policy world, and elsewhere. I want to devote the rest of this essay to establishing this point, largely through discussion of one individual who was present in both the educational councils of the NEA and the scientific enterprises supported by NSF and represented by the PSAC.

JAMES BRYANT CONANT, THE EDUCATIONAL POLICIES COMMISSION, AND NDEA

Focusing on one individual to make larger points about American education runs the risk of oversimplification and other distortions of the historical record. On the other hand, concentrating on an individual allows one to see larger developments through the eyes of an individual human being enmeshed in a series of institutions that are struggling in a variety of ways to contend with the events and forces that surround them. I have come full circle in my work on NEA, EPC, and NDEA which succeeded my biography of Horace Mann Bond to the point that I am now convinced that a close study of one individual, who was involved in the organizations as well as in the passage of the legislation, a biography to be specific, is the best way to build on my earlier studies of education in the mid-twentieth century world. Rather than belabor this point, let me simply restate that I have returned to a biographical approach in my work because I think it has the greatest chance of painting a full, complicated, and convincing picture of educational reality. In the rest of this essay, I want at least to suggest here, if not to establish, the thesis that James Bryant Conant was a pivotal figure involved in a distinct changing of the guard of the powerful individuals and groups in American education. He was pivotal because he was a member of both the group that lost power, the professional educators, and the groups that gained power, scientific and university interests.

The first point that I want to make about Conant is that he was one, perhaps the only one or certainly one of a very few, who was working with both American scientists and American educators in the middle of the twentieth century. To establish this, a look at Conant's early years as well as aspects of his career as president of Harvard University, is in order. James Bryant Conant was raised in the Boston suburb of Dorchester. Conant's father was an engraver, a craftsman who dabbled in real estate development to improve his and his family's economic situation. James Conant was a precocious young man who experimented with magic tricks as well as with those aspects of science that one with his talents and orientation would want to explore. Born in the late nineteenth century and schooled early in the twentieth, he attended the Roxbury Latin School for his six-year secondary education that followed his six years of elementary education. His secondary school was private and exclusive intellectually; rigorous competitive examinations were required for entry, but any boy[16] who passed the examinations and resided in or near Roxbury could attend without tuition expense. As Conant reminisced about his childhood and high school years, he stressed the non-elite aspects of his background and downplayed his family's ties to the past that might have been used to illustrate a higher social status than what he ascribed to himself.[17]

Conant was admitted to Harvard with advanced standing in chemistry and physics on the basis of a series of examinations in several subjects, including Latin and history, and the frequent and forceful recommendations from his high school science teacher at Roxbury Latin, who had recently earned a graduate degree in chemistry from Harvard. On the basis of his test scores, he won a Harvard scholarship that marked him as a student from whom much was to be expected academically. Conant did not disappoint those who held these expectations and he graduated with high honors and significant accomplishments in chemistry, as well as in non-scientific subjects and activities, in 1914. He went on to graduate study in chemistry and earned his doctorate and a place on the Harvard chemistry faculty in good order. As in his preparatory school, Conant was successful in non-scientific subjects at Harvard, as well as in extracurricular activities. As an undergraduate, Conant was suspicious of the "snobbery" that characterized much of the student culture at Harvard, dominated by elite Bostonians who zealously protected their status from the incursion of "others" of various backgrounds.

Conant was so advanced academically that the last year of his undergraduate study, the 1913–14 academic year, was largely spent earning graduate credits in chemistry. Following his graduation in 1914, he took only two years to earn his Ph.D., which was granted in 1916. He soon received an appointment on the chemistry faculty at Harvard and, after a brief interlude in the American chemists' pursuit of a nerve gas more lethal than that developed by the Germans in the World War I era, he proceeded in his academic career at Harvard, gaining tenure, promotion, and the chairmanship of the chemistry department all within a decade of his appointment to the faculty. He married his doctoral supervisor's daughter and thereby gained a set of social and cultural skills and orientations that he might have lacked. In 1933, in a surprise choice, he was picked as President of Harvard, a position he would hold for the next twenty years.[18]

As Harvard president, Conant was interested in the humanities and the social sciences, as well as his own field and other natural sciences. He worried as much about general education and the rest of the undergraduate curriculum as he did about advanced study in his own discipline, and other disciplines. He continued some scientific work while President and, more importantly for his eventual success outside of Harvard, participated in the weapons development program that occurred during the prosecution of World War II. Conant thus became a well-known leader of the American scientific enterprise as well as the president of arguably the most prominent university in the country.

As president, Conant instituted a national scholarship program which intended to open up Harvard College to students from a much wider range of backgrounds than the New England prep school origins that characterized the undergraduate student body under his predecessor. Conant's National Scholarship program was one illustration of the change in his view of American education away from reliance on schools like the Roxbury Latin School, which he had attended, toward consideration of the increasing enrollment in public high schools, especially in the areas outside of New England. Conant's increased understanding and appreciation of public high schools was enhanced by his encounters with two deans of the faculty of the Harvard Graduate School of Education. The first of those deans, Henry Holmes, Conant inherited when he became President of Harvard. Conant tried to justify his own secondary school experience as a democratic experience to Holmes, pointing out to the Harvard educator that the Roxbury Latin School was free to children of families living in Roxbury, and in other parts of the greater Boston area, who could pass the admission examination. Conant saw his own experience of success at Roxbury and at Harvard as an illustration of his "anti-aristocratic bias," and believed that he had communicated his position effectively to Holmes.[19]

While Holmes, and Francis Spaulding his successor as dean and the second person with whom Conant discussed educational issues, understood Conant's defense of Roxbury Latin, these men also managed to convince Conant of two things: first that the future of the nation depended more and more on the output of the public high schools rather than the prep schools like Roxbury Latin, and second, that the public high schools were seriously attuned to the success of all students who attended, not just those who were college bound. Thus, public high schools had a greater and more important job to do than did their preparatory peer institutions. In discussing his conversations with Spaulding, Conant noted that "I was directing my attention to those who were going to college; such students were not Spaulding's primary concern. My thinking was tied to the National Scholarship scheme; his thoughts were centered on the youth who attended high school without any intention of attending college." Conant's reminiscence of the situation, almost four decades after the conversations took place, was that "I had not come very far toward an understanding of 'public schools as instruments of democracy.'"[20] Yet that conclusion belied the distance that Conant had traveled along the path away from the prep school–Harvard College singular focus on college preparatory study as important and toward an appreciation of the value of the diversity represented in the student body and the curriculum of the public high school. Evidence of this wider perspective is contained in words Conant delivered to a California audience: he noted first that the way to provide "true democracy of opportunity . . . [was] to have all careers open to the talented" and added that intellectual was only one kind of talent that was to be appreciated and nurtured. Additionally, the "talent of the artisan" was to be appreciated and developed, as well as the talent of the academically oriented.[21]

One shorthand for distinguishing between the values held by Conant and by his two educational colleagues was that the former believed in a secondary school that widened its net to provide opportunity to talented students, whatever their background, while the latter saw that the main mandate for secondary education in a changing society was to provide education for citizenship for all those enrolled, whatever their abilities, backgrounds, or destinations. While Conant acknowledged the value of his own preference, he also acknowledged that "both concepts were exciting and important."[22]

While neither of Conant's educational colleagues subscribed fully to the progressive educational ideology that was becoming increasingly popular in educational circles in the 1930s, they both shared with progressives the suspicion of the value of the standard academic curriculum in secondary schools geared to college admission and the defense of citizenship education in a democratic society as an important goal. Conant's experience with educators who held values distinctly different from his own was intensified by his several terms on the Educational Policies Commission (EPC) where he became well known to the school superintendents and other college and university presidents who dominated the ranks of that body. Conant would serve multiple terms on the EPC beginning in the late 1930s and continuing into the 1960s. From his collaboration and interaction with the educators on the EPC, Conant learned a deep appreciation for the sentiments evidenced in the title and the substance of the already discussed 1945 EPC publication, *Education for All American Youth*. Conant approved of the EPC's emphasis on all American youth in the document, as well as the curricular diversification the group of educators thought necessary in order to meet the needs of this increasingly diverse student body.

Conant became much more vocally supportive of public schools as essential institutions in a democracy, during and after World War II. By the early 1950s, he had entered into a pointed controversy with advocates of private schools, particularly private religious schools. Conant's own recounting of the controversy began with a consideration of his visit to Australia in 1951. In that visit, he reported on the dominance, if not the numerical predominance, of private secondary schools, which received government financial support in most Australian states, and the harmful effects of the situation on the democratic character of Australia. More specifically, in comparing Australia and America, he noted that the

concept of a public school as a binding force in a community was an American idea—a product of the special history of the United States. I became more convinced than ever that public schools had been significant factors in the development of the United States. If one started with the assumption that there might be as many separate schools as there were religious denominations, the concept of a high school that served *all* youth in an area was destroyed.[23]

In 1952, President Dwight D. Eisenhower appointed Conant to the position of High Commissioner of occupied Germany. Conant concentrated on education, among many other areas, in his German efforts. He also kept in touch with the scientific community in the U.S. while he was overseas and continued to have great influence within the highest circles of the Eisenhower administration when he returned to the U.S. It should not be surprising that Conant's advice was sought in the development of NDEA by the administration and that he was in constant touch with the members of the President's Scientific Advisory Committee about both scientific research and educational issues related to it. As already mentioned, Conant also continued to be in touch with the American educational leaders in the EPC, as well as the top staff leadership of its parent, NEA.

The eventual demise of those educators as influential in the United States Office of Education (OE), as well as in other policy-making circles in American education, is a story too complex to be told here.[24] Suffice it to say that Conant was important in helping accomplish this power shift, though he never lost his contacts or favorable reputation with NEA and EPC leaders. This is remarkable, for during the 1960s, when John F. Kennedy was removing those educators from positions of significant influence in OE and replacing them with members of the traditional elites represented by Harvard University, Conant was also in the process of producing a rather scathing indictment of what he called "the American educational establishment" in his study of teacher education, *The Education of American Teachers.*[25]

FINAL REMARKS ON BIOGRAPHY AND AUTOBIOGRAPHY

The first thing I want to say in conclusion is that, for Conant, and many if not most Americans, education in the U.S. was a set of institutions that were distinctly related, and dependent on, each other. Thus, distinctions between K-12 and higher education, while necessary, also often hid the reality that American education was made up of interrelated institutions that needed to consider each other, understand each other, and depend on each other. Alas, the National Education Association, and most of those involved in departments, schools, and colleges of education that trained the teachers for those schools, did not understand this larger reality. Thus, in addition to the unionization of NEA as a factor involved in the decline of influence in larger policy circles for American educators, I would stress the importance of the reluctance of other groups within educational circles to understand their interdependence with institutions on other rungs of the American educational ladder. This failure to appreciate the importance of all involved in the educational enterprise at all levels seems to feed the isolation that higher education faculties often feel within schools or colleges of education. The tendency of higher education scholars and researchers to study only their own set of institutions without thinking at all about that relationship intensifies the isolation. Those of us in higher education should know better. I myself am now in a higher education unit but I am also involved in other units in my College of Education that sensitize me to the interdependence I wish my higher education colleagues appreciated. That is, we're all in this together and we will likely sink or swim together.

Finally, I want to stress that I have structured this essay so that it begins and ends with a biography. Going from Horace Mann Bond to James Bryant Conant was a long and complicated journey for me. Yet that journey represents, I think, the value of biography in the history of education and the history of higher education without essentializing it. Biography accomplishes certain scholarly objectives more effectively than other approaches. It was important to me during my Bond work, and receded in significance for me after that. Starting with my NDEA work, the importance of the study of significant individuals reappeared for me. The brief sketch of Conant here needs significant expansion. I am contemplating a full-scale biography. I hope that I have demonstrated, or at least suggested, the significance of biography for my own work, and for the work of others, in these pages.

QUESTIONS FOR DISCUSSION

1. This essay posits a productive relationship between a researcher's autobiography and his or her research. Can you imagine or do you know of situations in which such a relationship might be counterproductive? How would you deal with such a situation?

2. Much is made in the early part of this essay of the importance of the perspective of a biographer. Does this point of view mean that all perspectives in biographical study are inherently valid and productive? If so, why are they and if not, why are they not?

3. In this essay, administrative work is seen as an obstacle to scholarly productivity. Does this always have to be the case? Why or why not?

4. At more than one point in this essay, higher education scholars are urged not to ignore the relationship between higher education and elementary and secondary education in their research. How can acknowledging this relationship enrich higher education scholarship and how might it hamper it?

NOTES

1. Robert L. Hampel, "In Search of New Frontiers: How Scholars Generate Ideas," *Chronicle of Higher Education* (December 19, 2008), retrieved electronically at http://chronicle.com/weekly/v55/i17/a07201.htm
2. Wayne J. Urban, *Black Scholar: Horace Mann Bond, 1904–1972* (Athens: University of Georgia Press, 1992).
3. Craig Kridel, ed., *Writing Educational Biography: Explorations in Qualitative Research* (New York: Garland Publishing, 1998). My chapter in that volume was "Black Scholar: White Biographer."
4. Wayne J. Urban, *Why Teachers Organized* (Detroit: Wayne State University Press, 1982).
5. I would add that, when I was again a department head in the early years of the current decade, the time demands of the job were even more stringent and more inimical to scholarship than they had been earlier.
6. Bond's dissertation completed in 1936 at the University of Chicago was published: see Horace Mann Bond, *Negro Education in Alabama: A Study in Cotton and Steel* (Washington, DC: Associated Publishers, 1939). The book was reprinted by the University of Alabama Press in 1994.
7. David Stameshkin, "Review of Wayne J. Urban, *Black Scholar*," in *History of Education Quarterly* 33 (Summer, 1993): 250–52.
8. According to the Franklin and Marshall website, Dr. David Stameshkin is Associate Dean of the College. See http://www.fandm.edu.
9. Wayne J. Urban, *More than the Facts: The Research Division of the National Education Association, 1922–1997* (Lanham, MD: University Press of America, 1998); Urban, *Gender, Race, and the National Education Association: Professionalism and Its Limitations* (New York: Routledge/Falmer, 2000); and Ronald G. Henderson, Wayne J. Urban, and Paul Wolman, eds., *Teacher Unions and Educational Change: Retrenchment and Reform* (Oxford, United Kingdom: Elsevier, 2004).
10. Horace Mann Bond, *The Education of the Negro in the American Social Order* (New York: Prentice Hall, 1934).

11.	Wayne J. Urban, "Educational for All American Youth: A Failed Attempt to Extend the Comprehensive High School," in Barry M. Franklin and Gary McCulloch, eds., *The Death of the Comprehensive High School? Historical, Contemporary, and Comparative Perspectives* (New York: Palgrave Macmillan, 2007).

12.	Wayne J. Urban, Public Education and Religion: A Look at the Educational Policies Commission's *Moral and Spiritual Values in the Public Schools,* paper at the History of Education Society, Baltimore, Maryland, October 22, 2005.

13.	Wayne J. Urban, "*What's in a Name: Education and the Disadvantaged American* (1962)," paper at the International Standing Conference for the History of Education, Hamburg, Germany (July 26, 2007); *Paedagogica Historica* (January–February, 2009).

14.	For accounts of EPC history and hypotheses about its decline, see Wayne J. Urban, "The Educational Policies Commission, 1936–1968: Notes for an Autopsy," *The Sophist's Bane,* 3 (Fall, 2005): 15–30, and Urban, "Why Study the Educational Policies Commission," *Georgia Educational Researcher,* 13 (Spring, 2005), available on-line at http://coefaculty.valdosta.edu.lschmert/gera/vol3no1-GERA-Urban-specFEAT05.pdf.

15.	Wayne J. Urban, *More than Science and Sputnik: The National Defense Education Act of 1958* (Tuscaloosa: The University of Alabama Press, forthcoming, 2010).

16.	The term boy and also man or men was used by Conant in almost every discussion of higher education. It reflected the practice of the time in which higher education, especially but not only at Harvard College, was limited to males.

17.	The best sources on Conant's early years are the first chapters of his autobiography, James B. Conant, *My Several Lives: Memoirs of a Social Inventor* (New York: Harper & Row, 1970); and James G. Hershberg, *James B. Conant: Harvard to Hiroshima and the Making of the Nuclear Age* (New York: Alfred A. Knopf, 1993). The six-six plan of education that Conant followed was a nineteenth-century scheme that was superseded by the six-three-three plan which institutionalized the junior high school a decade after Conant had left school. Roxbury Latin was a preparatory school for college attendance, and Conant ranked at the top of his graduating class of 1910, scoring first in science but also quite high in tests of Latin, German, and History. Of the 21 members of his graduating class, 12 went on to Harvard and others attended Dartmouth, Amherst, Yale, and the Massachusetts Institute of Technology; Hershberg, *Conant,* 17–18.

18.	Ibid., Chs. 3 and 4.

19.	James B. Conant, *My Several Lives,* 181.

20.	Ibid., 191.

21.	Ibid., 192.

22.	Ibid., 193.

23.	Ibid., Ch. 34, "Are Private Schools Decisive?" quotation, 463.

24.	I discuss the changes in the Office of Education under Kennedy in *More than Science and Sputnik,* Ch. 6.

25.	James Bryant Conant, *The Education of American Teachers* (New York: McGraw-Hill, 1963).

4

"NO FOOD, NO DRINKS, PENCIL ONLY"

Checklists for Conducting and Interpreting Archival Research

Jordan R. Humphrey

For the last four hours, you've been sitting inside the university's archives reading through letters, notes, and diaries written by students in the 1920s. Your head is pounding, and your stomach growls, reminding you that you chose to skip lunch in order to continue working. Picking up a new folder, you begin to read another paragraph of barely legible hand-written text. Then you see it. There, scrawled in the margin of the letter, is the name "Sarah Marshall." Campus rumors of Sarah's involvement with the student government led you on this search, and you now have a piece of evidence that suggests that the rumors are true. The phrase "Ask Sarah Marshall about the meeting" implies that Sarah may have been, in fact, the first woman to sit on the traditionally all-male student governance board, and your thesis on the involvement of women in university student governance hinges on the truthfulness of this campus rumor. You realize you may have just found your historical "smoking gun."

Many of us will never experience the thrill of finding buried treasure, yet as historians we continually embark on our own form of a treasure hunt. Archival research is like a treasure hunt. An administrative memo leads to a letter from a student that then leads to a page from a faculty member's diary. The excitement that comes from following the clues that lead to the discovery of archival treasure is what brings most of us back to the archives time and time again. And many of us are drawn to the study of history because of our time spent conducting research in archives. Holding, smelling, and touching pieces of history and then using these pieces to re-create a moment in time is what drives many historians.

Archives hold the primary sources that are the hallmark of historical research and thus often serve as the principal sources of information for historians. Yet archival research can challenge even the most experienced historians. The path to finding buried treasure is not always an easy one to navigate. From the location of sources to the interpretation of evidence, archival research can be expensive, time-consuming, and frustrating. Archival research can be equally rewarding, however. Using examples from my own research, this chapter provides historians with the tools to successfully conduct archival research and then accurately interpret the sources their research uncovers.

These tools are provided in the form of checklists that researchers can use to help prepare for archival visits and maximize their efficiency during their archival research. A second checklist offers strategies for the interrogation of evidence uncovered within the archives.

PREPARING FOR YOUR VISIT TO THE ARCHIVES

My most recent research project required me to conduct archival work at Barnard College, an all-women's liberal arts college with ties to Columbia University. A colleague and I were working on a paper that explored the role of students in curricular change, and we identified two institutions—Barnard College and Harvard University—that had active student organizations involved in curricular change on campus. We divided the research work, and my colleague traveled to Cambridge to do research at Harvard while I traveled to New York City and Barnard College. Being graduate students, we had limited time and money to conduct this research so we chose to conduct our archival research during the week of our university's spring break. Such limited resources, therefore, made it imperative that we maximized our efficiency at our respective institutions. To do this, I developed a "to do" checklist for myself aimed at guaranteeing that I was prepared for and successful during my visit to the Barnard archives. Although in no way exhaustive or flawless, I offer the list below.[1]

1. Do Your Homework

Much of the work involved in archival research is done before one even travels to the archives. Aside from the identification of a topic and supporting literature, conducting research on your archival site can prevent pitfalls and frustrations during your actual on-site visit. The Internet is a great place to start your research on the archive you intend to visit.

Archives vary in size and type. Understanding the type of archive you will encounter during your trip helps reduce the possibility of surprises that may impede your research endeavors. There are generally two types of archives—public and private. Until recently, only public documents were held in public archives like the Smithsonian Museum or the Holocaust Museum, both located in Washington, D.C. This is changing, however. A number of college and university archives now maintain collections of public documents, which are in addition to their own institutional materials. The archives of Earlham College in Richmond, Indiana, house land deeds and county birth, death, and marriage records from around the country. These documents, in turn, have made the Earlham archives a Mecca for many genealogists.

Private archives, on the other hand, typically hold only personal papers, memoirs, family papers, etc. Traditionally, these are located on college and university campuses. Selected pieces of correspondence penned by Robert Frost can be found at Dartmouth College and manuscripts by William Faulkner and Thomas Jefferson's architectural drawings of Monticello can be found in the Small Special Collections Library at the University of Virginia. Some individual institutions also specialize in certain holdings. For example, the Special Collections Library at Penn State University maintains the only official holdings of the United Steelworkers of America and Bowling Green State University's Center for Archival Collections contains the National Student Affairs Archives.

Most archives offer online finding aids for their holdings. These databases catalog the specific holdings for each archive, and allow users to search through available materials before they get to the archives. Although often not exhaustive nor a complete representation of the archive's holdings, finding aids can allow you to identify the materials at each archive. Searching through these lists and then recording the call numbers of the materials you would like to use before you arrive saves both you and the archivist valuable time. Additional materials can always be pulled from the shelves of the archives during your visit, but providing advance notice of the materials you would like to see guarantees that the materials are ready and available as soon as you arrive to begin your research. I contacted the archivist at Barnard College weeks before my scheduled trip and provided her with a list of the call numbers for the materials that I wanted to examine. The boxes were waiting for me when I arrived, and I was able to begin my research as soon as I sat down. This saved me an incredible amount of time and allowed me to immediately get down to the task at hand.

Visiting an archive's webpage prior to your visit also allows you to check on the availability of the site to outside researchers. Some archives are an extension of a college or university library and therefore may not have a full staff assigned to the location. This can result in the archives being open for only limited hours during the day or on specific days of the week. Visiting scholars may also need to get special permission to use the institution's archives. Some archives are open to visitors while others require an appointment, a letter from your home institution, or other proof of your research status. The policies differ for every institution. Being aware of each archive's policies and availability helps ensure that you will be able to conduct your research when you arrive.

Data collection for my doctoral dissertation entailed conducting archival research at four different liberal arts colleges. My research agenda required spending between four and five days at each site, and my limited research budget required me to drive from State College to each location and back. Consequently, I needed to be very strategic about the time (and money) I allocated for each visit; I could not waste a moment or a dollar.

In planning for each of these four visits, I quickly discovered that each institutional archive in my dissertation maintains different hours of operations and different policies toward visiting scholars. For instance, two of the colleges—Dartmouth College and Earlham College—are open on the weekends, whereas the other two—Franklin & Marshall College and Hamilton College—are open only during weekdays. Also, the Dartmouth, Earlham, and Franklin & Marshall archives maintain visitor hours for the entire day, but the Hamilton archive is open only from 9 a.m. to 12 p.m., with hours extended by appointment only. Being aware of these differences became imperative as I scheduled my trips to each institution. Before I scheduled each trip, I contacted the archivist at each institution to confirm the archive's policy toward visiting scholars and also to confirm that the hours of operation on the archive's webpage were accurate. In two of the cases, after I contacted the college's archivist I was informed that the information I found online was incorrect; the archives were available on more days and for longer than I had anticipated. Recognizing these inaccuracies allowed me to better plan for my trip and conserve the funding I had received by packing five days of research into four days. (A word of caution—if you plan to conduct archival research at colleges and universities during the summer, it is essential that you confirm the availability of the site. A lack of students on campus and staff vacations can severely limit the availability of smaller archives.) Thus, recognizing the distinctiveness of the archives that you intend to visit will allow you to maximize your on-site time in addition to helping you avoid an unnecessary trip if the materials you need are not available or not available within the time frame in which you are working.

2. Contact the Archivist

My number one piece of advice on archival research is this: the archivist is your friend! No one knows more about the archives you are visiting than the on-site archivist. Identify the name(s) of these individuals prior to your visit and contact them as soon as you decide that you will be making a trip to their institution. First, these individuals can help you to schedule your visit. Second, the archivists can help you to locate the materials you need for your research. Providing the archivist with a general idea about the topic you are researching helps ensure that you will locate all the relevant materials within the archives. Although you, as the researcher, are largely responsible for identifying the materials for your research, the archivist can direct you to other materials that may prove to be equally significant to your topic. I never fail to be surprised by the materials that archivists bring to me once they have a better idea of the topic I am researching. On most occasions, the documents they produce are ones that I would never have identified on my own; there was no way for me to know that such documents existed. Again, a good rule to subscribe to is that no one knows more about the archives than the archivist. It is not a coincidence that the archivist is one of the most commonly thanked individuals in the works of historians.

3. Bring a Pencil, Not a Suitcase

Just like the variation in availability, different archives maintain different policies on what you can bring with you to conduct your research. Almost all archives require that you take your notes in pencil; this is to ensure that any accidental markings made on a document can be easily removed. So leave your pens at home, but be sure to bring plenty of pencils and erasers. Do not rely on your laptop. Although many of us cannot survive without our cell phones in hand and our laptops on our desks, not all archives welcome such technology. Be prepared to take notes the "old-fashioned" way. Take advantage of those technology-friendly archives, however. A mini-scanner or digital camera, in addition to your laptop, helps you to capture documents and photos that you may not otherwise be able to record. One of the best investments I have made as a historian is the purchase of a portable scanner. My scanner is small and fits nicely within my archive-friendly attaché bag. The scanner allows me to import documents directly to my computer and saves me the headache of making (or requesting) photocopies for the documents I want to take home with me.

Not all documents can be scanned, however, so you should also make yourself aware of the archive's policy on photocopying. Some archives will make photocopies on demand or will allow you to make your own photocopies, but this is always at a cost to the researcher. If photocopying is permitted, you should come prepared with plenty of quarters for the photocopiers. Other archives permit photocopying, but it is done only by and at the convenience of the archive's staff. If this is the case for the site you intend to visit, leave ample time between your visit and the time that you need the photocopied materials. I had to request that the photocopies I needed from the Barnard archives be mailed to me via an overnight service because I was working on a tight deadline and I was at the mercy of the archive's staff for my photocopies. Recognizing this policy ahead of time would have saved me a lot of headache and frustration, not to mention a few dollars of my precious research budget.

Finally, be smart about what you do and do not bring with you for your archival research. Some things you may not think about are: (1) wear layers—archives can often be chilly; (2) pack pain relievers—bringing a supply of ibuprofen, provided you are not allergic, helps to thwart the headaches that can arise from eye strain induced by long days of reading archived documents; and (3) have a protein or granola bar handy—you probably won't be able to bring this with you into the archives, but you will be happy that it is nearby when you realize you have missed lunch and you cannot find a vending machine. Ultimately, the rule "No Food, No Drinks, Pencil Only," is a good one to remember. Following this rule will ensure that you have all the materials you need (and not materials you do not need) to conduct your research.

4. Be Flexible

In conclusion, here are a few words of warning about preparing for your archival visit. Some trips will not go according to plan, so be flexible. Have a back-up plan in place in case a site falls short of your expectations and your research needs. Planning and preparation on your end does not guarantee that your archival destination will adhere to the same principle. Despite checking websites, submitting pre-visit requests for materials, and packing only what you need, even the best of intentions can still result in defeat. I offer a recent personal experience as an example of this.

I was about to begin the last leg of the research trip for my dissertation, and I had done all of the preparatory steps I recommend above. I recorded the archives' hours and visitor's policies; I confirmed and requested the materials that I believed to be part of the archives' holdings; and I exchanged numerous emails with the archivist to confirm my week-long appointment at the destination. Upon arriving at the institution's—which shall remain nameless—archives, however, it became apparent that my preparation was not going to bring the same results as it did at the previous three institutions I had visited. The archivist had forgotten my arrival date and thus had no materials ready for me to use. The archives appeared to be in complete disarray with boxes strewn throughout the small room, and the library's catalog that maintained the archive's collection was "down" for repairs for the entire week I would be visiting. With patience and time these administrative hurdles could be navigated; a lack of sources could not be, however. When the archivist began to pull the materials I had previously requested, I suddenly realized that the resources promised were not the resources provided; the primary sources that I *thought* would be in this institution's archives were not there or they were extremely limited. This trip was a bust! Thankfully, I had thought about possible substitute institutions before I started my research so I packed my bags, returned home, and began to research this new institution and its archives.

If I had failed to identify a substitute institution prior to my research trip, it is quite possible that I would have tried to make the best of the situation at the other institution and continued with my research. The fruits of this labor are questionable, however. Therefore, you should always be prepared to make a change to your research agenda. Very seldom will you need to implement this plan, but, just like the steps you have taken to prepare for your visit, having thought through alternatives helps to ensure that you can continue your research with as few interruptions as possible.

YOUR TIME IN THE ARCHIVES

In my pre-graduate student life I worked as an events planner for a liberal arts college. The mantra that helped me to succeed in my professional position is one that also helps me to maximize my efficiency when conducting archival research—(P)roper (P)reparation (P)revents (P)oor (P)erformance. Although my friends and colleagues continually mock me for subscribing to it, the five P's can make research (and life) much easier. As previously suggested, taking the time to prepare for your archival visit is almost as important as the research you want to conduct. A similar level of planning for your time in the archives can help you to avoid the pitfalls and frustrations that can often accompany archival research.

1. Hit the Ground Running

If you have taken the time to plan for your visit, then you should be prepared to hit the ground running when you arrive at the archives. Developing a plan of attack for your research helps ensure that you are prepared to begin your research. Know the specific dates, names, and types of resources you hope to examine while at the archives. If you have contacted the archivist prior to your arrival, boxes and boxes of archived materials may be waiting for you. Do not panic. Just dig right in.

2. Develop a "Triage Strategy"[2]

Develop a strategy for working your way through the archival materials. Essentially there are two methods of conducting archival research—tunneling and fishing.[3] Tunneling entails finding a run of documents—a specific set of dates, for example—and then examining the documents from beginning to end. During my research at Barnard, I found it particularly helpful to begin by examining all of the student curriculum committee notes from 1920 to 1935—my form of tunneling. When I found interesting comments or notations within a document, I made a note of it and then used the fishing method to investigate the notes I recorded. The fishing method therefore differs in that you look through different archived resources in search for materials that fit your hypothesis; it is much like throwing your fishing line into a lake to catch whatever swims up to your bait. These methods can be used independently of each other or in tandem. The key is to develop a "triage strategy" that works best for you. Every researcher eventually develops an understanding of the techniques and methods that work best for them and that fit their research skills.

If your research requires multiple visits, have a daily strategy or set specific goals for each visit. This helps to ensure that you make progress each day and that you stay on target to finish your research in the time you have allotted. Also, develop your own system of cataloging and recording information and then stick with it. A note-taking strategy that some researchers subscribe to is the "one page" rule. This unwritten rule recommends that you retype only documents that are one page (or less) in length and photocopy any document that is over the one page limit. If photocopying is permitted and fits within your research budget and time frame, copy everything you can. Traveling home with a ton of photocopied documents allows you to focus your attention on gathering materials while you are still at the archives, thus leaving the bulk of your analysis to be conducted at home. However, there is nothing worse than analyzing your documents from home and then experiencing researcher regret because you realize that there were documents you forgot or a research trail you failed to explore. Most of us have experienced this feeling. So, a little on-site analysis is warranted and can be beneficial, but do not spend the bulk of your time in the archives analyzing documents. Distance away from the materials and the strain of archival research can bring a better, more in-depth analysis of the documents. You can always schedule a return trip to the archives if you have failed to locate, record, or copy all of the materials you need.

3. Keep Your Topic in Mind, but Be Open to New Discoveries

The joys of conducting archival research often arise when you discover something unexpected—the archival diamonds in the rough. Sometimes these discoveries are not made until you are analyzing the documents at home following your visit. Other times, you locate the "smoking gun" or find the buried archival treasure while you are still on-site. This discovery can be the foundation for your thesis or can instead send you down a totally different research path. Be open to both. On the occasions when your discovery suggests a divergence from your current research agenda, follow that path, but continue to keep your topic in mind. The tangential trips we make as historians often help to create a more complete portrait of the story we are telling. Following too many paths, however, can lead to frustration and misuse of the precious time most of us have for our archival research.

I always make notes of other potential research topics on my laptop. Many of these have been uncovered during the course of my archival research, but were deferred because of their lack of a direct connection to my current research topic. For example, while conducting research on Penn State University during World War II, I discovered some newspaper articles that discussed the challenges some veterans faced upon their return to campus following their service in the war. The articles were related to my topic of the war, but I was interested more specifically in the institutional policies implemented during the course of the war. I thus made a note of the newspaper articles and the questions that the articles raised for me, and I have since returned to the questions through a qualitative study of the transition of Penn State veteran alumni after World War II. Consequently, you should not fear following a new path, but just be sure to leave plenty of bread crumbs so you can find your way back home!

ANALYZING THE FRUITS OF YOUR LABOR

You return home from your archival trip and now find yourself swimming in a sea of documents and historical evidence. The question then becomes: how do you turn your archival treasures into a sound argument or use them to recreate an historical event? Doing historical research is a lot like the old adage about making a sausage—sometimes you just do not want to know what goes into the process. Understanding the process, however, can make you a better historian. Despite the lists of recommendations provided above, locating your sources may be the easiest part of archival research. The hard part comes when you have to interrogate those sources. An advisor once told me that a person learns how to write history just by doing it. That may be true for some people, but for others a few guidelines may be helpful.

As historians, we must critically examine both the internal and external characteristics of each of our documents. Evaluating the external characteristics of each source entails asking where, when, and by whom each document was constructed. We must also ask ourselves about the authenticity of the document we are examining. Internal characteristics such as the intended meaning of the source; the accuracy of the reporting; and the positioning of the author should also be interrogated during our criticism of our sources. The process, therefore, can be complex and trying. Martha Howell and Walter Prevenier, in their book *From Reliable Sources: An Introduction to Historical Methods*, offer their own checklist to aid in the examination of primary and secondary sources.[4] I borrow four elements of Howell and Prevenier's list below and offer them as an aid as you interrogate your sources.

1. Genealogy/Originality of the Document

As historians, we first need to ask about the origin of the document we are analyzing; the originality of the document can have profound implications for the conclusions we draw from it. Is the document an original? A copy? A copy of a copy? The originality of documents can be hard to determine, however. I offer one of the sources I located at Barnard as an example of how one can test the originality of a source.

During the 1948–1949 academic year, members of the Barnard student curriculum committee developed and administered a survey that examined numerous facets of Barnard's liberal arts curriculum. I hoped that I could use the survey and its results as part of the basis for my argument about the increased technical competency and increased legitimacy of the student group. However, I first had to determine the originality of the document. As this was the only copy of the survey that survived, I had nothing to which I could compare the document. Writing scrawled in the margins of the mimeographed survey suggested that the document had undergone a number of revisions, but this same writing insinuated that the document I had was the final version of the survey. Numbers tabulated beneath each survey question also suggested that the survey was actually completed by members of the Barnard student body. To confirm this, I examined editions of the *Barnard Bulletin*, the college newspaper. One article within the *Bulletin* encouraged students to take the survey, and a second article published a few months later reported the findings of the committee's survey. Thus, from both the survey and the *Bulletin* I could establish that I was examining a copy of the original survey that was administered by the committee in 1948. In my case, I had already determined that no original was available so I knew that I had the best copy of the document available. You should always seek out the best text available, however. If the original is not available, try to locate the most "original" version.

"Placing" the document with other similar texts also aids in the authentication of the source. How does your document compare with similar texts from the same period? Are there glaring differences within the documents such as dates of the event, names of people involved, or details of the story being told? Exploring these questions helps to position your source within a broader context and allows you to determine if your source is the exception or the rule. If I aimed to address a research question about student surveys, then it would be prudent of me to analyze the 1948–1949 Barnard student survey in relation to other student surveys from the same period. Differences I may uncover could suggest something distinct about either of the two documents and may lead me to explore other documents or resources. Consequently, establishing the originality and position of your document serves to add legitimacy to the foundation upon which you build your argument.

2. Genesis of the Document

We must also always ask ourselves about the sources of our documents. Where was the source produced? Who produced it? When? Under what circumstances was the document created? Was the document written freely by the author or was it written under the coercion of someone? Asking such questions helps us to establish the genesis of the document.

I built much of the foundation for my argument on the role of students in curricular decision-making on the meeting minutes and annual reports produced by the Barnard Student Curriculum Committee that I discovered in the institution's archives. Determining the genesis of many of these was unproblematic given that most were signed, dated, and labeled. For example, the document labeled *Report of the Student Curriculum Committee of 1949* and signed by Margaret Mather, curriculum committee chair, leaves little ambiguity as to its purpose or author. I still verified both the purpose and the author with other archived documents, however. Previous annual reports submitted by the committee to Barnard's Undergraduate Association establish a precedent for the production of a yearly report. I could see that these reports actually were, as they suggested, published annually. Editions of the *Bulletin* also substantiated the information presented within the report. *Bulletin* articles reported much of the same information that was included within the committee's report. Finally, the Barnard yearbook confirmed that Margaret Mather was, in fact, a student at Barnard during the time in which the document was produced, and that she was the chair of the Student Curriculum Committee as the report insinuated.

Thus, for this document, the process of determining the genesis of the report was rather straightforward. For unsigned or undated letters, notes, or reports, identifying the source can be much more complicated. It is up to you as the researcher to become creative in the way that you determine the genesis of your source. Some details may never be uncovered. Others can just lie embedded within the lines or margins of other documents; hence the ways in which archival research can seem like a treasure hunt.

3. Authorial Authority

Questions about the genesis of a document lead to questions about the authority of the document's author. As historians, we must interrogate the voice behind the document. With what authority does the author speak? Was the author an observer or a participant? Is the account we are reading a first-, second-, or third-hand account? Is this first-hand account an accurate account of the event?

History is built upon truth *and* fallacy, and much of this is the result of the voices behind the accounts used to construct history. The proverb "History is written by the winners" suggests that the history we write can be influenced by the perspective from which our sources speak. A Saturday night in a college town illustrates my point.

Two students stumbling out of the local bar engage in a fight with another student walking down the street. Individuals inside the bar, individuals walking down the street, and individuals standing on the street corner all witness the altercation between the students. When the police arrive to investigate the fight, interviews of witnesses reveal a number of interpretations of the event. It then becomes the police officers' responsibility to determine which version of the story is the most accurate.

The job of a historian therefore is much like that of a police officer investigating a street fight. A historian must question whether the perspective offered by the document's author is an accurate (or truthful) record of the event. Not all misrepresentation of information is intentional, but we must work to unpack the truth from the fallacy— to reveal the event as it actually happened.

Historians of higher education often encounter issues of authorial authority because of the many individuals who find themselves within the walls of the ivory tower. Was the document written by a student? A faculty member? A senior administrator? Is the account of the student protest over the institution's chapel requirement as recorded within the president's memoir an accurate representation of the protest? Is a student letter to home that recounts the protest a more reliable account of the event?

Accounts of the desegregation attempts at Ole Miss (the University of Mississippi) serve as an example of the divergent perspectives that we, as historians, must question. One must ask how James Meredith's account of his days at Ole Miss differ from that of the student who tried to keep Meredith awake by bouncing a basketball in the room above Meredith's.[5] Does Mississippi Governor Ross Barnett's account of the riots on campus and subsequent federal troop invasion differ from that of the University president? From that of the rioting students? If either differs, then why? Which version is a more accurate account of what actually transpired? Our goal then is to tell history as it was observed by the winner, the loser, and the spectator from across the street.

4. Interpretation of the Document

Once you have determined the originality, genesis, and authorial authority of your sources, the art of piecing together your story follows. I use the word "art" intentionally. Your goal as a historian is to use your archived sources to create an objective rendering of the past. Assembling and ordering the facts of that argument or story to recreate the past requires a blend of both art and science. Just like the puzzles we all enjoyed as children, piecing together the past requires strategy, experience, a little luck, and even some finesse. We must first organize all the pieces of our puzzle and then find a starting and ending place for our story. Sometimes the pieces do not easily fit together, however, and you can struggle to tell a complete story. Often this is of no fault on your part, but rather just the consequence of historians' reliance on available primary and secondary sources. It then becomes a case of telling the story in the best way that you can; the story may be incomplete or lack causality. It happens.

I offer the research that I did on enrollment trends at Pennsylvania State College (now Penn State University) from 1890 to 1915 as a case in point. My intent was to use the enrollment data available from the university's archives to recreate the student body for each of the years of the study to test my hypothesis about enrollment trends at the college. I encountered a number of stumbling blocks during the course of my research, however. The first was due to the incomplete nature of the records that I used. The enrollment records from 1890 to 1905 included the names and hometowns of each student enrolled at Penn State, with names separated by class—freshmen, sophomores, juniors, and seniors. That was it. So I recorded each name and hometown and then identified the county in which each hometown was located. Using GIS software, I then plotted the enrollment density per county to create a map of Pennsylvania that showed the dispersion of enrollment throughout the Commonwealth. "Now, what?" I asked myself. I quickly realized I was stuck because I could not locate the census data that I needed to continue with the next step in my research. (The 1890 census data were lost in a fire.) I was then left with a decision—do I try to tell the story with the limited data I have or do I return to both my research questions and the archives? I chose the latter. Returning to the archives, I decided to explore another development at the college during this period—the adoption of intercollegiate football. My project then evolved into an exploration of the influence of football and the media on enrollment at Pennsylvania State College from 1890 to 1905. This was a much different story than I had previously intended to write, but the new story was significant nonetheless.

This example from my own research reflects the trials and tribulations that can result from historians' reliance upon the availability of primary sources to recreate the past. The paper that I produced lacked causality, but instead put forth a hypothesis about the influence of the emergence of intercollegiate football on enrollment trends at the College. My limited resources allowed me to go no further with my argumentation; I could only begin to tell the story of the changing enrollment at the College, and I had to accept that fact.

The primary sources I have uncovered in the course of my dissertation research have produced a very different result. At all four institutions, I have located an abundance of documentation on each institution during the war period. It has, therefore, proven much easier for me to recreate this time in history and to put the pieces of the puzzle together to tell the story of how these four institutions managed the strains produced by the nation's involvement in World War II.

CONCLUDING THOUGHTS

Archival research can be an investment of time, money, and sanity. Archival research can also be fun, exhilarating, and addictive. Perhaps all historians are a little like Sherlock Holmes or Indiana Jones. Re-creating the past requires the skills of a detective, the patience of a teacher, and the tenacity of an Olympian. Yet we are often rewarded for our efforts by the archival treasure we uncover and the stories we reveal. And every archival experience is different, thus making any standardized checklist imperfect. Developing your own checklists for your archival research allows you to feel confident about your experience and the work you produce from it.

The letters to home that extol the merriment of the 1766 Great Butter Rebellion at Harvard and the 1894 diary that recounts the previous night's fraternity initiation help re-create a time in the past that may never be replicated on campuses today. Archival research is just one step in the re-creation of history, but this research provides the building blocks needed to construct the foundation upon which each story and each argument is built.

Adequate planning before one even begins to conduct archival research can help maximize the efficiency of any scholar during their time in the archives. In addition, developing a strategy or plan of attack for your archival research can help ensure your research success. The analysis of your archival materials is then where the proverbial rubber meets the road. Interrogating the originality, genesis, and authorial authority of your documents as well as interpreting your documents helps guarantee that the story you tell is an accurate representation of the events as they occurred.

Therefore, employing a few select strategies during the preparation, implementation, and interrogation stages of your research ensures that your time conducting archival research will be successful *and* enjoyable. Once these strategies and checklists become routine, the fear and anxiety some can feel about archival research will dissipate. So, make checklists and then let your hunt for archival treasure begin!

QUESTIONS FOR DISCUSSION

1. What are the benefits and limitations of archival research as a methodology?
2. What is the relationship between archival research, qualitative research, and quantitative research?
3. Given the research strategies proposed above, how would you tackle collaborative research that uses archival methods with fellow students or faculty members?
4. How do you think technology will change or has changed the field of archival research?
5. What lingering concerns do you have about archival research?

NOTES

1. Parts of this list were adapted from research tips provided by: Barbara Heck, Elizabeth Preston, and Bill Svec, "A Survival Guide to Archival Research," (AHA Perspectives, December 2004) and AHA Committee for Graduate Students, "Some Trips and Suggestions for your Research Trips." Retrieved from http://www.historians.org/grads/ResearchTripTips.pdf.
2. AHA Committee for Graduate Students, "Some Trips and Suggestions for your Research Trips."
3. Ibid.
4. Martha Howell and Walter Prevenier, *From Reliable Sources: An Introduction to Historical Methods* (Ithaca, NY: Cornell University Press, 2001).
5. For more information read: Nadine Cohodas, *The Band Played Dixie: Race and the Liberal Conscience at Ole Miss* (New York: The Free Press, 1997).

5

THE LITERATURE REVIEW AS SCHOLARSHIP
Using Critical Reviews and Historiography

Linda Eisenmann

It may be rare for a scholarly invitation offered as flattery to result in real intellectual learning for the speaker, but I experienced such an unexpected moment a few years ago. A friend asked me to be a "virtual speaker"—that is, to join her class for an on-line "chat"—with her master's students who were studying one of my articles. My friend, who is not a historian, was guiding her class through the history of women in higher education, assigning them first the acknowledged landmark in the field, Barbara Solomon's *In the Company of Educated Women: A History of Women and Higher Education in America.*[1] Following their examination of Solomon, the students were reading my critical essay, "Reconsidering a Classic: Assessing the History of Women's Higher Education a Dozen Years after Barbara Solomon."[2] Starting from the recognition that Solomon's book had established a mid-1980s benchmark for knowledge about women's higher education, my article had reviewed the burgeoning scholarship appearing over the subsequent decade, comparing it to Solomon's study and showing where new work was extending her analysis.

The virtual chat found me sitting in my office in Boston entertaining questions from the students in Oklahoma, who, I gauged, would benefit from hearing how a "real historian" thought about her work. The discussion proceeded very smoothly, as the students asked questions about the article, including how I located my sources, how long it took me to write, how I chose the journal outlet, and how I viewed the current state of women's higher education. Relishing the role of expert, I became quite expansive in answering a question about how I came up with the idea for the article; that is, how I had decided to write a critical review of what Solomon had produced, coupled with an assessment of how the field had advanced in the dozen years following her landmark publication.

In responding, I first made sure that the students understood the import and impact of Solomon's book. Before *In the Company of Educated Women* appeared, historians looking for book-length examinations of women's movement into collegiate education had available only older, less historically sophisticated work. Thomas Woody's early compilation still serves as a significant source on both the founding of women's institutions and the growth of female enrollments, but his work was published in 1929.³ Thirty years later, Mabel Newcomer tackled the subject from a new perspective guided by the growth of women's collegiate participation and the post-World War II expansion of higher education.⁴ But no other single volume had attempted to gather and assess women's history in higher education since the post-1960s rise of the women's movement, the growth of social and feminist history, and the explosion of knowledge using those perspectives.

Solomon had spent years on her book, and I told the class some personal stories about her efforts, her approach, her ultimate pride in the work and its likely meaning for the field. This knowledge came, I explained with only a passing attempt at modesty, because I had been a student in the last class Barbara Solomon taught at Harvard before her retirement, a class offered at the very time her book was heading into print. I recalled how Solomon had graciously invited our small seminar on women's history to her home and had shared stories about her scholarly journey with our group of admiring scholars who hoped to follow in her footsteps.

At this point, I was stopped cold by a student's astounded reaction. "I can't believe you had that personal relationship with Dr. Solomon," the student typed. "You seem so mean to her in your article."⁵ Surprised by this passion, as well as the assertion, I asked the student to say more about my "meanness" in what I viewed as a scholarly, reasoned critique of what Solomon's book had accomplished.

"You were so critical," charged the student. "You picked on all the things Solomon missed and wrote an article about what should be added to the history she provided." The student was entirely accurate. I had indeed been critical, looking at the way Solomon had organized her history. She had, for instance, focused her work on women's *access* to higher education, because that was the unfinished story left over from Newcomer's 1959 work, when women were still struggling to find a place in academe. In fact, access and entrance had been the focus of most material written on women throughout the later-1960s, the 1970s, and the early-1980s, where the goal was to uncover women's stories and highlight their accomplishments in a world not very receptive to their experience.⁶ This recovery effort was important because few earlier historians had thought that adding women was either particularly necessary or likely to change basic historical contours.

Solomon, I had explained in my article, used her book to summarize and analyze what we knew about women's access, but she was not privy to the next stage of scholarship, which was offering a deeper analysis of women's *experience* and *impact* as collegiate students. I had approached my critical review by highlighting what Solomon had accomplished, and then analyzing where her approach left holes that the next generation of scholars would fill, such as more coverage of diverse populations and less-traditional college settings.

But clearly, the students on the other end of the Internet connection did not view critical review the same way I did. They saw critique as attack, and perhaps even a lack of respect for the original scholarly effort.

Even though I was not in my own classroom, I recognized a "teachable moment," and likewise acknowledged my own learning on the spot. I explained to the students that the type of critical review I had published was a significant part of the scholarly enterprise, and that all authors understand their published work as part of an ongoing intellectual conversation that is likely to challenge and change their findings. That's why peer review and publication are so important, I clarified, and so different from the personal scholarship of sharing comments in classroom discussions or submitting papers to professors. As students move through master's and doctoral work to the dissertation stage, then to their first conference presentations, and finally into the realm of published scholarship, they will begin to recognize—often with requisite twinges from rejections and negative comments—that scholarship is enhanced by public debate.

In fact, I suggested to the student who found me "mean," Barbara Solomon would not only have understood this fact, but she would have been proud that her book was the subject of a significant critical essay. It would demonstrate the importance of her analysis and its impact as a seminal work. She would understand that work on the topic would continue after her own, and would likely welcome later efforts to expand both her perspective and the direction of her analysis. It's true, I acknowledged, that every scholar secretly hopes her work will have lasting significance; who doesn't want to be the source cited in every footnote on our topic? But each of us also recognizes that scholarship grows through debate, change, and disagreement.

This experience with my friend's neophyte scholars helped me think more deeply about the nature of scholarly debate and one's responsibility to advancing the field. I have always had a penchant for writing critical reviews. Doing so helps me organize scholarship and see where new material builds on old, as well as where new work sends our understanding in different directions. My propensity to examine scholarship in this way probably means that I am a "lumper" rather than a "splitter."[7] This dichotomy in analytical approaches suggests that some people look for patterns in material, privileging similarity over difference. "Lumper" historians, for instance, would recognize that arguments, analysis, and evidence are different across scholarship, but they would highlight the themes and the streams of development among a set of works on the same topic. Solomon's history "lumped," for example, by following the theme of access across the rise of female academies, the opening of the first women's colleges, and the granting of early Ph.D.s to American women. Similarly, her focus on financial aid for women, which had not been much studied, furthered the idea of access by demonstrating how financial and familial support was critical to women's collegiate opportunities.

A historical "splitter," by contrast, might emphasize the varied movement into higher education by women in different racial, socioeconomic, religious, and geographic groups. As Solomon shows, African American women had many fewer collegiate opportunities than White females, and their early colleges more often resembled advanced high schools. Likewise, women in the American Northeast encountered considerable numbers of female-only institutions which had been created to keep women outside the already-established men's colleges. Yet, as settlement moved westward, coeducational and public schools became much more common because of their efficiency and lower cost. These individual cases are the work of "splitters." *In the Company of Educated Women* actually covers both approaches, or better said, both lumpers and splitters can find evidence for their thinking in Solomon's book.

My subsequent review attempted to categorize the state of historiography at the time Solomon wrote and then again as it leapt forward with the growth of scholarship on women's educational history. I would argue that such critical reviews, in their attempts to take the pulse of a field, are important historiographic benchmarks for both experienced and new scholars.

Historiography has come to encompass many meanings, including the way we write history. This aspect concentrates on the methods we use, the sources we explicate, and the theories we depend on. Thus, in women's educational history, the use of a feminist or a postmodern perspective could direct historiography in a certain way. Historiography can have a simpler meaning as well, referring to the body of work focused on a particular topic, traced over time. This is the sort of historiography Solomon used, as she outlined and organized the changes in women's collegiate history era by era. The historiography of my critical review took Solomon's work one step further by organizing the themes in her chronological explication, noting which items were bolstered by copious evidence and which areas remained underdeveloped.

At this point, any student or scholar who has written a literature review might be wondering what the difference is between their exercise and the historiography I am discussing. After all, every doctoral student is required to gather and review the literature in her or his field, and most dissertations contain the obligatory Chapter 2 which walks through what others have said about the topic. Traditional journal articles likewise contain a literature review section with an admittedly smaller sweep that focuses on previous scholarship, and which serves as the base for the evidence being presented.

But too often, a literature review turns into a pro forma exercise, a dutiful recounting of what others have said about our topic. Further, when it is seen mainly as a way to establish our own credentials, writing a literature review can be loaded with temptations. Some scholars, for instance, cannot resist the lure of padding the long reference list or that first summarize-the-field footnote. Others, especially new scholars, let the literature review roam too far beyond what is needed, sending the scholar and the reader in too many imprecise directions. Worse yet, the new scholar may become overwhelmed with the amount of extant writing on the topic, provoking the sense that there is no new approach or no creative application still available in the field.

The best reviews of literature go beyond these pitfalls. When I advise doctoral students at the start of their work, I always recommend that they search for a good literature review or critical essay by an established scholar. The literature review can become scholarship in the hands of an expert. Before spending countless hours reading whatever they can find on their topic, students can be helped by seeing how an experienced scholar has already examined and categorized the field, analyzed its changing contours, challenged the existing approaches, and offered new directions. My advice boils down to this: look for the lumpers and then see where you can be a splitter. That is, use the work others have done to categorize and analyze your field, and then choose a particular place where your own scholarship can contribute and thrive.

Like most historians of education, I have pursued a few different strands of inquiry over time. Much of my work has examined women's experience in education, especially at the collegiate level. I have written about the role of a women's coordinate college nestled uncomfortably within a more-established men's university. I have explored the growth of women as faculty members, dealing with the challenges of a professionalizing field. I have examined how post-World War II philanthropy made halting attempts to support women's issues. Some of my work explores subjects outside women's concerns, including how market forces affected the growth of teacher education in one state and how religion has had a much greater impact on higher education than extant histories tend to recognize.

But one strand of my writing has always returned to historiography: surveying a field, assessing its strengths, analyzing its changes, and commenting on its present and future directions. My mind seems to need to turn that basic inquiry—which every good scholar conducts at some stage of research—into public analysis that becomes part of the formal scholarly debate. I'd like to think that this propensity makes me a good critical reader rather than the "mean scholar" described by the Oklahoma student.

The critical review of Barbara Solomon's book was my first significant effort at public historiography, and it was prompted by talking with other scholars about how they were using Solomon's work in their teaching. Finally having available such a good summary of the field should, I suspected, have an impact on how we teach the history of education. I invited a group of historians of higher education onto a conference panel to explore how we used Solomon's book in our classrooms, including what we found especially useful and what seemed to be missing. The panel was well attended, provoking spirited discussion with the audience.[8]

Intrigued by the ideas we generated, I asked my fellow panelists if we might turn our discussion into an article that would reach a wider audience. No one else expressed energy for the task, but each encouraged me to do so. Thus, the first part of my critical review acknowledges and explores our joint thinking about the impact and uses of Solomon's book. The second half of the article, where I take intellectual risks in suggesting where our field is going and where it might grow, came at the prompting of the journal editors. They liked my original article, but for their generalist readers, wanted me to go further in assessing the field and prompting new directions. They were inviting me to take on the role of expert, which I did, with some nervousness at claiming such public authority.

I didn't quite recognize my growing propensity for historiography until somewhat later, after I had spent several years as a lexicographer of sorts. I was invited by Greenwood Press to create a *Historical Dictionary of Women's Education in the United States*, and the editors generously allowed me to shape the scope, detail, and contents of the book.[9] For a lumper like me, this was an ideal opportunity. I spent time once again reviewing the literature, trying to choose about 250 representative terms—individuals, institutions, events, concepts—that would convey the history of women's education as experienced by American women over time. The individual entries in the volume would be the work of splitters, but my lumper persona would need to fit it all together.

After honing the list and reading the submissions of 100 different authors, I worked to portray the larger picture. First, I created a timeline of women's educational history, using this visual task to highlight patterns. Then, I used the book's introduction to organize my thinking, and opened with a summary statement: "The story of women's education in the United States is a continuous effort to move from the periphery to the mainstream in both formal institutions and informal opportunities."[10] In other words, looking at the individual entries and seeing their relationships across the timeline showed me how women had initially searched for education wherever they could find it: in colonial dame schools for early literacy; in early academies that helped prepare them for teaching; in women's groups that supported their non-formal learning. Only eventually, slowly, and sometimes grudgingly, were women welcomed into established centers of education. The *Dictionary*'s introduction allowed me to trace the themes chronologically, as well as to comment on the way we historians had built our historical understanding about women.

Two years after the *Dictionary* appeared, I was invited to give a keynote presentation to the British History of Education Society, on a topic of my choice. The knowledge gained from completing the *Dictionary* was still bouncing around in my mind, but I

-wasn't quite sure I had yet formalized everything I had learned. I asked myself whether, having had the chance to work with dozens of scholars, I might be in an ideal position to say more than the timeline and the ten-page introduction had offered. If I applied a more systematic historiographical lens—especially one that recognized the United States as its own subject—perhaps I could provide a deeper assessment of women's educational development.

For my presentation to the British Society, I first re-read all the entries in the *Dictionary*, looking for patterns. I created a concordance, keeping track whenever one entry appeared somewhere else in the book. From that review, one tidbit struck me: the term "suffrage" appeared most frequently, in nearly one-fifth of the entries. Speculating on what this might mean, I first worried that I had overrepresented the suffrage period; certainly, the Progressive Era with its public advances for women traditionally attracts a large share of historians' attention. Or, perhaps historians have privileged the suffrage movement because it presented such a moment of celebration for women. Looking more deeply, I realized that the frequent appearance of the term likely came because work on women's suffrage extended for decades before and after the actual ratification of the Nineteenth Amendment in 1920. For instance, the 1848 Declaration of Rights for Women spoke about the need for women's suffrage seventy years before; after the amendment passed, women's use of their vote remained a continuing concern for decades.

In considering what the power of the suffrage movement might mean for women's history, I recognized how the cause had banded women (and their male advocates) together. They had formed groups, built networks, created organizations, and raised money, all in the effort to secure full voting rights for women and to enhance their civic participation. I began to notice the appearance of those same methods across the whole array of women's work in education. That is, in the particulars of various non-suffrage stories, I could see women forming groups, creating networks, building organizations, and raising money. Taking a further step back, I began to identify four frameworks that helped explain, or at least organize, women's educational efforts: religion, money, networking, and institution-building. My lumper self was again at work.

In the article I published from that keynote talk, I developed my thinking about the four frameworks, showing how they help us understand women's educational history.[11] Although I analyzed all four frameworks, I argued that institution-building was ultimately the most potent.

Religion, I contended, has played a surprisingly significant role in women's education. Early advocates like Catherine Beecher and Emma Willard were the first to put together the need for teachers with women's ability to instill values in the young. In their analysis, early-nineteenth century society needed "Christian female teachers" to extend the country's mission, yet women would need formal schooling to do the job well.[12] Similarly, at the college level, religion animated the creation of nearly every college before the mid-nineteenth century; even afterwards, students' religious background influenced their ability to attend institutions of their choice. Catholic families, for instance, were slower to see the need for their daughters to pursue advanced education, retarding participation for Catholic women until well into the twentieth century.

Money—or, more precisely, the need to secure it—also focused women's educational efforts over time. Without financial independence, women were consigned to inadequate schooling, or they advanced only at the sufferance of institutions that were already established. The nineteenth-century Seven Sisters women's colleges, for instance, grew into significant centers for women because their financial security was assured by generous donors committed to women's education.

Networks cohered women's efforts in everything from creating kindergartens to establishing parent–teacher organizations to organizing philanthropy. I explored the examples of the abolitionist movement and the college settlement movement to show how women used similar methods across different causes.

Each of these frameworks characterized a great deal of women's educational effort over time. But the fourth framework—institution-building—exerted the greatest impact. I examined how women built institutions for three reasons: to provide the basics of education, to support women's career needs, and to advance social reform agendas. They worked together on all sorts of goals, using their networks, raising money, and organizing around their religious concerns. But only after they successfully reified their work into tangible institutions did women firmly establish their place in education. Physical buildings, including female academies, normal schools, and women's colleges demonstrated women's seriousness, as did organizations like the American Association of University Women and the National College Equal Suffrage League. When the institutions took actual form, the networking and financing of women advocates were formalized and strengthened. Overall, the article took the *Dictionary's* theme—women moving from margins to mainstream—and argued that the creation of formal institutions marked and established their advances.

Both my critical review of Solomon's book and my article analyzing the educational frameworks had wide chronological scope. Since Solomon presented 300 years of women's efforts at higher learning, my review likewise covered that sweep. The *Dictionary* covered an equally long chronology, adding layers of informal education (the Girl Scouts, the League of Women Voters) and other levels of schooling (kindergartens, dame schools) to the study of higher education. Although such reviews obviously carry a challenge in covering so much material, the very sweep obviated me from claiming expertise in each and every area. My next major historiographic effort would use a far narrower lens, and it came in a field where I was, indeed, trying to establish myself as a specialist.

In 2006, I published my first major book, *Higher Education for Women in Postwar America, 1945–1965.*[13] I had been working on the project for many years, watching it morph over time from a thoughtful but bounded study of Radcliffe College's Bunting Institute (a major research center for women established in 1960) to a wide-ranging examination of post-World War II colleges, associations, policy-making bodies, and research efforts.

The impetus for the book came from my five years' experience as assistant director of the Bunting Institute in the early-1990s. The Institute was a fabulous place with a wonderful history. It was the brainchild of Mary Ingraham Bunting, who started the Institute almost immediately upon becoming president of Radcliffe College in 1960. A women's advocate in a non-feminist era, Bunting understood (from personal experience and professional commitment) the challenges facing highly-educated women in the academic world. Her Institute provided a Harvard affiliation, office space, and a stipend to women with doctorates whose academic or professional careers had been stalled because of family or other responsibilities. Bunting hoped the year at Harvard/Radcliffe would reinvigorate their careers by providing time for work, establishing networks, enhancing scholarly visibility, and boosting personal confidence.

By the time I worked at the Institute, thirty-five annual groups of "fellows" had experienced this generous opportunity; thus, our institutional archives contained records on hundreds of women—including their original applications, their published work, their self-reflections, and their participation in several Institute studies. My initial plan was to apply an updated historical lens to the Bunting history, as well as to figure out how a program started before the new women's movement had managed to stay attuned to women's needs across several decades.

After a few years of writing and publishing about the Institute, I began to widen my range of inquiry. I saw that it wasn't enough just to investigate the Bunting Institute; I had to explore it contextually. What had been happening in traditional higher education that would help me understand the Institute's place? Since Mary Bunting was not alone in her work on women, what did other "pre-feminist" efforts tell us about the postwar status of women's issues? And, since higher education never develops in a vacuum, how did the larger postwar environment affect colleges and the adults who attended them?

I decided that the book needed to be much bigger, and decided to include three aspects related to postwar women. First would be my initial focus: the educational programs—like the Bunting Institute—created to influence women's collegiate and professional opportunities. A second focus would examine the era's research about women that provided a knowledge base for the programs. And third would be the policy-making bodies and practitioner organizations that used the research and supported women's advances. The story of the Bunting Institute would become a much smaller component in a wide-ranging look at postwar women.

Historians of women had tended to ignore, or perhaps not even notice, the attention to women by researchers, policymakers, and educators throughout the postwar period. Because advocacy for women looked so different and so much less bold than what would come after the mid-1960s, many historians overlooked the era's quieter advances, inquiry, and efforts on behalf of women.

Imagine my surprise, then, in finding acclamation about the depth of postwar women's research from one of Mary Bunting's colleagues. Esther Raushenbush, president of Sarah Lawrence College and a contributor to John F. Kennedy's President's Commission on the Status of Women, had hailed work of the era. "There was an explosion of interest, attention, and research about women in the 1950s—their role in society, their education, their personal dissatisfactions," she claimed.[14] Clearly, I needed to learn more about this "explosion" and how it affected the contours of women's lives and education.

The blessing of a sabbatical gave me a year to read and pull together what I was learning, not only about higher education, but the postwar period in general. I regularly and repeatedly "lumped" my findings, filling folders with "bibliographic essays," "historiographical thoughts," and "ideas for writing." At some point during the sabbatical, I realized that the first part of my expanding book needed to be a critical review of the literature. My months of searching were showing me how scattered the literature was. New work was beginning to extend our understanding of postwar higher education, but little of it included women. At the same time, work was expanding on women in the larger society, but none of it deeply explored education. And, no historian had yet put the two together.

Part of my decision to recraft the book could be considered altruistic. Certainly, I could save other scholars the time I had spent gathering, assessing, and organizing so much material. Another part of the decision was the sound scholarly recognition that readers deserve to know the context for the arguments one is making. But I also began to realize that in the field of postwar women's higher education, there was no established base of knowledge, no agreed-upon framework, and no standard analysis of women's efforts and accomplishments. By using the first part of the book to offer such an analysis, I would be laying claim to an original interpretation.

However, offering the initial interpretation in a field has its dangers. I thought back to my discussion with the Oklahoma students where I argued that scholarship grows through public debate, and that all scholars must be willing to have their work critiqued and even overturned. Here was my chance—and my challenge—to practice what I had preached.

I decided to divide the critical review into two chapters. The first would summarize and analyze the growing literature on postwar women generally, and the second would look more specifically at developments in higher education. The postwar period has suffered from our easy assumptions about its limitations and constraints, as well as a mistaken thought that the whole period prior to the radical late-1960s was identical. Until more recent scholarship began to problematize the era, it was tempting to assume that television depictions like "Father Knows Best" (now perhaps better symbolized by "Mad Men") were representative portrayals of postwar family life and gender relationships.[15] As I reviewed the growing evidence from more substantive literature, I recognized that postwar women had, themselves, been subject to some of these expectations, even if they didn't always fulfill them.

I organized the material into what I called four "ideologies" that characterized women's postwar milieu: patriotic, economic, cultural, and psychological. Each of these terms characterized advice given, measures applied, and ideals flouted by women. The patriotic ideology, for instance, asked women to heed the good of the country, as they had during the war. Women should defend "the home front," and if that meant ceding wartime jobs so that returning veterans could enter the work force, women should respond patriotically. The economic ideology pushed women to see their role as financial helpers in the family, rather than permanent or primary wage earners. If workplace policies subsequently developed that disadvantaged women, they must understand their secondary place. Culturally, women were validated as wives and mothers. If they contributed outside the home, it was best done as volunteers in schools or civic clubs. The psychological ideology followed the tenets of Freudianism, focusing on women's reproductive role and presumed limited sexuality.

In each of the four areas, many postwar women actively resisted the ideologies or subtly worked around them. Just as historians discovered that nineteenth-century prescriptive literature about "woman's proper sphere" was more rhetoric than practice, postwar women, too, grew in ways outside the ideologies.[16] The Kinsey reports, for example, showed that nearly one-half of American women admitted having premarital sexual intercourse during an era that considered such behavior unacceptable and even unimaginable.[17] Likewise, many women succeeded professionally in an era that did not welcome or support their long-term career efforts. And most of the ideologies were directed at White, middle-class women in the postwar period; poorer women and women of color were either ignored in societal thinking or lacked the choices proffered to their middle-class counterparts.

The ideologies allowed me to organize material about postwar women. And, by declaring them "ideologies," I was arguing for the power of these viewpoints in people's lives, even when they might not believe or accept the strictures. In highlighting the areas of patriotism, economy, culture, and psychology, I was suggesting an interpretation of how women's beliefs and efforts were channeled during the period.

My second chapter reviewed the historiography of postwar higher education. I began to think of women as the era's "incidental students" because my examination showed how rarely they were considered in decisions about educational policy or practice, even though they regularly constituted nearly one-third of the student body. The impact of the G.I. Bill, along with the rise of the research university, overshadowed women's increasing movement into postsecondary education. They were marginalized both as students and as faculty. I traced the few researchers who had studied women, either as "economic utilitarians" supporting women's presence in the job pipeline, as "cultural conformists" who spoke for adapting curriculum to women's presumed roles, or as "equity based planners" who argued for expanded opportunities.

In many ways, these two opening chapters do not match the rest of the book. They are wide-ranging reviews of the literature that contain no original scholarship on archival sources. However, my subsequent two sections do present that type of scholarship, digging deeply into particular aspects of postwar women's efforts. The middle chapters, for instance, discuss the early research captured by the Commission on the Education of Women of the American Council on Education, the approach to advocacy practiced by women's groups (especially the American Association of University Women and the National Association of Women Deans and Counselors), and the early policy formulations of Kennedy's President's Commission on the Status of Women. Part III returns to the original idea for the book, examining the Bunting Institute alongside several other programs addressing the needs of non-traditional female scholars and students.

I believe the book works as a whole because there is solid original research to support the interpretation offered in the opening chapters. But in many ways, this book's literature review was more challenging to write than my earlier critical essays. Because the previous pieces surveyed such a wide sweep, I could be excused for not being expert in many of them. But by focusing on an era and a topic where I was producing original research, I faced the tougher scholarly challenge of claiming expertise. Because no one had yet written a volume specifically on women in postwar American higher education, I took the plunge of offering the first interpretation.

Several years later, as scholars and teachers use the book, my task now is to handle scholarly critique with the grace I expected of Barbara Solomon. Viewing Solomon's work with professional distance, I imagined her ability to weigh my review with equal scholarly detachment, admitting where she might have done more or said something differently. After all, a good review can explicitly encourage scholars to pursue a particular direction or fill certain holes. For instance, Solomon's relative lack of attention to philanthropy opened the way for new work showing how foundations affect educational developments.[18] Her brief mentions of the normal schools and academies encouraged new work exploring their importance for women.[19] Likewise, my interpretation of the postwar era should prompt the next scholars to test the staying power of the ideologies or counter the notion of women as "incidental students." Perhaps the next analyses will find better examples than the Bunting Institute to make a claim for compensatory efforts. Or, perhaps my reading of the President's Commission on the Status of Women as ignoring the real potential of educational change will be proven wrong.

If so, I should be pleased. If any historiographic analysis is meant to be challenged—if it is indeed a sort of planned scholarly obsolescence—I should welcome challenges to my interpretation and be ready to dig deeper into the data. Nevertheless, it's always nice to be in the footnotes.

QUESTIONS FOR DISCUSSION

1. If historians can be categorized as either "lumpers" or "splitters," is one approach more useful to the field than the other? Does identifying as either a "lumper" or a "splitter" determine one's own scholarly questions?
2. How does a literature review become an act of scholarship? Is it possible for a student's literature review to be such scholarship, or can only an established scholar produce one? Could both "lumpers" and "splitters" write successful literature reviews?
3. How can a scholar avoid "critique as attack"? That is, how does a scholar (including a student) provide critical analysis and remain respectful?
4. In considering the ideologies surrounding postwar women's behavior, how does a historian distinguish rhetoric about women's role from women's actual practice? What sort of material would allow a historian to make this distinction?
5. Are the four frameworks for understanding women's educational history—religion, money, networking, and institution-building—potent analytical tools? Should any of them be omitted or replaced with another framework?

NOTES

1. Barbara Miller Solomon, *In the Company of Educated Women: A History of Women and Higher Education in America* (New Haven: Yale University Press, 1985).
2. Linda Eisenmann, "Reconsidering a Classic: Assessing the History of Women's Higher Education a Dozen Years after Barbara Solomon," *Harvard Educational Review*, vol. 67 (Winter 1997): 689–717.
3. Thomas Woody, *A History of Women's Education in the United States* (New York, NY, and Lancaster, PA: Science Press, 1929).
4. Mabel Newcomer, *A Century of Higher Education for American Women* (New York: Harper, 1959).
5. I have paraphrased the student's comment, but only slightly.
6. See, for example, Gerda Lerner, *The Majority Finds its Past: Placing Women in History* (New York: Oxford University Press, 1979).
7. The notion of "lumpers" and "splitters" has offered a handy way to explore two varying analytical perspectives. The dichotomy was popularized in Isaiah Berlin, *The Hedgehog and the Fox: An Essay on Tolstoy's View of History* (London: Weidenfeld and Nicolson, 1953).
8. The panel was "Ten Years after a Classic: Historical Research and Teaching on Women's Higher Education a Decade after Barbara Solomon," annual meeting of the American Educational Research Association, San Francisco, April 1995. The other contributors were Carolyn Terry Bashaw, Geraldine Joncich Clifford, Patricia Palmieri, Linda Perkins, Sally Schwager, and Mary Ann Dzuback.
9. Linda Eisenmann, *Historical Dictionary of Women's Education in the United States* (Westport, CT: Greenwood Press, 1998).
10. Ibid., p. xi.
11. Linda Eisenmann, "Creating a Framework for Interpreting U.S. Women's Educational History: Lessons from Historical Lexicography," *History of Education*, vol. 30 (5), 2001: 453–470.
12. Beecher extols the need for "Christian female teachers" in "The Evils Suffered by American Women and American Children: The Causes and the Remedy," reprinted in Nancy Hoffman, ed., *Woman's "True" Profession: Voices from the History of Teaching* (Old Westbury, NY: The Feminist Press, 1981), p. 51.
13. Linda Eisenmann, *Higher Education for Women in Postwar America 1945–1965* (Baltimore: Johns Hopkins University Press, 2006).

14. Esther Raushenbush, *Occasional Papers on Education* (Bronxville, NY: Sarah Lawrence College, 1979), p. 407.

15. "Mad Men" is a television drama series, premiering on the AMC network in 2007, depicting the early-1960s work and home lives of workers at a Madison Avenue advertising firm. It explores the gendered relationships and limitations facing both the male and female characters.

16. An early discussion of "woman's proper sphere" appeared in Nancy F. Cott, *The Bonds of Womanhood: "Woman's Sphere" in New England, 1780–1835* (New Haven: Yale University Press, 1977). Since then, considerable scholarship has explored women's use of and resistance to that sphere.

17. Alfred C. Kinsey, Walter Pomeroy, and C.E. Martin, *Sexual Behavior in the Human Male* (Philadelphia: Saunders, 1948) and Kinsey and Staff of the Institute for Sex Research, *Sexual Behavior in the Human Female* (Philadelphia: Saunders, 1953).

18. See, for instance, Andrea Walton, ed., *Women and Philanthropy in Education* (Bloomington: Indiana University Press, 2005).

19. See, for example, Christine A. Ogren, *The American State Normal School: An Instrument of Great Good* (New York: Palgrave Macmillan, 2005), and Nancy Beadie and Kim Tolley, eds., *Chartered Schools: Two Hundred Years of Independent Academies in the United States* (New York: Routledge Falmer, 2002).

Section II
Using a New Historical Lens

6

HORIZONTAL HISTORY AND HIGHER EDUCATION

John R. Thelin

"True Confessions" is hardly a term one associates with serious scholarship. But it is time I owned up to the undeniable fact I've had a love affair with the American college and university campus for over a half century. This syndrome has given my research an energy and passion that makes archival exploration and writing continually exciting. However, even I have had to admit that love is blind. My preoccupation with the campus, ranging from its physical beauty to its enduring and endearing histories, prevented me from seeing that the magnificent colleges and universities are not isolated institutions. My belated insight has prompted me during the past fifteen years to observe and appreciate another, often under-appreciated, part of the story of higher education. I call this added dimension "Horizontal History" and use it to look at American higher education by analyzing the complex array of organizations that cut across the educational landscape both to provide services and impose constraints on colleges and universities. I hope this will assist higher education scholars and participants to leaven the conventional way we tend to read and write—and, hence, think and conceptualize—about the history of American higher education. Most observers are subject to a peculiar stigmatism in which vision is focused first and foremost on *vertical* institutions; namely, the monumental campuses of colleges and universities. The danger of this preoccupation is that it overlooks the more complete ecology of higher education that includes the roles of foundations, consortia, associations, accrediting bodies, state bureaus, and federal agencies, which have contributed funding, incentives, and regulations to the American campus. This chapter does not represent a "world turned upside down"—but it requires at least a 90 degree tilt to look at the integral roles that horizontal institutions have played in the ways that colleges and universities work.

THE ROOTS AND BRANCHES OF AMERICAN HIGHER EDUCATION

Colleges and universities are, of course, the remarkable steeples that dot the landscape of American higher education. This is both a literal and symbolic dimension, as architecture has long been impressive and important in American life, whether in the

18th century or the 21st century. In standing tall, the bricks and mortar (and stonework and reinforced concrete) of more than 3,000 colleges and universities are the vertical monuments and workplaces whose success has made higher education in the United States the envy of the world. Little wonder, then, that they shape the dominant institutional imagery of our national commitment to academic pursuits and advanced learning.

Less obvious but essential is that the prototypical American campus has historically relied on a network of related organizations and institutions which are less visible because they cut horizontally—often low to the ground or even below the surface, out of public vision. The roots of "horizontal institutions" run deep in American higher education in part because of a tradition of institutional autonomy and decentralization, best characterized by the absence of a central federal ministry of education. To fill this void, colleges and universities have long depended on a fluid network of philanthropies and voluntary associations to carry out the primary goals of teaching, research, and service. The perspective of "horizontal history" is attractive because it places colleges and universities into the context of the broad, distinctive nonprofit sector—a phenomenon well established in the United States that is virtually absent from other nations worldwide. Second, "horizontal histories" are metaphorically the networks and synapses by which individual institutions are joined, providing multiple connections in which the collective cooperation contributes to each campus's distinctive definition of self-promotion and self-protection.

An important corollary is that the concept of "horizontal history" is also useful for providing a continual reminder that colleges and universities compete with a variety of other societal institutions and organizations for voluntary support. Hospitals, art museums, insane asylums, orphanages, schools for the deaf, schools for the blind, symphonies, and performing arts groups all have been claimants for philanthropic resources from individuals and foundations since the colonial era. And over time, new kinds of nonprofit activities have surfaced to join with colleges in appeals to donors. Hence, tracking the horizontal history shows the strength or weakness of higher education's stature at any given time.[1]

The essential characteristics that have shaped higher education's "horizontal history" in the United States are two-fold: first, the generosity of Americans in providing financial support for a variety of social and educational causes; second, an American penchant to be joiners, to form voluntary associations for numerous activities and for a variety of motives. Throughout this chapter, I shall refer to these cardinal principles. First, however, it is important to acknowledge legacies of philanthropy and voluntary support from European roots dating back to the late medieval period and the Renaissance.

GETTING AND SPENDING AND SAVING: SOME LEGACIES FROM THE CONTINENT AND ENGLAND

"Horizontal history" as part of institutionalized philanthropy in the United States draws from historic roots in Western European Civilization. In the Renaissance Italy of the 15th and 16th centuries, the commercial innovation of double entry bookkeeping allowed merchants to keep an eye on the accuracy of income and expenditures. This attention to enterprise also provides traces of the deep roots of charity as part of

Western European capitalism. Historians, for example, in looking through financial ledgers and journals noted the recurrence of the entry, "Domini Deo" marbled into receipts for purchases of lumber, olive oil, and spices. "Domini Deo" was no typical durable good—it meant "Given to God" and signaled that profit-minded merchants also placed high priority on their debt and responsibility to provide for charities.

Early in the 19th century the French bureaucrat Alexis de Tocqueville emphasized the generosity of Americans in their voluntary support of numerous social services. De Tocqueville's official charge was to survey prisons across the young United States—but, in fact, he also observed and analyzed a diverse array of philanthropic and charitable initiatives to support all kinds of innovations—illustrative of an American impulse for innovation, a belief that societal problems could be solved, and that private initiatives rather than government agencies often were the preferred medium.

This cultural strand of generosity in the American character was a local synthesis that drew from a formal legacy from England. The endowments of educational groups enjoyed historic sanctity and protection. Indeed, central to and distinctive of the English heritage was statutory endorsement of the notion of *perpetual endowments* plus, often, the added benefit of exemption from royal taxation. This provision is sufficiently pervasive today in the United States that the danger is that it is taken for granted as an assumption and universal practice. In fact, these privileges of private endowments were deliberate, not accidental. And the statutory provisions of the English crown were not necessarily followed elsewhere.

If, for example, in the infant United States of America its leaders had looked to France rather than England in drafting essential laws, the legal environment for philanthropic organizations would have been wholly different. This conjecture is not far-fetched, given the influence and attraction "Les Philosophes" had on and for such Americans as Thomas Jefferson and Benjamin Franklin, both in their vicarious readings and in their memorable, albeit often hedonistic, assignments to Paris. Most important was that the 18th-century French minister of finance, Turgot, pursued a campaign for modernization and industrialization of the national economy which relied heavily on prohibiting perpetual endowments along with their tax exemptions. This was a high stakes policy deliberation. In France, allowing monastic orders as well as academic institutions to build endowments for perpetuity was depicted as a government license to hoard large sums of capital which would better serve the nation if invested in the national economy. Hence, endowments were confined by law to a life span of five years.[2]

In England, the prevailing logic was that endowments were sacrosanct for several reasons: first, respect for the private property of selected institutions—such as the colleges that comprised Oxford and Cambridge Universities as well as various clerical and monastic orders. Whatever benefits England and the British Empire gained from such largesse, it also extracted a price. The best example of this was in Henry VIII's heroic dispute with the Church of Rome. Most attention usually goes to his anger and impatience with the Roman Catholic Church's restrictions on divorce. Yet not far behind was his long-festering complaint that the Church and its various monastic and clerical orders maintained a tax-exempt stronghold on large parcels of real estate along with lucrative endowments. The trade-off, perhaps, was that it was the Church and its administrative unit of "the parish" that became the major provider of charitable services to the nation's poor and indigent. In other words, strong measures to enhance and exempt the private sector served as a proxy or alternative for the Crown to be obligated to use tax monies to fund and administer what we currently consider local social services.

On balance, Mother England carried the day with her errant American colonial children, which not accidentally included the powerful region proudly known as "New England." Not only was this Anglo-Saxon philosophy and legal precedent of perpetual and protected endowments transferred to the American colonies, it was reaffirmed and strengthened in judicial decisions following the creation of a new nation, the young United States of America. A landmark case was the *Dartmouth College v. Woodward* decision rendered by Chief Justice John Marshall in 1819. This Supreme Court decision is usually hailed as important for the history of American higher education because it allegedly protected the sanctity of college charters. However, less obvious and less celebrated is that it also was a magna carta for nonprofit and philanthropic organizations in the United States. Its crucial, defining element was *not* exclusively "the college." Rather, it referred to the broader category of *eleemosynary* institutions—of which, so the Justices argued with some legerdemain, colleges were defined as "charitable foundations." A more accurate depiction would have been to say that colleges were part of the philanthropic orbit in that they simultaneously gave *and* received charitable services. These mixed roles often became a source of confusion and even conflicts of interest in colleges' and universities' relationships with the public—and with government agencies.

FROM INDIVIDUALS TO INSTITUTIONS

Perhaps the most crucial juncture in the horizontal history of American higher education has been the transformation of individual activism into systematic, formal, and enduring philanthropy. In other words, it is the legal, economic, social, and historical process whereby individual generosity and priorities become institutionalized. One reason this transformation was significant was the observation and complaint by many leaders in American society that a dependence on scattered individual donations tended to fritter resources, to be spasmodic, transient, and uncoordinated. It was a testimony to American individualism and the right to use one's discretionary dollars and time to support (or not support) one's favorite educational or charitable entity or service. That was off-set by its uncertainty and inefficiency. So the incentive to create horizontal associations was to provide a setting for "commonwealth" and a vehicle by which decisions about priorities and goals could be constructed and then harnessed.

One recurrent characteristic of "horizontal history" is that it allowed philanthropists the effective option to pursue broad goals as distinguished from being confined exclusively to building and funding "vertical" institutions. This meant, for example, that an organization could solicit donations to provide annual scholarships for students across the region or nation, regardless of the college they attended. In other words, the scholarship foundation was not tied to a single college, but allowed financial aid portability so long as students honored the pledge of professional service. Or, another variation was that a foundation could be created whose broad goal was to support some specific field such as engineering or agriculture at many colleges, as distinguished from focusing on facilities programs at a single campus.

FOUNDATIONS AND FOCUSED FINANCIAL AID

An excellent early example of the power of a "horizontal" organization to influence both colleges and the subsequent contributions of college alumni is the American Educational Society (AES). The scope of these scholarship programs sponsored by the AES and other religious organizations in the 19th century were both substantial and exceptional. Historians David Allmendinger (1975), Helen Horowitz (1987) and Rupert Wilkinson (2005) estimated that in the early 19th century at Yale along with the newer Hilltop Colleges of New England (Williams, Amherst, Dartmouth, and Bowdoin) as many as 25% to 30% of their students received AES financial aid.[3] Wilkinson (2005) noted that by 1838, about 1,100 students—roughly 15%—of undergraduates in New England colleges were AES scholarship beneficiaries.[4] Thanks to the well-funded and deliberate program provided by the AES, numerous alumni of Protestant liberal arts colleges who had pledged to serve as Congregationalist missionaries carried out their lifelong work in distant, allegedly heathen sites far from New England—a vocation and location which most likely would not have come about without the scholarship program.

The AES contributed almost all the major principles and precedents that have shaped American student financial aid for the next two centuries. It included a major agency (in this case, the AES—an incorporated foundation) whose endowment provided resources to award financial aid to a large number of students at numerous colleges. It demonstrated that philanthropy meant a reciprocation of a student both giving and receiving. It combined merit and need in evaluating applicants. And, it spawned a formidable bureaucracy that required applicants to fill out numerous forms and affidavits. The scholarship program cast its net beyond a single institution by compiling a slate of approved colleges where students were allowed to enroll. At the same time, its conditions narrowed eligibility to those who met explicit criteria of religious affiliation, sound academic performance, and professional commitment.

The AES scholarship program contributed an important precedent in that it illustrated how an incentive (making going to college affordable) could be used as the means to accomplish another end—namely, spreading a particular religion to under-served locales via a learned clergy. It also provided a pioneering example of how donors could be encouraged to support funding of services and educational outcomes, rather than the usual inclination to dedicate monies to construction of college buildings. The AES plan required student repayment of sorts in the form of specified services. And, although it started out by awarding only scholarship grants, over time the program vacillated—including loans as well as grants. It was, in sum, a truly American "package deal." As such, it provided the defining elements of large-scale student financial aid that would surface time and time again, either by private foundations or by other agencies in partnership with students and colleges. Its success in attracting and educating a large number of Congregationalist ministers provided a model for other denominations. The Presbyterian Education Board, founded in 1866, the Methodist Episcopal Church Board, established in 1864, and the Evangelical Lutheran Board, founded in 1885, represented extensions of the original AES model.

Though AES and its comparable church board programs represented the peak of organized philanthropy for student financial aid in the first half of the 19th century, it did not typify how most colleges arranged for scholarships and loans to make higher education affordable and attractive. Apart from the AES, student financial aid well into the mid-20th century can be characterized as a widespread yet uneven and unconnected "cottage industry." Thus, although the AES was unusual in its own time, it provided a model for foundations and federal agencies to emulate in the 20th century.

NOBLESSE OBLIGE: NORTHERN PHILANTHROPY AND SOUTHERN EDUCATION

A strategic advantage of a horizontal institution was that it could prompt and prod colleges to take on projects and endeavors that most likely they would not have been willing or able to pursue if left to their own accord. By this litmus, then, the role of philanthropic organizations in the Northeast stands out in taking on the unusual, unexpected task of funding and guiding higher education in the South—both for African-Americans and Whites, though usually not together, in the latter half of the 19th century.[5] This involved evolution over time, with a shift from emphasizing the abolition of slavery to providing basic educational opportunities for African-American freedmen after the Civil War. Most notable for their regional focus on higher education in the South in the late 19th century were the Peabody Fund and the Slater Fund. Later, in the early 20th century, the foremost focused contribution came from the Rosenwald Foundation, whose funding was made possible by the Sears Roebuck & Company, which was dedicated to building safe, sturdy schools for African-American students in states where education of the races was not only separate but decidedly unequal in providing facilities and resources for Blacks. Large-scale philanthropy based in New York City also became a fertile source of support for college education for another under-served group: poor White students in the mountain regions designated as Appalachia. An example of this initiative was the generous support for Berea College in Kentucky which, to this day, has sufficient endowment so that eligible students who fulfill criteria of financial need and geographic home do not pay tuition or room and board.[6]

THE GREAT FOUNDATIONS AND THE QUEST FOR STANDARDS AND STANDARDIZATION

During the late 19th and early 20th centuries, higher education in the United States was a prime beneficiary of one of the most prosperous eras in the nation's commercial and industrial expansion. Both by good fortune and design, colleges and universities received an inordinate proportion of the private donations generated by this unprecedented individual and corporate wealth. What is interesting is to contrast the giving patterns of the decades 1870 to 1900 with those of the next decades, roughly 1900 to 1920. The earlier decades were dominated by large donations to "vertical" institutions—i.e., individual campuses. This is best illustrated in the names of new great universities— Vanderbilt, Clark, Carnegie Institute, and Stanford. In contrast, after 1900, the wealthy industrialists modified their philanthropic plans by opting instead to create foundations that honored the namesake. Hence, one finds the proliferation and influence of the great foundations—Carnegie Foundation for the Advancement of Teaching (CFAT), the Rockefeller Foundation, the Sloan Foundation, and later, the Ford Foundation.

This shift from campus to foundation signaled a change in philanthropic mission and focus—from building a great campus to having a foundation act as catalyst for nation-wide innovations in higher education.[7]

The CFAT, for example, took on the simultaneous roles of providing a generous pension plan for retired college faculty, known today as TIAA-CREF. In so doing, it required colleges to agree to conditions of curriculum, admissions, and size. On balance, it used the carrot of a retirement plan in tandem with the stick of new standards whose intent was to rid American higher education of small, weak, academically lax, and financially risky church-related colleges. Later, especially after its generous incentives had depleted much of its endowment, the CFAT placed increasing emphasis on being the critical analyst of American education on topics ranging from the problems found in medical schools to advocacy of state coordination of public higher education.[8] It was no less than the de facto Ministry of Education.

The other major endowment from corporate wealth, the Rockefeller Foundation, established its own policy agenda.[9] This included establishing and funding the General Education Board (GEB) in 1902, with a succession of major gifts over the next decade. The GEB took on a wide range of regional and national educational issues, and con-tinued to provide generous funding well into the 1950s. One interesting venture of the Rockefeller Foundation in the 1930s was to stimulate interest in serious social and behavioral science research via establishment of a major funding agency, the Social Science Research Council (SSRC).[10] Related to the awarding of grants to promising professors and projects, the SSRC acted as a testing ground for systematic use of stat-istics and social indicators—projects which were watched closely by federal agencies and ultimately led to establishing indicators for economic data collection.[11]

ACRONYMS AND ASSOCIATIONS

Philanthropy and charitable support was not the only characteristic of "horizontal institutions" in American higher education. One of the best illustrations and explan-ations for the importance of horizontal history is found in the creation and prolifer-ation of national scholarly associations, starting around 1887 and gaining momentum for over a half century and into the post-World War II era. Indeed, the phenomenon enjoyed yet another sustained period of popularity and growth starting in the 1970s. As historian Hugh Hawkins noted, this penchant for college and university representatives to "band together" was part of a larger movement in late 19th- and early 20th-century American public life—a manifestation of the belief that forming associations contrib-uted an antidote to waste, corruption, and inefficiency.[12] It was, as historian Robert Wiebe observed, a deep-rooted "search for order" in the chaos of American life.

Colleges and colleagues sought national alliances because they provided an antidote to a chronic weakness of the campus as a "vertical institution": namely, its insularity and isolation. The relatively small size and often the homogeneity and conformity of a single college or university may have been effective for perpetuating the institution's culture, but it was not well suited to fostering exploration in scholarly fields across a broad swath. The networks of scholarly exchange, via newsletters, correspondence, refereed journals, conferences, and research paper presentations invigorated scholarship. It's not unreasonable to say that it helped create the scholarly and academic professions in a substantive way. It was also the impetus for forming intercollegiate athletic conferences whose aim ostensibly was to bring together the presidents and athletic directors of like-minded colleges and universities—and to provide a structure for both organizing and regulating the conduct of college sports.

It is important to note that some of the oldest scholarly associations in the United States initially had little if any connection with colleges. Rather, one was more likely to find in the early to mid 19th century that the prototype member was the "man of letters" or independent, amateur scholar in natural science, bibliography, ornithology, and so on. Crucial to the connection of associations and academe was the founding of The Johns Hopkins University in 1876. Its pioneering work in this area included founding the first university press in the nation, and its numerous departments were given encouragement and funding by the university administration to provide editorial homes for many scholarly journals of national academic disciplinary organizations. The idea and organization gained increasing membership among a new generation of professors at a variety of colleges and universities. Some of the early groups faced a few problems of adjustment and embarrassment. For example, the American Sociological Society leaders had to regroup when, at their first conference, they confronted a large banner bearing their acronym. Immediately they changed their name to the American Sociological Association, with its more refined acronym. But such incidents were minor distractions as scholars flocked to join kindred colleagues across the nation to present papers, referee manuscripts, and publish journals in their respective fields.

Above the level of departments and disciplines, institutions formed alliances that were tantamount to influential clubs. The pioneer in this trend was the Association of Land Grant Colleges and Universities, formed in 1887 due to the leadership of George Atherton, president of Pennsylvania State College. Despite the federal largesse of the Morrill Act of 1862, the harsh truth was that most of the land grant colleges in the Midwest and Mid-Atlantic states struggled to create viable academic programs and attract qualified students. Advanced programs and graduate degrees, along with scholarly research, languished. In response, Atherton rallied his fellow presidents of land grant institutions to establish an office in Washington, D.C. Over the next four decades this formidable association was successful in having the U.S. Congress approve and fund large-scale programs for research and development. The second Morrill Act of 1890, followed by the Hatch Act and the Smith-Lever Act, represented the programs that allowed the land grant universities to flourish in the early 20th century.

The most prestigious horizontal organization was the Association of American Universities (AAU), established in 1900. Its 20 charter members represented the apex of universities committed to advanced scholarship. The collective aim was to showcase all that was worthy in American universities, especially to a critical audience of professors at European universities who tended to look askance at the quality of academic degrees conferred in the United States. The AAU also became the voice of prestigious universities in evaluating the stature of Ph.D. programs offered by American universities. Close behind was the larger and more inclusive umbrella organization, the American Council of Education (ACE), an association whose membership included presidents of colleges and universities. Over time the national associations of institutions would gravitate toward an official presence in Washington, D.C. This culminated in the 1970s with the Kellogg Foundation providing construction funding for a large building called "One DuPont Circle" as the gathering point for numerous higher education associations.

THE POST-WORLD WAR II ERA AND THE ORGANIZATION OF INDEPENDENT COLLEGES

In the years immediately following World War II, American higher education's horizontal sector underwent significant changes in response to changes in state and federal programs, regulations, and tax laws. At the state level, the growing popularity of providing public universities with annual state subsidies from tax revenues created justifiable fear among independent or private colleges and universities that their institutions would be at a disadvantage in acquiring resources and providing scholarships and programs for students and faculty. The net result was that private colleges formed new statewide associations to be increasingly attractive to private donors, including a new wave of charitable foundations established by major business corporations. The state institutional associations also provided independent colleges an educational and lobbying voice within their respective state legislatures and with Congress in Washington, D.C. A pioneer in this state association movement was the Association of Independent Colleges of Indiana, led by the president of Wabash College. Soon thereafter, strong comparable associations of independent colleges and universities were formed in California, New York, Illinois, and eventually, over 25 states.

What was remarkable about this groundswell of horizontal organization and cooperation was that it resurrected the influence of private colleges and universities in two distinct yet ultimately related ways. First, it enhanced the collective fund raising of these institutions in their appeal to individual donors and, most novel, corporate and industrial donors. Second, it gave the private colleges a prime seat at the public policy table of state and federal legislative deliberations. How did these two strands develop and then merge? This grass-roots movement at the state level was so successful that eventually it led to inter-state cooperation among colleges and associations. It culminated in the creation of a national organization in the early 1970s called NAICU (National Association of Independent Colleges and Universities) and its lobbying wing, incorporated as NIICU (the National Institute of Independent Colleges and Universities). The net result of these innovations between 1950 and 1975 was that private colleges and universities were assured of having a voice and a seat at the table in state and federal legislation and programs involving higher education public policies. Illustrative of the effectiveness of the movement was that when the 1972 reauthorization of the Higher Education Act introduced large-scale federal student financial aid programs, there was ample provision for students at independent colleges to be eligible to receive financial aid from the Pell Grants and a variety of student loan programs.

One of the most imaginative and innovative examples of cooperation among independent colleges and universities came about in 1946 with the creation of the United Negro College Fund (UNCF). In response to the financial adversity facing historically Black colleges, the UNCF established offices in New York City to launch numerous campaigns for raising awareness of—and donations to—their member institutions. In an era when public relations was gaining sophistication, the UNCF wisely appointed and then relied on trustees who had been drawn from the ranks of established executives and influentials from major companies whose headquarters were in New York City. Furthermore, UNCF directors and staff enlisted the support and fund-raising skills of corporate executive spouses, resulting in a high-profile foundation. When the 1954 Supreme Court decision in *Brown v. the Board of Education* signaled the gradual deterioration of legally segregated campuses, the UNCF responded with yet another generation of effective national initiatives. Most enduring and effective was its motto, "A mind is a terrible thing to waste . . ." What the UNCF showed time and time again was that promoting an educational ideal, as distinguished from asking directly for a donation, was a key to enduring large-scale philanthropy.[13]

LAST BUT NOT LEAST: THE FORD FOUNDATION

After World War II, when many of the famous major foundations were completing long-term projects and scaling down their dedication of resources, the Ford Foundation was a significant exception to the trend. Founded in 1936, it did not really enter into major national and international initiatives until the early 1950s. Despite this relatively late start, the Ford Foundation was influential and even controversial. Its higher education initiatives included the Fund for the Advancement of Education, whose charge was to promote innovation that would help colleges and universities go beyond "business as usual" in curricula. In 1955 the foundation awarded $210 million to 630 private liberal arts colleges, with such aims as raising faculty salaries. To encourage habits of self-help, the Ford Foundation often required matching funds from its institutional grant recipients. Also illustrative of its bold academic reform initiatives was a project to transform the content and quality of the prototypical Masters of Business Administration (MBA) degree. The strategy was to generously fund MBA programs at five prestigious universities and encourage these programs to incorporate course work in such fields as economics, sociology, political science, and statistics into the MBA framework. The long-term hope was that these five pace-setting institutions would be sufficiently influential so that programs elsewhere would follow their example of curricular rigor. Other major ventures funded by the Ford Foundation emphasized pursuing genuine democratization of American institutions through such programs as the National Merit Scholars Corporation, the Fund for Adult Education, the Fund for the Republic, and a Center for Advanced Studies in Behavioral Sciences. The concerns raised by the Ford Foundation about the efficacy of American education in the early and mid 1950s anticipated the concerns of the United States Congress which surfaced in 1957 when the Soviet Union's launch of Sputnik sounded alarms about the relatively deficient state of schooling, especially in sciences and mathematics in the United States.[14]

THE CRISIS OF THE NONPROFITS

One reason it is logical to include discussion of federal agencies as part of higher education's horizontal history is that the private, voluntary associations and foundations often defined themselves in response to the relative strength or weakness of government involvement in higher education. For example, in an era before federal income taxes or federal regulation, the great foundations filled a void by acting as the de facto ministry of higher education, both in setting standards and in allocating resources and rewards. The important change for foundations was that after World War II, the federal government made a belated yet large and growing entrance into programs dealing with colleges and universities. For the first time, there was a widespread and enduring array of research and development projects that numerous federal agencies announced in requests for proposals sent to faculty at universities. The residual implication was that in the years after 1950, when the federal government opted to support an area of research, its resources were sufficiently large that federal research then tended to dwarf the research programs sponsored by foundations in the same field.

The new deal of external research for universities was that foundations were relegated to a smaller role in funding. It was not, however, necessarily a less significant role. The informal compact and working relation was that the private foundations tended to act as the "distant early warning systems" of high-powered research. In other words, foundations would be the source of funding for imaginative, visionary pilot studies. Later, the federal agencies would selectively adopt and then expand the topics and projects which earlier had been pioneered by foundation grants.

This symbiotic relationship worked reasonably well from about 1950 to 1980. However, by 1980 such astute analysts as Waldemar Nielsen warned of a "crisis of the nonprofits."[15] Once the bone and sinew of social and educational philanthropy in the United States, the foundations were battered by simultaneous problems. First, more than a decade of double digit inflation combined with a weak economy created "stagflation"—and eroded foundation endowments. Second, local and regional foundations were often the victims of regional and demographic change. What was called the shift from the "Rust Belt" to the "Sun Belt" meant that, for example, there was an excess of nonprofit organizations in such areas as the upper Midwest and a shortage of them in the Southwest. Some measure of relief came about with revisions in tax laws and, above all, the increasing interest of President Ronald Reagan's administration in encouraging "privatization" of charities and philanthropies, including higher education.

CONCLUSION: SUCCESS AND EXCESS

What has surprised me most about higher education since I started to pay attention to its affiliated foundations, agencies, and philanthropic organizations is my realization that often the sideshows run the circus. My concerns about higher education's "horizontal history" have often ironically been, in part, a function of that sector's success. Foundations and educational associations tended to be asked to do more, demonstrating the logic that one good turn deserves another—and another. Within almost every college and university, one finds, since the 1980s, enhancement of its development and fund-raising staff so as to make optimal connection with foundations and potential donors. It also has meant the increasing appeal of the incorporation of new charitable groups, usually with the designation, "Friends of the . . .", a blank which could be filled with the name of almost every campus activity and interest, from athletics to zoology. By the 1990s the Internal Revenue Service guidebooks listed more than 70 categories of nonprofit organizations—testimony to the popularity and complexity of the nonprofit sector. Alexis de Tocqueville's observations in the early 1800s were ratified in the early 21st century, as higher education's horizontal institutions demonstrated that Americans continue to be a nation of joiners who gravitate toward formation of voluntary associations to provide funding and perhaps solutions for myriad higher education issues and problems. And, most sobering is that recognition in 2009 that even these seemingly indestructible institutions of philanthropy and endowments have their foibles and weaknesses. Although the "boom years" of hedge funds and endowments with double-digit annual investment returns inflated colleges and universities with a sense of abundance between 2002 and 2007, the abrupt collapse of Wall Street banks and investment firms has spread to colleges and universities with drastic and dramatic consequences. Foundation officers customarily like to make awards that allow colleges and universities to do good work. But foundations without money to give away are sad places. Perhaps an essential lesson from the study of philanthropy and higher education is that in lean times the university budget becomes a truly philosophical document in which presidents, board members, faculty, staff, students, alumni, and donors are forced to make decisions about what is essential and what is expendable in our colleges and universities. For me, I now have renewed appreciation in the 21st century for the thrift and stewardship displayed by John Harvard and his fellow colonial college builders in the 17th and 18th centuries. Even though American higher education is characterized by success over five centuries, I find the periods of adversity to be enlightening.

QUESTIONS FOR DISCUSSION

1. Do our colleges and universities in the 21st century warrant the same privileges and exemptions they have enjoyed over several centuries? In other words, are colleges and universities today sufficiently complex and commercial that the notion of exemption from property taxes or the entitlement to allowing donors to claim gifts to colleges as income tax deductions are still sound, reasonable policies? What do you think would be appropriate, wise practices today?

2. Imagine that you are the head of a well-endowed philanthropic foundation. What are the priorities and projects you would rank most worthy for funding at colleges and universities? Are there customary requests from colleges and universities for foundation awards that you do not think are any longer compelling—even though they might have been appealing to earlier generations of philanthropists? Explain your logic and choices with specific examples.

3. For many years you have valued wise stewardship and giving in your personal choices. This morning you have just received the unexpected news that you have won the Powerball lottery. Explain how you would plan to carry out your enduring values of giving and support. How would gifts to your undergraduate Alma Mater fare within your vision? What are other societal and cultural endeavors you would like to consider?

4. A strong tradition in American higher education and the nonprofit sector has been that endowments are to be nurtured wisely and carefully. Do you think it's a good idea for a college or university to insist that gifts and donations must be placed in the institution's perpetual endowment? If so, why? Are there other variations or alternatives on being steward of wealth and institutional service you would like to consider?

5. You are the President of a college or university. Your Director of Financial Aid informs you that a careful review of institutional records show that each year many scholarship funds intended for student aid go unused. That's because the donations are bound by criteria and purposes that usually cannot be fulfilled today. How might you correct this restriction on existing funds? What would you recommend for policies and practices to avoid such financial paralysis in the future?

6. You are the mayor of a major city who faces a tough re-election campaign in about a year. Your office, along with the city council, has received two proposals for

consideration—both of which are requesting incentives from the municipal government in the forms of property tax exemptions for perpetuity, along with your approval of a municipal bond issue to cover estimated construction costs of $50 million per project. Your budget director advises you that the city treasury can accommodate one, but not both, proposals. The first proposal is from a National Football League franchise in a neighboring city that may wish to relocate to your city. But to do so they require property tax exemption plus the municipal bonds of $50 million for constructing their new stadium. The second request for the same privileges and exemptions comes from the local university, which proposes to build a new performing arts center. Which project would you recommend for city approval—and why?

7. A prosperous and grateful alumnus of your university has proposed to you in your role as President that he wishes to make a major gift of $150 million for a new state-of-the-art complex for varsity football and basketball. At the same time your Provost and Vice President for Finance have cooperated on a report indicating that budget shortfalls for academic and educational programs indicate that the university will not be able to fulfill its customary pledge on need-based student aid; furthermore, several faculty positions will have to be eliminated. How will you respond to the generous alumnus donor?

NOTES

1. John R. Thelin, *A History of American Higher Education* (Baltimore and London: The Johns Hopkins University Press, 2004).
2. Robert Wiebe, *The Search for Order, 1877–1920* (New York: Hill and Wang, 1967).
3. David Allmendinger, *Paupers and Scholars* (New York: St. Martin's Press, 1975).
4. Rupert Wilkinson, *Aiding Students, Buying Students: Financial Aid in America* (Nashville: Vanderbilt University Press, 2005).
5. Eric Anderson and Alfred A. Moss, Jr., *Dangerous Donations: Northern Philanthropy and Southern Black Education, 1902–1930* (Columbia and London: University of Missouri Press, 1999).
6. Robert H. Bremner, *American Philanthropy* (University of Chicago Press, 1988) (2nd edition). Jesse Brundage Sears, *Philanthropy in the History of American Higher Education* (Washington, DC: U.S. Government Printing Office, 1922).
7. Ellen Condliffe Lagemann, *Private Power for the Public Good: A History of the Carnegie Foundation for the Advancement of Teaching* (Middletown, CT: Wesleyan University Press, 1983).
8. Ellen Condliffe Lagemann, *Private Power for the Public Good: A History of the Carnegie Foundation for the Advancement of Teaching* (Middletown, CT: Wesleyan University Press, 1983).
9. Merle Curti and Roderick Nash. *Philanthropy in the Shaping of American Higher Education* (New Brunswick, NJ: Rutgers University Press, 1965).
10. Donald Fisher, *Fundamental Development of the Social Sciences: Rockefeller Philanthropy and the United States Social Science Research Council* (Ann Arbor: University of Michigan, 1993).
11. Roger Williams, *George W. Atherton and the Beginnings of Federal Support for Higher Education* (University Park: Pennsylvania State University Press, 1989).
12. Hugh Hawkins, *Banding Together: The Rise of National Associations in American Higher Education, 1887–1950* (Baltimore and London: The Johns Hopkins University Press, 1992).
13. Marybeth Gasman, *Envisioning Black Colleges: A History of the United Negro College Fund* (Baltimore and London: The Johns Hopkins University Press, 2007).
14. Waldemar A. Nielsen, *The Big Foundations* (New York and London: Columbia University Press, 1972).
15. Burton A. Weisbrod, *The Nonprofit Economy* (Cambridge, MA: Harvard University Press, 1988).

7

PHOTOGRAPHS AS PRIMARY SOURCES

Michael Bieze

Photographs should be a challenge for anyone including them in their efforts at writing and teaching history. They are both fact and fiction, intimately connected to their subject and yet cut off and de-contextualized. On the one hand, they resonate with an aura that mysteriously brings us in contact with a person, place, or event. On the other hand, we know that we are only glimpsing a dislocated fragment of the real thing. It reminds one of the old lines from the 1923 Irving Berlin song about how, in the absence of a person, all that remains is their picture: "What'll I do with just a photograph to tell my troubles to?"

Just what to do with photographs does not trouble everyone. Most often, their insertions into articles, books, and lectures follow no discernable guidelines or common practices—except that of ornament to set a tone or let us know what someone looked like. Examples are not hard to find. Look at the recent article by Kelefa Sanneh on Booker T. Washington in *The New Yorker*.[1] A large reproduction of a portrait of Washington floats within the text of the brilliant essay (Figure 7.1).[2]

The photograph only connects to the article with a caption paraphrasing a line in the text: "Washington fended off black rivals and White supremacists with almost equal fervor."[3] Tucked along the margin, in tiny print, is a citation acknowledging the photograph comes from the Library of Congress (LOC), letting us know that it was fished out of that massive, easily accessible source of images. Archivist Linda Ries describes her dismay at the way some historians, having completed a manuscript, seek photographs to embellish text. I cringe at the finished product: images used simply to break copy, rather than as an integral part of the story. Oftentimes they appear in a cropped format, without captions or miscaptioned, have no attribution or misattributions, and lack proper citation information so readers do not know where the originals are kept. This is a disservice to the integrity of the image and the intended audience.[4]

The Sanneh article follows the familiar pattern of selecting an image after the text is written, offering a visual accompaniment void of context. Stripping the photograph of its historical, semiotic, and aesthetic context is, as we will see, of particular concern when dealing with the subject of this photograph, African Americans.

Figure 7.1 Walden Fawcett, Booker T. Washington, Three-quarter Length Portrait

Source: Library of Congress.

Using photographs as historical evidence requires that we ask probing questions. Does it matter that the photographer of Figure 7.1, Walden Fawcett, was a White journalist working in Washington, D.C. who practiced his profession during the dawn of the era of the writer-photographer? What does this image share with those photographs produced by other White photographers such as Julian and A.W. Dimock, Clifton Johnson, and John Tarbell, all of whom shared an interest in depicting life in the South during the early Progressive era?[5] Does it matter that Booker T. Washington carefully constructed a public image and never used the Fawcett image from his stops in Washington, D.C., instead favoring one by Addison Turner, a Black photographer whose career he helped to launch (Figure 7.2)?[6]

Or that the pose, a variation of the one Gertrude Kasebier used in Washington's *Up From Slavery*, falls within certain portrait conventions of the day?[7] Stripped of historical references and aesthetic context, a photograph becomes iconic, symbolic, and timeless. In other words, it becomes a-historical. Roland Barthes's famous line "the image always has the last word," speaks to the danger created when images appear to be representative or significant. In the case of the Fawcett photograph, viewers are lured by the poetic expression of the tattered edges evoking Washington's many battle scars from the political arena. While such visual embellishments serve to amplify or extend the tone of the text, they frequently do so by distorting the historical meaning of the image. At the very

Principal Washington.   Mrs. B. T. Washington.

Principal Washington's Home, Tuskegee Institute, Ala.

Figure 7.2 A.P. Bedou Postcard, Principal Washington's Home, Tuskegee Institute, AL

least, the use of photographs as evidence should undergo the same rigor and standards used when citing textual sources.

This chapter offers practical strategies, not a theoretical discourse for researchers using photographs as historical evidence. Since my own work examines Booker T. Washington's varied uses of the medium to promote himself and the Tuskegee Institute's mission, the case study offered in this essay follows the life of one well-known photograph of Washington from its original publication through later reprintings over the course of nearly one hundred years. In doing so, I draw upon the important work of Alan Trachtenberg, which first opened my eyes to seeing a photograph as fundamentally changing in nature as it reappears in different publications.[8]

The Fawcett photograph shows how acquiring photographic images with such ease offers new possibilities and presents new problems. History is both an art and a science, an expressive representation of the past grounded in reliable sources. Increasingly, primary sources, the bedrock of historical writing, include photographs. Understanding how to use photographs, themselves part art and part science, as a primary source in the writing and teaching of history matters more today than ever before. With the advent of PowerPoint, Photoshopfi, and instant accessibility to an ever-expanding number of digitized photographs in databases and web sites, inserting pictures into an article, book, or classroom presentation is just a few clicks away. As photographer and professor Dona Schwartz writes in a succinct overview of the history of photojournalism and facts, "The 1980s ushered in revolutionary changes in photographic technology that opened a Pandora's Box of issues concerning the medium's credibility and future of photojournalism."[9]

Similarly, the potential for unintentional manipulation and distortion of the past is changing how history is communicated in unprecedented ways. There is nothing new about illustrating history texts with images or manipulating images to sell an idea or a story. That practice is centuries old. Before the advent of photography, history texts inserted various kinds of prints and reproductions of paintings. However, the present era of instant acquisition of photographs is fundamentally new and different. Since photographic images are more readily available and too often thought to be factual than functioning within a highly complex context, their various meanings often go unnoticed—or entirely new meanings are created that bear little connection to the original reason for existing. Historian John Lewis Gaddis reminds us that, in the historical consciousness, there is always a tension between the "literal and the abstract, between the detailed depiction of what lies at some point in the past, on the one hand, and the sweeping sketch of what extends over long stretches of it on the other."[10] But the process begins inductively with reliable sources. This is especially important when working with photographs. The ones that we see reproduced may be representative, the ones most easily available from an on-line collection, or simply the only ones to survive.

The researcher turning to the literature on the use of photographs as historical evidence finds a rapidly growing, complex, and often confusing body of writings. About thirty or so years ago Susan Sontag argued, "the language in which photographs are generally evaluated is extremely meager."[11] Today, one finds the research on the photograph grafting methodologies and approaches from disparate fields including art history, linguistics, philosophy, anthropology, history, sociology, and the work of archivists. It is still a field of inquiry being defined and thus provides a challenge to researchers. That said, I have found a few books to be helpful in my own research and thinking about photographs. First and foremost is Alan Trachtenberg's *Reading American Photographs*, which remains a standard text on reading photographs as social history. Cara Finnegan's *Picturing Poverty: Print Culture and FSA Photographs* expands many of Trachtenberg's essays.[12] She offers an extremely useful framework of five principles for interpreting photographs:

(1) documentary photographs are not merely "evidence," but are by their very nature rhetorical; (2) photographic meaning is not fixed or univocal, but neither is it relativistic; (3) photographs cannot productively be separated from texts they accompany, nor should they be viewed as merely supplements to those texts; (4) photographs created for public purposes are best studied in the contexts of the print culture through which they circulate; and (5) all images, including photographs, are products of a particular visual culture that values and privileges certain forms of visual expression over others.[13]

Peter Burke's *Eyewitnessing: The Uses of Images as Historical Evidence* provides a clear and thoughtful art historical overview of iconography or the interpretation of images.[14] Robert M. Levine's *Images of History: Nineteenth and Early Twentieth Century Latin American Photographs* offers a deeply insightful, comprehensive set of practical questions for historians to consider when examining photographs as evidence, such as:

- Does the publication in which a photograph was published offer information about how contemporaries saw the image?
- Is the image representative or anachronistic?
- Is there corroborative evidence beyond the visual image?

- Were photographs taken in a certain way to achieve a desired effect?
- How can "official" ideology be distinguished from reality?[15]

Finally, Collier and Collier's *Visual Anthropology: Photography as a Research Method* offers a variety of ways to glean meaning through different models of analysis, particularly ethnographic.[16]

For the researcher examining the dynamics of power and photography, a number of works analyze how to read photographs as exerting control or containing resistance. On the one side are those works emphasizing photography's role in subordination, a tradition running from Walter Benjamin through Susan Sontag and John Tagg. In this line there are a number of works, including *Colonial Harem* by Malek Alloula that focuses on the fantasies or projections those in power place upon their subjects.[17] On the other hand, several works explore the complexity of power and agency and find resistance and self-representation within photographs. Examples of these works include Shawn Michelle Smith's *Photography on the Color Line*, Judith Fryer Davidov's *Women's Camera Work*, and David Levering Lewis and Deborah Willis's *A Small Nation of People*.[18]

THE PHOTOGRAPH AS A PHYSICAL ARTIFACT

At the most basic level, a photograph is both a physical object and an image. Some photographs were created as prints and others for publication purposes. In either case, when chosen by a contemporary author, the original photographs are appropriated or lifted from one source—a book, journal, an archive (now often on-line), and inserted into a project. In this way, the physical or material culture dimension of the photograph is cut off leaving the researcher without important information that may be helpful. This may be as basic as the information written on the back of the image and on the front along the edges missing from the digital scan, or knowing how the original format was designed for a particular audience.

As a physical object or artifact, a photograph may be considered in several ways including the medium and the iconic or talismanic potential. First, a photograph exists in a medium. They appear as tintypes, albumen prints, stereographs, silver gelatin prints, Cibachromes, or any number of other formats. Different formats tell us about the historical period, the expense of the project, and limits of a particular technology. Subsequently, one can see that as primary sources, words and images are not interpreted in the same way. It may be the case, as W.J.T. Mitchell and others argue, that interactions between text and images are ultimately inseparable. However, the fact remains the format of a photograph was a consideration when it was created. In contrast, the type of paper used for a correspondence rarely contributes meaning to the words.

Photographs are protean, sliding not only between categories of art, science, journalism, and promotion, but also media. The original printing method of the photographic image can be of great importance. For example, Richard Benson's recent exhibition at the Museum of Modern Art in New York, *The Printed Image*, convincingly argues that photographs belong to the tradition of reproductions emerging from printmaking, and the medium matters. In the words of the author,

We can be sure, though, that the form of the picture is the dominant influence on how we understand it, and that is where my interest lies: not so much in meaning as form . . . When the picture-making system is photography, though, everything becomes muddled, because even in original work—photographs taken out in the world—the mind of the maker has to share the driver's seat with the form of the picture as it is shaped by the technology of photography. And when a photograph is reproduced, things get still more difficult, because such reproductions can only be made by rephotographing the photograph. It then becomes hard to tell whether the person doing the reproduction or the technology itself might be in charge.[19]

Finally, as physical objects, photographs have a history. One should try to ascertain the name of the photographer, the date of the creation, the size of the work, whether it was part of a series, and the medium or format (metal, type of paper, glass, etc.). If possible, also include the technical dimensions such as shutter speed, aperture, depth of field, use of filters, and film speed because this information tells us many things about the intent of the image maker.

Secondly, photographs also have the power, as physical objects, to be viewed as talismanic, iconic, and scientific—all at the same time. The literature on this aspect of photographs may be found in what is described as its indexical dimension, that is, literally referring back as a mirror to the original source or subject matter. Roland Barthes's description of the photograph as "literally an emanation of the referent," captures both the mystery and science of the medium.[20] Stated another way, photographs are a screen that records the reflection of light off of surfaces, suspending them as if we are seeing a mirror reflecting an instant in time. As an object that records transient light from a subject that no longer exists one can see how photographs have the capacity to become magically iconic. Look around and you see how often photographs are placed at funerals, in people's homes, in government spaces, or in clubs to suggest the presence of someone not physically in the room.

In the early 20th century, Booker T. Washington's image was presented wherever he appeared, as well as in countless homes as a savior, on the buttons worn with his picture by members of the National Negro Business League, in Black schools, or even looming behind Paul Robeson in the background of Oscar Micheaux's film *Body and Soul.*[21] I would argue that this talismanic power often appears in high school and college history books when authors insert portraits of famous men and women without any substantiation. Without a visual context, pictures of the famous become an aura, as if looking into their eyes we somehow make a connection or know them better. Or, as argued by Margaret Stetz, the Victorian era's crisis of faith "witnessed the substitution of the human face for the Divine."[22] Unwittingly, this practice resurrects the great man approach to history.

THE PHOTOGRAPH AS IMAGE

Along with being a physical object (unless it only exists digitally), a photograph is an image. Once copied and divorced from the physical photographic format, the image becomes a replica which can be altered, cropped, change color, or even have words added. My approach to interpreting photographs is a combination of social context method from art history that considers the triad of artist, patron, and audience, with Barthes's mode of "the triple context of the location of the text, the historical moment, and the cultural formation of the reader."[23]

The first consideration for me is the historical context of the photograph. Included in such analysis is the discussion of the artist (his or her training, style, motivations, gender, race, technical abilities), the patron (his or her degree of control in the creation of the photograph), the conventions and history of photography at that historical moment, and the political, religious, philosophical, economic, and other social forces which may have contributed to the image. With respect to conventions and aesthetics of the image, art historians recognize that no universal criteria exist. Cultures vary in their standards of beauty, aesthetics, conventions for posing figures, and depictions of power, to name a few. For example, concepts of art such as Japanese *kokoro* or Indian *rasa* have no equivalents in the West. Works such as Stephen F. Sprague's "Yoruba Photography: How the Yoruba see Themselves," offer researchers a starting place for such considerations.[24]

Second, I consider the original placement or siting of the photograph. Was it made as a high art print, for reproduction in a mass journal, shown in an elite publication, or some other site? Booker T. Washington carefully crafted his image along race lines, controlling photographs and the type of journal they appeared in. Finally, one may consider the intended audience. Who would have understood the varying messages in the photograph? In the case of Washington, he activated different visual codes along race and class lines. Jim Crow America bluntly carved audiences into Black and White, rich and poor with different lenses for each. As a consequence, Washington and his audiences spoke to one another through strict race codes, which included visual images. In towns such as Tuskegee, Alabama, members of each race lived in different parts of town, were buried in separate cemeteries, read different newspapers, and brought different experiences and expectations to what they read and saw.

A CASE STUDY: AN A.P. BEDOU PHOTOGRAPH OF BOOKER T. WASHINGTON

In order to clarify the issues noted so far, I will use a certain photograph of the Tuskegee Institute principal to point out some of the challenges facing historians using photographs. The photograph is by the noted African American photographer A.P. Bedou (1882–1966), a man who served as Booker T. Washington's official photographer during the last year of his life (1915). Washington, an early master of the new modern media including photography, film making, and glass slide lectures, employed Bedou to promote the mission of Tuskegee through the creation of many different types of photographs. Following the life of these photographs in different publications will reveal the complexities of using photographs to illustrate ideas rather than being critically examined as primary sources in the same way as text sources.

THE BASIC CONSIDERATIONS: ARTIST, TITLE, DATE, MEDIUM, SCALE, SUBJECT MATTER, STYLE

Figure 7.3 is a reproduction of an often utilized A.P. Bedou photograph of Booker T. Washington.[25] Among Bedou's responsibilities was documenting Washington's speaking engagements in the region of the country known as the Black Belt. This work was commissioned by Washington, who vigorously controlled his depiction in the national press. When evaluating photographs as primary sources, historians should initially want

Figure 7.3 A.P. Bedou, Booker T. Washington Speaking to an Audience in New Iberia, LA

Source: Library of Congress.

to know the photographer, when it was made, the medium, the scale, the source of the image for citation, and the basic subject matter. Bedou took this 6 ½ × 4 ½ silver gelatin print, which can be found in the Tuskegee University Archives and the Library of Congress, as a record of Washington's April 1915 tour through Louisiana.[26] The researcher must consult multiple sources in order to corroborate the information since it is often misidentified. While Bedou frequently produced pictorialist studio photographs, controlled campus shots, and promotional materials such as postcards, this photograph was made using a snapshot aesthetic in order to express the action of Washington as a charismatic orator. As we will see, there was conscious aesthetic choice being made for the project.

MEANING AS CONTINGENT UPON PLACEMENT AND
HISTORICAL CONTEXT

For me, the question of the meaning of a photograph begins with its original placement in a gallery display, a journal article, or book illustration. The Bedou photograph of Washington first appeared in print in the June issue of the progressive journal, *The Survey*.[27] Later known as the *Survey Graphic, The Survey* was a nationally distributed Progressive era reform magazine committed to the professionalization of social work. Found in *The Survey* at this time were articles on child labor, the work of Jane Addams, unions, illiteracy, prison conditions, health issues for the poor, the horrors of World War I, women's rights, and the struggles of African Americans. The article on Washington, "Loosening up Louisiana," was a main article, which was advertised a week earlier as a "special feature of the next issue."[28] Bedou's cover photograph for the article, for which he was given credit in the journal, shows a large Black audience wearing buttons with Washington's image (Figure 7.4).[29]

The main theme of the article was how a team of Black leaders joined with Washington in a goodwill tour, bringing to the masses the Tuskegee principal's familiar message of advancement through economic empowerment and forging business alliances with White neighbors. While the article highlighted White attendance at some of the Louisiana stops, the photographs in the article show segregated audiences.

Figure 7.5 shows Washington in profile as a fiery orator, fists clenched, hat off, dynamically delivering his talk to an American flag-waving, densely packed Black crowd.[30] Washington had hired Bedou to chronicle such trips and to use images with articles and books marketing his ideas. Bedou's photograph in *The Survey* falls within the tradition of photojournalism that not only documents an event, but is also motivated by the desire to change social conditions. Audiences of *The Survey* in 1915 would have understood it as belonging to the world of contemporaries such as Jacob Riis and Lewis Hine.

Only a few months after *The Survey* article was published, Booker T. Washington died. Soon, two new books produced by Tuskegee insiders used the Bedou photograph. In the first one, the Bedou photograph appears in a 1916 reworking of Washington's first autobiography, *The Story of My Life and Work* (Figure 7.6).[31]

In the later version, now titled *Booker T. Washington's Own Story of His Life and Work*, we see a slightly different angle of the event.[32] We now realize, because of the shift in angle, that a series of photographs had been taken. In other words, Bedou took several shots and thus enabled authors slightly different choices for their works. We also learn from the caption that the event took place in New Iberia, Louisiana. Within months, Emmett J. Scott, Washington's longtime assistant, and Lyman Beecher Stowe, grandson of Harriet Beecher Stowe, published a biography of Washington's life titled *Booker T. Washington: Builder of a Civilization*.[33] *The Survey* article itself is quoted (without any identification of the source) in the chapter on race relations. However, the Bedou photograph is the sole illustration used in the next chapter, "Getting Closer to the People," a shift in emphasis toward the Black audience.[34] The Bedou photograph, this time shown as part of a series from the Louisiana tour, is described in the list of illustrations as "Mr. Washington in typical pose speaking to an audience" (Figure 7.7).[35]

Bedou is not credited for having taken the pictures, having fallen out of favor with the Tuskegee administration. He had been replaced as Tuskegee's official photographer by another African American artist, C.M. Battey. Since Emmett Scott was a member of the

Figure 7.4 A.P. Bedou, Cover of *The Survey*, June 19, 1915

Washington entourage with Bedou during the Louisiana tour, the omission is quite telling about their falling-out. Unlike the use of the photograph *The Survey*, the Bedou image in Scott's book helps to show how Washington never drifted far from the everyday world of the Black farmer, laborers, and the poor who lived in simple cabins.

LATER PRINTINGS OF THE BEDOU PHOTOGRAPH

The Bedou photograph, along with much of the holdings of Tuskegee University on Booker T. Washington, would eventually move to the Library of Congress and be

266

The Survey, June 19, 191?

Photo by Bedou

LOOSENING UP LOUISIANA

The story of a missionary junket carrying the gospel of co-operation, educational and economic, to black folk and white

By

William Anthony Aery

HAMPTON INSTITUTE

BOOKER T. WASHINGTON IN ACTION

Fifty thousand Negroes and hundreds of whites attended the outdoor meetings arranged through Hampton and Tuskegee Institutes.

GEORGIA now stands alone. This spring, for the first time, a group of Negro leaders, under the head of Booker T. Washington, accomplished an "educational tour" through the black parishes of Louisiana.

The general feeling had been that public opinion in neither Louisiana nor Georgia had reached the stage for the massmeetings and the general gospel of co-operation, educational and economic, which characterize these missionary junkets out from Tuskegee and Hampton. But on the invitation of not only representative Negro citizens, but of the governor of Louisiana and mayors of several cities, the venture was made; and for the first time in their lives hundreds of white men and women listened to Negro speakers.

Mr. Washington confessed that he and his party of twenty-five colored men, when they started on their pilgrimage, had something of the feeling of the little girl whose family were going on a trip. The night before she prayed as usual:

"Now I lay me down to sleep
I pray the Lord my soul to keep.
If I should die before I wake,
I pray the Lord my soul to take."

Then she added, "Good-bye, Lord, for two weeks. We are going down to Louisiana."

Great outdoor audiences of thousands upon thousands, however, white and colored, all friendly, prosperous and orderly, convinced Mr. Washington and his associates that the Negro in Louisiana is making progress in the essential things of life and that sympathetic contact of the races in Louisiana is more widespread, if less widely reported, than the spirit of modern violence or racial antagonism.

In this tour of the state these objects were kept in view: (1) to observe conditions among Negroes; (2) to say a word to promote greater progress among Negroes; (3) to bring about, if possible, more helpful and sensible relations between white and black.

Within four days, Mr. Washington spoke to over 50,000 of his own people, and hundreds of interested white men and women listened eagerly to his helpful message of progress and co-operation.

Meetings were held in New Orleans, St. Bernard Parish, New Iberia, Crowley, Lake Charles, Lafayette, Southern University, Baton Rouge, Alexandria, Gibsland, Shreveport, and Mansfield. Everywhere Mr. Washington and his party were met at railroad stations by crowds of black people; other crowds of white citizens gathered to see him and to hear him expound his gospel of industrial opportunity and racial good-will.

Negroes came on mule back, in carriages, and in wagons, long distances—ten, twenty, thirty, and even forty mi[les]. They gathered in thousands at rail[way] stations to see the "wizard of Tus[ke]gee." They stood for hours to get a chance to hear the most distinguished member of their race tell them of pro[g]ress and of the opportunities in the Southland. There were literally m[asses] of people and vehicles. Good-nat[ured] policemen were sometimes nearly c[ar]ried off their feet in the effort to k[eep] a path open through the eager thro[ng], but there was no trace of disord[er.] Everyone was happy, sober, recep[tive.]

Equally encouraging was the atti[tude] of white people—men and women [of] distinction in southern life. M[ayor] Behrman of New Orleans said to [Mr.] Washington: "The work you are d[oing] for the uplift of your people means [so] told good to the great state of Louis[iana] and to the whole country. Nowhere [has] your race greater opportunities tha[n in] Louisiana. If the people of the [Negro] race will follow your teachings, [it] will help materially to bring about a [con-]dition that will mean much for Lou[is-]iana, the South and the nation."

N. C. Blanchard of Shreveport, ex-governor of Louisiana, said in [intro-]ducing Mr. Washington to an aud[ience] of over 10,000 white and colored c[iti-]zens: "I am glad to see this good [at-]tendance of white people, represen[tative] white people at that; for his hono[r, the] mayor, is here, and with him are [many]

Figure 7.5 A.P. Bedou, Photograph of Booker T. Washington Speaking to an Audience in New Iberia, LA

Figure 7.6 A.P. Bedou, Washington Speaking at New Iberia, LA, On His Last State Educational Tour

Figure 7.7 Photographs of Booker T. Washington during His 1915 Louisiana Tour

organized by Louis Harlan, Washington's biographer of record. Harlan's two-part biography of Washington, the best-known account of the Tuskegee leader, contains several photographs.[36] Harlan recognized Washington's shrewd marketing strategies without specifically dealing with the many photographers employed to sell the Tuskegee philosophy. The Bedou photograph is included in Harlan's book, which even identifies its maker.[37] However, Bedou himself does not appear in the text of the book or in the index.

In the monumental fourteen volumes of *The Booker T. Washington Papers*, scant reference is made to the complex aesthetic world of artists, poets, musicians, and photographers hired by Washington as part of his program. Consequently, the hundreds of references to these artists are not available in the LOC finder guide to the collection.[38] Harlan's portrait of Washington is that of a devious trickster working behind the scenes, and had little room for the aesthetic projects of the Tuskegee principal. Since Harlan's work set the standard for both the scholarship and cataloguing of most of the Washington primary text and visual sources, his points of emphasis and omissions held great weight for future research.

Robert Norrell's new biography of Washington, *Up from History*, is a response to Harlan. Norrell counters the body of research that resulted from casting Washington as the accommodationist counterpart to W.E.B. Du Bois, with a look at Washington as a man circumscribed by racism.[39] The Bedou photograph is included in Norrell's book and serves as the back dust-jacket image. Norrell appropriated the photograph from Scott and Stowe's book for his chapter on Washington's development as a public speaker during the 1890s (even though the image is from a very different period in Washington's life).[40] Bedou is not identified as the photographer on the jacket nor in the text. The purpose of the photograph is to present an archetypal image of Washington as a public speaker who reached diverse audience with his disarming humor, simple charm, and plain talk. However, at the time of the Bedou photograph, Washington was a much more outspoken advocate of Black history, achievements, towns, campuses, Black Diaspora, and depictions in film and popular culture. Who could have imagined that the man on the stage in Atlanta in 1895 would tell a Black audience at Western University, nearly twenty years later: "It is indeed true that many of our own race go to institutions where they study all races, history of the Jews, history of the Greeks, history of the Germans, but they never study the history of our own race."[41] The image of Washington in the Bedou photograph bears little resemblance to the early phase of Washington's life compellingly described by Norrell.

The Bedou photograph also appears in several history publications, including *The American Pageant*, a popular book used as a United States history survey by Advanced Placement high school and university courses. This well-known, thoroughly researched book is richly illustrated with reproductions of paintings, political cartoons, ephemera, and photographs. The Bedou photograph in *American Pageant*, is reproduced with this caption:

> In a famous speech in New Orleans in 1895, Washington grudgingly acquiesced in social separateness for blacks. On that occasion, he told his largely white audience, "In all things that are purely social, we can be as separate as the fingers, yet one as the hand in all things essential to mutual progress."[42]

The text of the caption reveals a major problem with the vast, easily availability of images. Washington's 1895 Atlanta Cotton States Exposition speech should have been the intended reference. However, that event occurred in Atlanta, not New Orleans. The mistake was made, in part, by taking the LOC's misidentification of the work as Washington speaking from a stage in New Orleans, *ca.* 1912, not New Iberia in 1915. While Washington spoke to a segregated, primarily White crowd in Atlanta, the Bedou photograph in *American Pageant* shows a sea of admiring Black faces. This is a case of embellishing an existing narrative with an image rather than examining the historical meaning of the photograph. This misappropriation allows us to see the importance of critical examination of photographs. Certainly Washington on the stage in 1895 Atlanta, the first Black man to speak to such a White audience at an event in the South, did not strike such a forceful pose. Instead, the ever-cautious Washington would have employed his mask of subservience. This particular use of the Bedou photograph to serve as a record of an event that was not photographed opened my eyes to a number of proxy images in history texts; that is, stand-in images for events that were not documented by the camera. In our world of image abundance and surveillance, we sometimes forget that many important events were never documented by a camera. That historical reality does not stop us from sometimes creating them.

SPECIAL CONSIDERATIONS IN AFRICAN AMERICAN SCHOLARSHIP: ACCESS TO PHOTOGRAPHS

I am sympathetic to all of the authors of the works cited because finding information on A.P. Bedou and other early African American photographers can be very difficult. While Deborah Willis's *Reflections in Black* offers an invaluable starting point in the study of the lives of Black photographers, little is known about even the well-known ones.[43] As mentioned, the first questions facing researchers working with photographs is simply: who took it and when was it taken? During the period from the invention of photography in the 1830s through 1920s, these can be very difficult questions to answer. Washington rose to prominence at the very beginning of an era in which photographers began to copyright images with blind stamps or a signature. Consequently, few Washington photographs bear the name of the photographer. Even when they do, as in Figure 7.2, Bedou put his name on an image of Washington he appropriated from Addison Turner. In addition, photographs at the time were often sold to various distributors who, in turn, placed their marks on the photographs, erasing the photographer from history or leading to misidentification. Moreover, Black photographers were rarely employed by the mainstream news agencies. Finally, I have found through genealogical research that Black photographers sometimes passed as White in census reports.

The second issue concerning the use of photographs during this era concerns providing an accurate date. Most of Washington's photographs, except those by nationally known artists such as Frances Benjamin Johnston, are not dated.[44] Even when they are dated, sometimes the date on the photograph is not the date of its creation but that of a later copyright. Along these lines, photographers sometime published the work of others and added their own later date.

The third issue confronting researchers concerns access to the original photographs. Many works exist today only as reproductions, resulting from the fact that many Black colleges did not have the resources or archives to collect and preserve works. Also, Black artists were simply not acknowledged in the same way as those in the mainstream, and their stories were not frequently recorded. Only last year the majority of works by the other major Washington photographer, C.M. Battey, came to light. Battey, one of the great photographers of the 20th century, who is known primarily as the teacher of photographers such as P.H. Polk, had been represented by a handful of works. Miraculously, in 2008 hundreds of his photographs were found in an attic of a home in Tuskegee.

The places to start looking for photographs of and by African Americans are the LOC, the Schomburg Library and other Black research libraries, Black history museums, university collections, and art museums. Even then, there are major hurdles. For instance, Tuskegee's archives were closed for a few years. Some Black colleges no longer exist. I vividly remember driving through Alabama in search of Kowaliga Academic and Industrial Institute, a Black college run by William Benson. To my surprise, it now lies under the surface of Lake Martin. Writing Kowaliga's full story is nearly impossible.[45] Many photographs and other materials remain in the private collections of African American families and private collectors. Of these, I have found that several of the works that have survived are in a poor condition, meaning that they will not be part of any museum exhibitions and the publications which disseminate the works into the historical narratives.

Subsequently, I have come to understand why a handful of images tend to get reused again and again. There is always the danger of forgetting that there are complicated reasons why things survive or gain importance. The most beautiful, or representative, or important images are not always the ones we get to see and access. The critic Holland Cotter said it best:

> Many of our masterpieces owe their origins to the distinctly immoral ambitions of power politics, their survival to prosaic strokes of luck, their present pre-eminence to institutional marketing, scholarly attention and popular sentiment. Even so, survival can be chancy. Fine things get tossed out and crummy things kept all the time.[46]

The lessons for academics are that, when dealing with photographs, many works are still waiting to be made public, making it very difficult to be sure if the known works are truly representative. Do not think that the entire catalogue of images is just a mouse click away, that photographs should be added after the writing is complete, and that photographs in a publication are the same as the originals. Change the size, alter the medium, and add a caption, and the photograph is transformed into something different than when it was produced and seen by its intended audience.

Because there are so many challenges facing those interested in working with African American images, researchers must be open to some non-traditional ways of finding images. They must learn to think outside of the academic box and traditional holdings. Over the years I have learned of many Black families who use their collections of photographs to teach history in their communities. They feel that local education is a better use of the works than placing them in an institutional archive. I could not have conducted my research without the generosity of many families who made their private collections available, or told me about other people to contact so that I could see their collections. For example, Gerald Norwood of Wichita, Kansas, is a passionate collector of Black history. Last year, he returned a lithograph, based on a Washington photograph, which had been used in publicizing Washington's appearance in Wilson, North Carolina to a Black and White audience at the Colored Graded School. The lithograph was framed with photographs supplied by Washington's oldest living descendant, Margaret Washington Clifford. Citizens of Wilson raised the money for the work to be displayed in the Black center, the Round House Museum. This small local event, a news item only reported in *The Wilson Daily*

Times, took place in the overlooked world of Black history community educational efforts.[47]

So how does the novice researcher find such works? Get off the computer and go outside. There was a great story in the paper last year about scientists being baffled by a gathering of whale sharks in the Gulf of Mexico. All kinds of theories were being offered. Then, one of the scientists actually asked the local fisherman what they knew about it. Their answer stunned him. "They said, We see whale sharks all the time," he recalled. "These guys see a lot of stuff out there, and they never think to contact us, and we had not been contacting them."[48] Contact people, hear their stories, and see what they have to share.

QUESTIONS FOR DISCUSSION

1. Like many historical events, Booker T. Washington's 1895 Atlanta Cotton States Exposition speech was not documented with any photographs. In the absence of any images, historians have substituted other photographs to serve as visual proxies. Find another example of an historical event that was not recorded with a camera. What kinds of images are chosen to offer a visual record or dramatization of the event? How do these images either enhance or distort our understanding of the historical event?

2. I recommend Robert M. Levine's *Insights into American History: Photographs as Documents* (Pearson Education, 2004) as a great starting point for teaching students how to think about photographs as a primary source. The book provides a concise set of questions, based on a variety of themes, for analyzing the meaning of photographs. From my experience, Levine's chapter on family snapshots is the place to start because the students begin by reflecting upon their own history. Here are a few of his discussion questions:

    What was the occasion for this picture?
    Who suggested that the picture be taken?
    Who took the photograph?
    Are the people in the snapshot arranged in any discernable way?
    Are the spatial relationships in the picture determined by cultural mores or are they accidental? (Levine, 161)

NOTES

1. Kalefa Sanneh, "Annals of Politics," *The New Yorker*, 2 February 2009, 26–30.
2. Walden Fawcett, Booker T. Washington, three-quarter length portrait, *ca.* 17 June 1908, LC-USZ62–128954.
3. Sanneh, "Annals of Politics," 27.
4. Linda Ries, review of *Picturing the Century: One Hundred Years of Photography from the National Archives* by Bruce I. Bustard, *The Public Historian* (Spring 2000): 99.
5. For example, see John H. Tarbell, "My Experiences Photographing the Negro in the South," *New England Magazine* (December 1903): 463–478. See also Thomas L. Johnson and Nina J. Root, *Camera Man's Journey* (Athens, GA: The University of Georgia Press, 2002).
6. A.P. Bedou postcard, Principal Washington's Home, Tuskegee Institute, Ala. Courtesy of Collection of Margaret Washington Clifford, Atlanta, Georgia. The Portrait of Washington is by Addison Turner.
7. Michael Bieze, *Booker T. Washington and the Art of Self-Representation* (New York: Peter Lang Publishing, 2008).

8. Alan Trachtenberg, *Reading American Photographs* (New York: Hill and Wang, 1989), 253ff.

9. Dona Schwartz, "Objective Representation: Photographs as Fact," in *Picturing the Past: Media, History and Photography*, ed. Bonnie Brennan and Hanno Hardt (Urbana and Chicago: University of Illinois Press,1999), 174.

10. John Lewis Gaddis, *The Landscape of History: How Historians Map the Past* (New York: Oxford University Press, 2002), 15.

11. Susan Sontag, *On Photography* (New York: Dell Publishing, 1973; 1977), 138.

12. Cara A. Finnegan, *Picturing Poverty: Print Culture and FSA Photographs* (Washington, DC: Smithsonian Books, 2003).

13. Ibid., xv.

14. Peter Burke, *Eyewitnessing: The Uses of Images as Historical Evidence* (Ithaca: Cornell University Press, 2001).

15. Robert M. Levine, *Images of History: Nineteenth and Early Twentieth Century Latin American Photographs as Documents* (Durham, NC: Duke University Press, 1989), 77–90.

16. John Collier Jr. and Malcolm Collier, *Visual Anthropology: Photography as a Research Method* (Albuquerque: University of New Mexico Press, 1986).

17. Malek Alloula, *The Colonial Harem* (Minneapolis: University of Minnesota Press, 1986).

18. Shawn Michelle Smith, *Photography on the Color Line: W.E.B. Du Bois, Race, and Visual Culture* (Durham, NC: Duke University Press, 2004). Judith Fryer Davidov, *Women's Camera Work: Self/Body/Other in American Visual Culture* (Durham, NC: Duke University Press, 1998). David Levering Lewis and Deborah Willis, *A Small Nation of People: W.E.B. Du Bois and African American Portraits of Progress* (New York: HarperCollins Publishers, 2003).

19. Richard Benson, *The Printed Picture* (New York: The Museum of Modern Art, 2008), 2–3.

20. Roland Barthes, *Camera Lucida* (New York: Hill and Wang, 1981), 80.

21. *Body and Soul*, prod. and dir. by Oscar Micheaux, 86 minutes, Micheaux Film Corporation, 1925, Silent Film.

22. Review of *Beyond Oscar Wilde: Portraits of Late Victorian Writers and Artists from the Mark Samuels Lasner Collection*, text by Margaret D. Stetz. *The Chronicle of Higher Education*, 13 September 2002, B20.

23. John Storey, *An Introductory Guide to Cultural History and Popular Culture* (Athens: The University of Georgia Press, 1993), 80.

24. Stephen F. Sprague, "Yoruba Photography: How the Yoruba See Themselves," in *Photography's Other Histories*, ed. Christopher Pinney and Nicolas Peterson (Durham, NC: Duke University Press, 2003), 240–260.

25. A.P. Bedou, Booker T. Washington speaking to an audience in New Iberia, Louisiana, 1915. Booker T. Washington Collection, Library of Congress (LC-USZ62–131995). Identified in the LOC as Booker T. Washington speaking from a stage near New Orleans, Louisiana, *ca.* 1912.

26. See Louis R. Harlan and Raymond W. Smock, eds., *The Booker T. Washington Papers*, vol. 13 (Urbana: University of Illinois Press, 1972–1989), 281, "An Account of Washington's Tour of Louisiana in the *Chicago Herald*," 26 April 1915. See also, Richard Powell & Jock Reynolds, eds., *To Conserve a Legacy* (Andover: Addison Gallery of American Art, New York: The Studio Museum of Harlem, 1999), 165.

27. William Anthony Aery, "Loosening up Louisiana," *The Survey*, 19 June 1915, 266–269.

28. *The Survey*, 12 June 1915, 258.

29. A.P. Bedou, cover of *The Survey*, 19 June 1915.

30. A.P. Bedou, Photograph of Booker T. Washington Speaking to an Audience in New Iberia, Louisiana, *The Survey*, 19 June 1915, 266.

31. Booker T. Washington, *The Story of My Life and Work* (Atlanta: J.L. Nichols & Co., 1901). Illustration by A.P. Bedou, "Dr. Washington speaking at New Iberia, LA., On His Last State Educational Tour." In Albon L. Holsey, *Booker T. Washington's Own Story of His Life and Work* (J.L. Nichols & Co., 1915), 338–339.

32. Albon L. Holsey, *Booker T. Washington's Own Story of His Life and Work* (J.L. Nichols & Co., 1915), 338–339.

33. Emmett J. Scott and Lyman Beecher Stowe, *Booker T. Washington: Builder of a Civilization* (New York: Doubleday, Page & Company, 1916; reprint 1918).

34. Ibid., 136–137.

35. Photographs of Booker T. Washington from his 1915 Louisiana tour. In Emmett J. Scott and Lyman Beecher Stowe, *Booker T. Washington: Builder of a Civilization* (New York: Doubleday, Page & Co., 1918), 136–137.

36. Louis R. Harlan, *Booker T. Washington: The Making of a Black Leader, 1856–1901* (New York: Oxford University Press, 1972), and Louis R. Harlan, *Booker T. Washington: The Wizard of Tuskegee, 1901–1915* (New York: Oxford University Press, 1983).

37. Harlan, *Booker T. Washington: The Wizard of Tuskegee*, 270–271.

38. Booker T. Washington Papers in the Division of Manuscripts of the Library of Congress, Library of Congress, Washington, D.C.
39. Robert J. Norrell, *Up From History: The Life of Booker T. Washington* (Cambridge, MA: Harvard University Press, 2009).
40. Ibid., 137.
41. Harlan, "A Speech at Western University," 4 March 1914, *Booker T. Washington Papers*, vol. 12, 466–468.
42. David M. Kennedy, Lizabeth Cohen, and Thomas A. Bailey, *The American Pageant*, 13th ed. (Boston: Houghton Mifflin Company, 2006), 575.
43. Deborah Willis, *Reflections in Black: A History of Black Photographers 1840 to the Present* (New York: W.W. Norton, 2000).
44. See Bettina Berch, *The Woman behind the Lens: The Life and Work of Frances Benjamin Johnston* (Charlottesville: The University of Virginia Press, 2000), 59–69.
45. For photographs of the school see Oswald Garrison Villard, "An Alabama Negro School," *The American Monthly Review of Reviews*, December 1902, 711–714.
46. Holland Cotter, "Framing the Message of a Generation: Cultural History is Being Written, and Revised, Right Before Our Eyes. It Can Be a Disturbing Sight," *The New York Times*, May 31, 2009, Arts & Leisure, 1.
47. Adrienne Gaskins, "Donations Help Unveil Washington Print," *The Wilson Daily Times*, 1A–2A.
48. Jim Tharpe, "Whale Sharks Mysteriously Gather," *The Atlanta Journal Constitution*, 17 August 2008, A3.

8

QUANTIFICATION AND COGNITIVE HISTORY
Applying Social Science Theory and Method to Historical Data

Jane Robbins

The undervaluing of history is one of the great paradoxes of academic and practical life. History gets little respect in this country—until, of course, we need it: the banks implode, disaster strikes, a government betrays, a shocking crime is committed. Suddenly everyone is asking, what happened, how did it happen, or why did it happen? We want to know who was involved, and who did or said or knew what? These are historical questions. They can only be answered by locating and digging through the historical record.

In that I was once one of those people who had little regard for history, I am an accidental, one might even say reluctant, historian. My interests lie in the area of governance and management in higher education; because my work is concerned with the behavior of universities as institutions, I am naturally interested in institutional theory, organizational economics, and leadership and ethics. But it was impossible for me to look at, or analyze, the current state of the university without wondering how it got there. I began to realize that history is not merely a subject or discipline, it is a *methodology*—a tool for uncovering the back-story on today's news, and for understanding the roots and consequences of policy and practice—a way to answer all those process questions of who, how, and why.

The specific question that led me to history was: By what process did the patenting of scientific research in universities become institutionalized? I was particularly curious about the underlying decision making by university leaders—the question, in effect: What were they thinking?

I came to call this *cognitive history*. I wanted to trace the process of reasoning and deciding about patenting science in a systematic way, one that would extract and make meaning of the relevant data from the historical documents within a theoretical framework. This meant that I would be treating the text as data in a manner more conventionally associated with empirical research in the social sciences, and I began to think about whether, and how, such data might be quantified or represented.

In an age when even history, and historians, are not immune to the ever-encroaching, knee-jerk insistence on quantification, particularly from funding sources and journals, and when historians are being bypassed by departments of higher education in favor of quantitative specialists in the social sciences, it is worth asking to what extent, in what form, and under what circumstances quantification of historical data adds value. Einstein once famously remarked that "Not everything that counts can be counted, and not everything that can be counted, counts." This bears remembering. As historians, we need to be able to defend what we do or do not do, and to ensure that others understand when the calls for quantification make sense, and when they not only do not, but may also mislead or distort the record, thus undermining or ignoring the truly valuable "uses of history."[1] The question of quantification in history is a particularly timely topic for higher education, for two reasons. There is funding pressure for using empirical methods in educational research, particularly to calculate what are called "treatment effects."[2] At the same time, the central method of empirical work in the social sciences, null-hypothesis testing, is increasingly under attack within its own fields for producing limited and irrelevant—even wrong—findings. Critics argue that in complex fields of human endeavor, empirical results produce "excessive truth claims based on partial analysis and both unrealistic and biased assumptions," and that the scientific method is not sophisticated enough to be rigorously applied to issues involving the complexity of human nature and the role of intentionality and choice.[3] In strategic management and organizational studies, fields that share many issues of concern with the field of higher education (especially performance improvement and a search for reasons for success or failure), and where an active search is on for more realistic and integrative methods, leading scholars argue that in focusing on scientific research, business schools are quickly "institutionalizing their own irrelevance."[4] We want to be sure that we don't follow them off the cliff.

Based on observation and experience (including trial and error) since first raising my own question of how best to approach historical data to make evidence more explicit, I've come to some conclusions about the potential for, and value of, quantifying and representing historical data, and of combining social science theory with history. The telling of history does not, except in a very narrow sense, lend itself to positivist methods. However, numbers and quantitative analysis can be useful for abstracting or representing complex information, and in certain instances to confirm traditional historical analysis or to generate *qualified estimates* of the effects of a particular historical process or decision (although not the historical or decision making process itself). In that sense, quantification is supplementary or complementary to narrative, not a substitute for narrative; its greatest utility may be in its iterative relation with the historical text, each raising questions about, and providing a check on, one another. A clear contribution of the social sciences, however, is their established theories, which can assist in the framing of historical problems, the interpretation of historical data, and the drawing of connections between history and the present.

In the following two sections, I discuss and illustrate some of the pros and cons of conventional quantification and empirical analysis of historical data, and my own conception of cognitive history within a social science theoretical framework. Taking a cue from the positivists, I ask whether quantification offers any particular parsimony to history that cannot be achieved by traditional historical methods.[5] By parsimony, I mean two things: *efficiency*, defined here as economy and convenience of communication; and *effectiveness*, defined as providing greater precision and greater credibility or understanding. Ideally, we want any quantification methods we use to yield both measures of parsimony, while preserving history's unique ability to convey the big story.

TRADITIONAL QUANTIFICATION IN HISTORY

The most common use of quantitative data in history is counts, which address the "how many?" question. Counts can be shown in tabular or graphic form to indicate either absolute numbers or proportions, or trends or change over time; they may be periodic or continuous series, and may show the added value of percentage change or other difference measure. A simple example is shown in Figure 8.1, a trend line in funding of university research and as a percentage of GDP from 1965 to 2005.[6] Similarly, we could count the number of female or African American students attending medical school during the 19th century; the proportion of faculty off the tenure track since 1970; the percentage change in colleges requiring a year of geology for all students since 1900; or anything else for which we would like to understand or show a sense of absolute or relative growth, change, or proportion.

In looking at Figure 8.1 or similar examples, we can acknowledge that this is an efficient form of communication of data to the reader. Rather than provide every dollar amount for each year, which would require a long and dull run-on paragraph, and then for the reader to have to adjust each amount to present value and calculate percentages, the graph in Figure 8.1 does it for us: this is a convenient and economical representation of the history of funding. But is it more effective than the historical narrative? In this case, the answer is mixed. On the one hand, no, because it does not indicate anything about how or why the trend came to look as it does. For that, the text is needed to identify and make connections among historical reasons for funding growth, such as government programs, economic conditions, and the emergence of new industries. This is true even when the data are suggestive, because what they suggest often depends on some other, prior knowledge of the reader, whereas a narrative does not. On the other, a qualified yes, because it lends credibility to the text—it is specific evidence of the claim of growth—and also heightens, through the drama of representation, the magnitude of that claim. I say "qualified" only because the source of the counts matters: were they

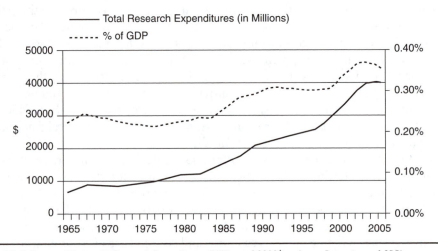

Figure 8.1 College and University Research Expenditures (Millions of 2000$ and as a Percentage of GDP)

Source: Roger Geiger, "Culture, Careers, Knowledge, & Money: Change in American Higher Education since 1980" (Keynote address presented at *Deutsche Gesellschaft für Amerikastudien*, Jena, Germany, June 4, 2009). Reproduced with permission.

pulled from primary historical records, or secondary reports or databases, which may be unreliable or replicate prior errors, or may contain adjustments to the data of which we are unaware? So, counts may be efficient, but they are not, on their own, effective as substitutes for the contextual narrative, and do not necessarily increase our understanding. But they may provide complementary evidence that enhances credibility, and as a visual representation may increase the impact of the data on the reader.

A variation on counts is survey data, which may serve as a large-scale permutation on, or supplement to, oral history. Diamond and Hurley report the results of a survey of women who went through the Higher Education Resource Services (HERS) administrator training institutes program between 1976 and 2003, and generated descriptive statistics from the responses on a wide range of questions related to their backgrounds and career experiences.[7] Table 8.1, for example, shows the percentage of respondents who experienced different primary obstacles to their careers, and who reported no obstacles at all.

As with Figure 8.1, this is an efficient form of communicating historical data; it also enhances credibility as, although it is subject to the vagaries of memory and bias implied in all self-reported data, it is from a primary source, and is more precise than generalizing from, for example, anecdotal reports or limited interviews. Surveys as oral histories are not always possible and have their own sampling and other methodological issues but this example suggests that they can add value to a history based on institutional documents alone, and offer a relatively efficient means for investigating the individual, human dimension of recent history.

Beyond counts and their variants, historians have usually—even logically—shunned quantitative methods of *analysis* such as regression because these modeling methods have as their object something that many historians would find internally inconsistent: prediction. Historians report on and interpret the past, and despite the colloquialism that "history repeats itself," are not so literal or so certain: history tends to make you less, not more, sure. So the positivist concepts of standard errors, dummy variables, and statistical significance may seem dangerously simplistic to us; as Barbara Tuchman put it, "Prefabricated systems make me suspicious and science applied to history makes me

Table 8.1 Percentage of HERS Alumnae Reporting Perceived Obstacles to Career Advancement, by Type and Decade of Attendance (Response limited to *one* obstacle per respondent)

Obstacle/No obstacle	1976–1984 (N=201)	1985–1994 (N=395)	1995–2003 (N=603)	Total (N=1199)
No obstacle	40	42	34	37
Education/Degree	11	10	12	11
Appropriate Training	3	4	5	4
Experience	8	10	12	11
Personal Motivation	1	2	2	2
Geographic Mobility	7	7	9	8
Family Responsibility	8	11	8	9
Discrimination	13	9	10	10
Other obstacle	7	6	8	7

Source: Adapted from Nancy Diamond and Sam M. Hurley, "Preparing Women for Academic Leadership: The Higher Education Resources Services (HERS) Institutes, 1976–2003" (paper presented at AERA Annual Meeting, San Diego, CA, April 13–17, 2009). Reprinted with permission.

wince."[8] Historians generally believe that explanatory generalizations emerge from the narrative, rather than from brute force methods.

Historians are, however, interested in causality, another use of scientific methods. Can traditional quantitative methods of analysis such as regression contribute to predicting or identifying the causes and effects of historical events? Put another way, can they be used to identify the effects of history? Let's consider an example—first noting that economic, labor, and policy history are the primary areas where regression is used, and much less than one might expect. Goldin and Katz have extensively explored the question of the relationship between technological change, education, and inequality.[9] Drawn from the central chapter of their book, Figure 8.2 shows actual versus predicted college wage premiums versus those with a high school diploma, calculated as the log of the ratio between the two groups, for the years 1915–2005 for two of five model specifications in an ordinary least squares regression; the actual regression results for all five models are provided in a table.

Is this efficient and effective, as defined earlier? That, it turns out, is a complex question. On balance, I would have to say no—and at the same time, to say that I find careful, detailed empirical studies like this extremely valuable. While a complete review is not possible here, let me try to explain that seemingly internally inconsistent statement. At first glance (and that is part of the problem), Figure 8.2 does appear to meet the test of both efficiency and effectiveness: we see that the college wage premium is roughly where it was 90 years ago; that it declined until the mid-20th century and then increased; and that there were two periods of unusual departure from the overall trends.

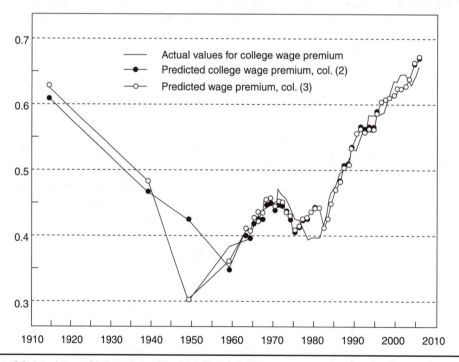

Figure 8.2 Actual versus Predicted College Wage Premium: 1915–2005

Source: Claudia Goldin and Lawrence F. Katz, *The Race Between Technology and Education* (Boston, MA: Belknap Press of Harvard University Press, 2008), 300.

The graph communicates all this in what looks to be a very precise manner; its initial impact is high.

Does it enhance the credibility of the text, however, or is it the text that is needed to determine the credibility of the regression results? In this and other regressions, abstracted tabular and graphic results require extensive evaluation of the research design on the part of the reader, as reliance on the regression results alone could be misleading (those "partial truths" mentioned earlier). In this sense it is not particularly economical either: the abstraction cannot be taken at face value, but requires a lot of work to understand the discontinuity and noncomparability of data sources and the choices and compromises made in the construction and adjustment of data sets; sampling and sample differences across time; creation of dummy variables for unknown information; the size of and explanations for standard errors. This means, in effect, understanding multiple estimates on which the final estimates that we see represented here are based.

For Figure 8.2, an entire book, including several appendices, is necessary to judge the credibility and utility of the results contained in that one graph. *This kind of judgment is to be distinguished from judging the credibility of the application of the methodology;* they are often conflated, but are separate questions. Thus, an analysis can be done as thoroughly and meticulously as possible, within the accepted norms of the method, and the results may still be viewed with skepticism *because* of the method and the simplifications, substitutions, excluded variables, and adjustments it *necessarily* entails.

For a historian, however, even results that must be viewed with caution, and that have clear limitations, can provide specific insights and motivate questions for more in-depth historical analysis; often, another source of questions can be found in the researchers' own conclusions and explanations. Regardless of the questions that regression, well-designed or otherwise, may raise, however, it is the *uses* of work like this that are of concern. It may all be well and good as long as you understand what you actually are dealing with, and have studied the work carefully. But policy makers will read or be presented with the conclusions (including summary graphs), not the caveats and details, and statistics on their own may readily be used as "proof" by those with a policy agenda—including in a manner other than intended by the author. In this instance, we have to read across several hundred pages to learn that the demand for skilled workers has remained relatively stable for more than 100 years; that the large spike in the wage premium in the past 25 years was due to a large decline in the growth rate of the relative supply of educated workers; and that, had that supply not slowed, the wage premium would have *fallen*. We also learn that the return to white collar work was highest before 1914; that the wage premium for high school is much lower now than it was before 1915; and that the primary reason for the collapse of the high school wage premium was oversupply, an effect of the successful high-school movement (Goldin and Katz, 101, 121, 304). This is all very interesting, and raises a number of important questions, including ones about the internal consistency of the authors' own ultimate conclusions and recommendations. But none of this fascinating story can be readily seen in the culminating Figure 8.2 or, for that matter, the many useful tables and charts scattered throughout the book. Even if we accept the construction of the regression analysis, the implications of these other statements suggest possibilities quite different from the regression results in isolation.[10]

In sum, quantification of historical facts seems to enhance the historical narrative. Analyses using regression and other methods that aim to show cause or prediction using historical data should be carefully scrutinized; oddly, these "scientific" methods of studying history for causal purposes may be less, not more, objective than traditional history of narrative construction. No method, of course, is truly objective; all are partial, limited, and subject to human bias. But the method must suit the complexity of the questions and the objects of study, and the data should be as close as possible to what Tuchman called "contemporary with the subject."[11] To paraphrase Bendix, we want to be careful that pressure for empiricism in higher education history does not become a fetish to the detriment of reason.[12]

COGNITIVE HISTORY: AN ILLUSTRATIVE CASE OF THEORY, METHODS, AND INTERPRETATION

Cognitive history is a blending of cognitive and institutional theory and methods with a historical approach to studying institutional change. By institutional change, I mean any change that alters an institutionalized way of operating; this can be a process, program, strategy, structure, policy, culture, or any other facet of organizational or social life.

One way of conceiving of cognitive history is as a method within the method of history for targeting and abstracting a particularly useful kind of historical evidence—language or rhetoric—that reflects thought over time. It is a form of tracing "the history of the history" of events or outcomes by uncovering, revealing, and parsing in detail the underlying narrative of thought. By focusing on agency in the unfolding of events, and on the reasoning, decision making, and communication of actors in the change process, it produces a history that moves beyond the "what" and "when" to explanatory details of the "who, how, and why." It is particularly useful for answering questions of how specific circumstances came to be; who (whether individuals or groups) was instrumental in shaping those circumstances; and the validity of contemporary claims and assumptions about those circumstances, particularly their consequences. It is also an excellent means for studying increasingly visible questions of individual and institutional ethics, and the historical underpinnings of policy and of organizational mission or structure.

Cognitive history thus directly responds to the critiques of empirical studies of organization as process- and people-free, and to calls for a more agency-oriented approach; a view of change as mobilized and driven by political and entrepreneurial methods; an understanding of change as arising out of an inherited set of actors and complex arrangements; and an emphasis on judgment, the semantic content of problems, bias, and emotion ("hot cognition").[13] In these ways, cognitive history serves traditional history well: it reflects Mark Bloch's view that "historical facts are, in essence, psychological facts," and that "it is human consciousness which is the subject matter of history," allowing us to find explanations for how and why changes occur in the "peculiar propensities of collective sensibility."[14]

Here are four foundation guidelines to my approach to cognitive history, illustrated with the original institutional question that led me to this method.

1. Cognitive History Begins with a Question about a Contemporary Situation or State, and Works Backward to Locate Its Source, then Forward to Document Its Evolution

Early in my doctoral studies I became interested in university–industry–government relations through reading about the growth of research universities. Having come to graduate school after a long career in business, I quickly recognized the essentially commercial nature of many university activities and relationships as far back as the mid-19th century. As I started to conduct my own research, I stumbled on the issue of university patents, and became fascinated: here was an ostensibly established activity not only purely commercial, but also contrary to the dominant idea of the university as a generator of knowledge for all; moreover, the higher education literature was silent on the subject. This was in itself curious considering its fundamental connection to university mission and governance, but principally I wondered: How did the current practice of patenting research in universities come to be taken for granted?

I immediately understood that this question of institutionalization was a historical question—that its answer or any beginning of an answer meant that I would be doing a historical dissertation. From preliminary research, I knew that another "taken-for-granted" notion—that university patenting had begun with the passage of the Bayh-Dole Act in 1980—was not accurate. It seemed to me that Bayh-Dole was in fact the culmination of a much longer process, not a sudden paradigmatic change. I wondered: how long? where and why did it start, and with whom? I came to the conclusion that the history I was interested in was the history of the thinking behind an accepted policy—the process of decision making, the arguments made, and the reasons given that led to a decision that has had fundamental, and continuing, effects on university operations, university culture, university relations with government and industry, and indeed, on science itself. This shift in focus in the historical narrative implied a shift in attention toward those documents that most closely constitute the concretization of thought: the writing and speaking of individuals in the moment.

2. Cognitive History Pays Special Attention to Documents that Memorialize Thinking and Make Reasoning Explicit

In cognitive history, private correspondence, meeting transcripts, hearings, briefs, working papers (e.g., study and committee files that serve as background to published reports), and other material that memorializes thinking forms the *basis* of analysis. These kinds of internal documents reveal the interactions among decision makers that contain the motivation for and the product of the change process, or its resistance and stagnation; they "inevitably contain much of the self-analysis necessary for making important decisions."[15] I consider summary documents such as secretarial or trustee minutes, final reports, budgets, newspaper articles, and so on, to be important but secondary productions, and use them primarily for fact-checking, supplementing, or sourcing other documents; the cognitive historian drills way down.

Archival data is ideal for the study of reasoning. It allows for a long time frame, crucial to answering questions, such as my own, of process dynamics (including environmental change or change in agents) and their effects on thinking. It also permits the analysis of the direct discourse of prominent figures that were involved in politically or emotionally charged issues—both of which were true of my topic of patenting science.

Once I had determined that I wanted to focus on thinking, I realized that, to cover a meaningful period of time—under my working-backwards principle I had determined 1917 to be the year of the first recorded university-owned patent—and to be able to draw anything close to a generalization for the field of higher education as a whole, I needed a "way in." It was obviously not possible to travel to every major research university and locate and study the kinds of documents I sought at the depth required (although I have done a lot of that). I searched for, and ultimately found, a lens through which to conduct a field-level analysis for the relevant period: patent policy committees of the National Academies of Science (NAS). These proved to be an extensive goldmine of meticulous, if arcanely catalogued, records of just the sort I wanted. There are reasons for this, and why I have come to view cross-sectoral committees as outstanding sources of data for cognitive history. First, committee members are not all in one location, so must correspond, and even argue, about their positions and their reasons for their positions by mail, often at length. Second, committees periodically meet, and when they do, their deliberations are often recorded in full, resulting in never-before-published, confidential transcripts. Third, cross-sectoral committees often function within a pivotal association or other group that is a communication hub for all members, allowing both scope and scale; this was true of the NAS, a network linking universities, the government, and industry. A bonus was that the files contained much of the secondary articles, news, and other references as well.

Through the NAS records, I had access to such data entirely focused on patent policy in science and universities for the years 1917–1966. In telling the story of university patenting, I wanted to extract and abstract the reasoning. I looked for a means to that end, and found it in discourse, rhetorical, and content analysis approaches.

3. Cognitive History Uses Social Science Tools for Analysis

The evidence contained in a historical narrative focused on thought and communication can be methodically parsed using techniques of language analysis developed from research in language-focused fields such as law, philosophy, communications/media studies, psychology, and political science. These sharpen and abstract the historical evidence for drawing organizational conclusions; offer a means of evaluating and summarizing an extended historical process; and provide a check against overall historical interpretation. Depending on the particular questions or topics being pursued, these techniques might include structural argument analysis (useful for identifying bias, fallacy, and types of reasons and appeals) or integrative complexity analysis (frequently used to analyze ideology in political speech). Thematic content analysis, including computerized analysis, allows another form of abstraction and analysis, including the quantification and modeling of argumentation; the analysis of thinking on a particular issue over time; the analysis of implicit values; and the role of individual background and influence on decisions. All forms of content analysis lend themselves to the study of strategic persons or groups, and differences in perspective or justification, thus addressing one of the critiques of empirical studies of organization.[16]

I have experimented with, and continue to be interested in, all three of the above methods—all well-suited to archival data. I describe here a simple example that serves to illustrate their use and my assessment of their value to understanding the history of higher education—in the instant case, the history of university patenting.[17] I applied each of the three methods to a 114-page confidential transcript, stamped "Not for Publication," of a conference on patent policy convened by the NAS in 1935. My motivation to analyze the transcript in depth stemmed from the fact that the conference was *strategic*—intended to induce a specific policy change by convincing attendees of its merits—and the proceedings were *complex* in a way that the planners had not quite bargained for. In short, the conference was in effect a protracted debate. By analyzing the arguments themselves and their integrative complexity (the first two methods), I sought to better understand not only the soundness and underlying justifications of the arguments but also their moral and ideological underpinnings. By analyzing the transcript with computerized content analysis (I used WordStat/Simstat developed by Provalis Research), I believed that in approaching the document as a whole (rather than in pieces, as with the other two methods) and converting the text to numerical data, I might see something that would be difficult to discover by coding exclusively by hand or with qualitative software. I also was interested in trying to graphically display the arguments.

Through close reading and manual coding I had identified five conference themes or debate points: (1) a mandate to control patents versus dedication to the public; (2) licensing exclusively versus broadly, and litigation; (3) individual versus university "rights" to determine the disposition and control of science; (4) individual versus university access to profits from patents, and the relationship between patents and research funding; and (5) centralized versus decentralized control of patents and various mechanisms of control. To analyze specific arguments, I used a composite of methods drawn from Golding, Rieke and Sillars, and others.[18] This type of argument analysis focuses on form rather than content, breaking the argument down into parts, and then identifying argument characteristics. You can systematically identify, by person and argument, the claims and subclaims, warrants (justifications), backing (support), qualifiers, rebuttals, reservations (answers to rebuttals found in the original claims), types of reasons (e.g., instrumental), types of claims, kinds of arguments or reasons, underlying moral presuppositions, appeals, assumptions, and fallacies, to the extent that they are present. The results of this type of analysis can be numerically represented by person and group, and compared: for example, whose/which arguments lack warrants or backing? How many fallacies did person x use in arguing compared to person y? What proportion of arguments used instrumental reasoning? Moral reasoning? How many participants used the claim of x or argued y prior condition? What was the dominant justification used? And so on.

Measures of integrative complexity are related to argument analysis in that they are aimed at the structural, rather than the content, characteristics of thought as memorialized in verbal material. They specifically target complexity in decision making, my area of interest, and as such are excellent for analyzing policy debates and public rhetoric generally. Integrative complexity analysis is performed on a sample of material, usually a minimum of five paragraphs similar in form, purpose, and style, and in which the basis or rule structure of the speaker's/author's reasoning is completely apparent; there are several rule-out criteria for sample selection. Samples are scored from 1 (low complexity) to 7 (high complexity) on two components: differentiation, or the extent to which the speaker/author is aware of and articulates different aspects to or considerations in the subject at hand, including alternatives to his or her own position; and integration, or the extent to which these views are synthesized, balanced, abstracted into a larger idea, or otherwise conceived of and treated as independent. Bias is a characteristic of argument, and integrative complexity provides a measure of ideological position and fairmindedness, or credibility in argument. Low scores are generally accepted as measures of dogma or beliefs in the rightness and authoritativeness of one's position, possibly of defensiveness in response to attack. Higher scores are generally associated with more balanced, open, and pluralistic views of issues, and perhaps with accountability.[19]

The third method, computerized content analysis, uses digitized text as a basis for quantitative analysis. Once the data has been loaded into the software program in proper form, and tagging (e.g., of speakers) is complete, a wide range of analyses can be constructed, including regression. My own goal on this piece of analysis was visualization and confirmation. From frequency analysis of the entire document and a carefully developed "dictionary" of terms, I used the program to produce a number of graphic representations of the text. Cross-tab data were used to develop concept maps and correspondence plots of themes and conference speakers.

For space reasons, only a few examples of results understandable out-of-context are provided here. Table 8.2 and Figure 8.3 show the integrative complexity scores of key participants in the patent conference on samples drawn from the conference transcript.

At the low or "simplistic" end are conference organizers and NAS patent committee members, including Karl Compton and Vannevar Bush, both of MIT and both members

Table 8.2 Integrative Complexity of Selected Participants, 1935 Conference on Patent Policy

Speaker	Score
Bastin	3.0
Blake	4.7
Bush	1.0
Compton	1.0
Howell	2.0
Hutchison	4.0
Jewett	5.0
Merriam	5.0
Pegram	5.0
Poillon	1.0
Rossman	1.0
Schwitalla	1.0
Weidlin	2.0
Whitehead, R.	1.5
Wilson, E.B.	6.0
Wilson, R. E.	1.5

Source: Jane Robbins, "Solving the Patent Problem" (Ph.D. diss., University of Pennsylvania, 2004), 330.

Low (1, 2)	Moderate (4)	High (6, 7)
K. Compton	E. Bastin L. Hutchison	F. Blake F. Jewett
V. Bush		
J. Rossman		J. Merriam E. B. Wilson
A. Schwitalla		
H. Poillon		G. Pegram
R. E. Wilson		
R. Whitehead		
E. Weidlin		
W. Howell		

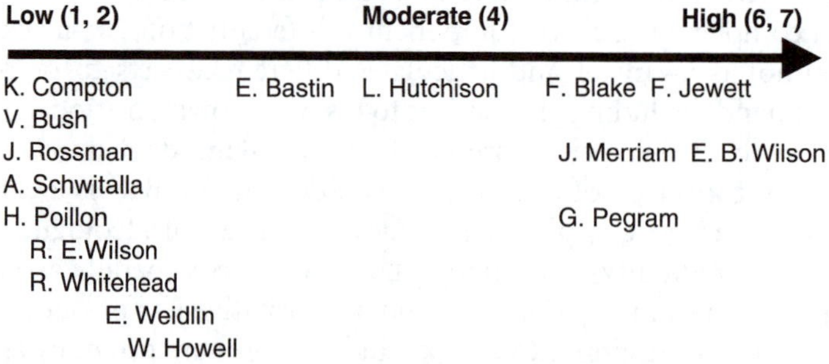

Figure 8.3 Participant Scores on Integrative Complexity Continuum, 1935 Conference on Patent Policy

Source: Jane Robbins, "Solving the Patent Problem" (Ph.D. diss., University of Pennsylvania, 2004), 330.

of the Scientific Advisory Board (SAB) and connected with its own patent committee; Joseph Rossman, U.S. Patent Office examiner and editor of the Patent Office Society journal that was a major communicating mechanism on university patent policy; and Howard Poillon, President of Research Corporation, the "mechanism" preferred by the committee to manage university patents. Among those at the high end are prominent professors of medicine, public health, and physics, and, most interestingly, Frank Jewett, member of the NAS patent committee, President of AT&T's Bell Telephone, and member of the SAB patent committee. The worldly Jewett advocated a far more nuanced, balanced, and cautious approach to the patenting of academic research than his fellow committee members, and was often at odds over the years with those who took a more monolithic stance. Figure 8.4 shows a dendogram, the result of a hierarchical cluster analysis of themes according to co-occurrence at the sentence level of the transcript; this indicates, among other things, that a prominent topic of debate was patents as altruistic or patents and their relationship to the public good (or not), with a particular focus on medical discovery. Figure 8.5 is a simple word-count graph indicating that there was almost no discussion of science itself, including the concepts of discovery and growth of knowledge, compared to discussion of scientific research as an activity—the funded research enterprise. Of numerous concept maps and correspondence plots generated, Figure 8.6 shows the positions of key conference participants on the issues of universities or university scientists taking profits from patents, and whether research outputs should be controlled through patents. The precise reading of correspondence plots, including correlation, is a function of the distance and angles of categories and participants from the origin; however, readily apparent to any reader are the views and similarity of views of speakers; the split in views, and, again, Jewett standing relatively alone and taking a more balanced position.

I personally find all these techniques useful as supplements to the historical narrative, both for my own understanding and discipline as a historical researcher, and for the reader. Scrutiny of arguments, by tracing their replication, change, or persistence over time, is one way of understanding how decisions take hold and persist, and the moralization of policy rhetoric. In my own work, it has been particularly useful for seeing

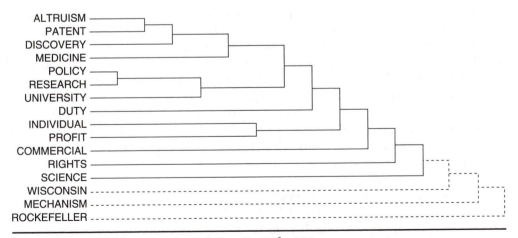

Figure 8.4 Dendogram of Conference Themes, Sentence Level ($R^2 = 0.81$)

Source: Jane Robbins, "Solving the Patent Problem" (Ph.D. diss., University of Pennsylvania, 2004), 325.

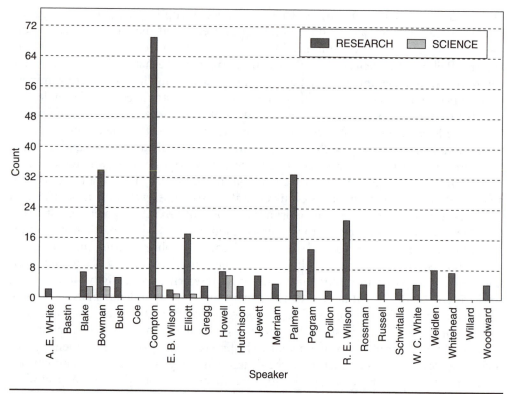

Figure 8.5 Focus of Discussion: Research Activity and Scientific Issues

Source: Jane Robbins, "Solving the Patent Problem" (Ph.D. diss., University of Pennsylvania, 2004), 329.

where *organizational mantras*—pat, semantically consistent statements of purpose and justification for accepted activities—came from, even with whom they originated. It is, thereby, an outstanding means of concretizing mimetic processes; *communicative isomorphism* is my term for convergence of practices or structures among loosely coupled institutions (like universities) that occurs largely through the vehicle of verbal and written communication. Argument, integrative complexity, and content analysis all help avoid errors of attribution and hindsight in evaluating the thinking and actions of people involved in organizational or policy decision making; they are a good check on your own work or biases. Content analysis results such as shown here are actually the equivalent of descriptive statistics—but rather than use them in an exploratory way, I have used them to confirm and add credibility to my own analysis. But the method can be used to get started as well. Finally, I like these methods for their representational nature; they abstract and present historical data in a form that is accessible to both the historian and the nonhistorian reader.

4. Cognitive History is Framed and Interpreted within the Context of Social Science Theory

When we pursue "how" and "why" questions we are implicitly if not explicitly moving into theoretical terrain. While the word "theory" has often been misunderstood and misused by historians, and theory has generally been absent from higher education

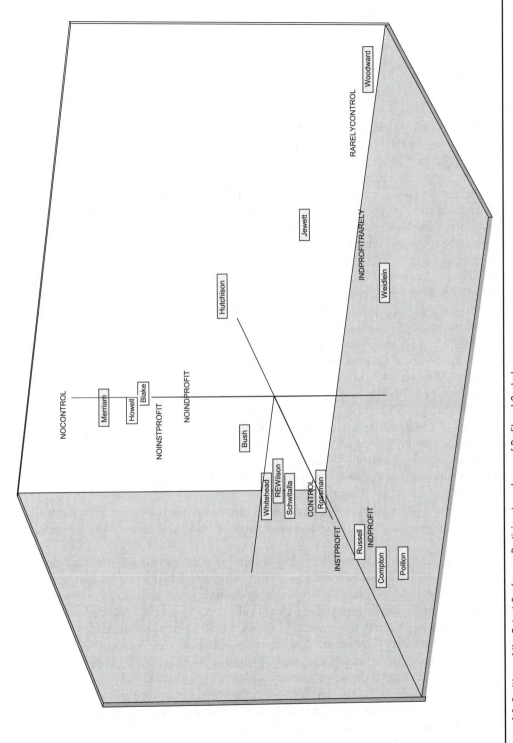

Figure 8.6 Positions of Key Patent Conference Participants on Issues of Profit and Control

Source: Jane Robbins, "Solving the Patent Problem" (Ph.D. diss., University of Pennsylvania, 2004), 328.

history, I want to make a case for making theory both an *explicit* input to the design of historical organizational study and an ultimate output goal of our research. Clark Kerr, who considered the university a "remarkably understudied institution," contributed to this theoretical goal with his multiversity perspective, and earlier still James Conant asserted that we cannot define what a university is (a theoretical question) except through its history.[20] I have explored alternative theoretical perspectives of the university using history and theories of the firm and the state, and am currently studying university presidents over time within a leadership and policy theory perspective.[21] But more attention to theory is needed if we want to both further hone our craft and develop more valuable—and valued—interpretations of its results.

Not only is theory the gold standard of research in the social sciences (of which, from time to time, history has been considered one—and, I would argue, is implied by conceptualizing history as a methodology), but compelling, coherent theoretical works tend to become the "classics" of scholarship because of their broad and lasting utility. In fields that study strategy, politics, and organization, history has been a dominant method of constructing the lasting foundations of the fields, and is a natural avenue to theorizing about the institutional field of higher education. Rather than view theory as related to universal law, I prefer to think of it as a form of communication; an abstraction of collected observations into a cognitively manageable form; a summary of the thinking that has gone before, any generality of which is testable and malleable over time; a chain of reasoning; a fount of questions, salient constructs, definitions, and items to attend to, a springboard to new hypotheses and methods—and a gift to future scholars in training. While theory *building*—as opposed to the use of theory to frame or interpret research—will not be a reasonable or responsible outcome of every piece of research, I believe it should be an intellectual objective for our field tantamount to finding the Holy Grail. The history of higher education is an especially apt, even ideal, site for organizational theorizing given the now-accepted view that institutions are boundaryless, and the concerns of higher education as interdisciplinary.[22]

In cognitive history, theory serves the double purpose of an input—a way to frame my questions—and an output—a goal of trying to induce something generalizable about universities as institutions. I reiterate that the latter is not always possible, but I want to look and see what, if anything, can be abstracted from the historical story that either confirms or alters what we know about institutional behavior. This played out in my work on the question of how universities came to patent science in the following ways.

To begin, I was interested in addressing the critiques of organizational studies as ignoring people and process, particularly cognitive process. I had some background in information-processing theories and expert–novice differences in problem solving, so when I noticed in my preliminary research that the NAS repeatedly referred to issues around patenting as "our patent problem," I decided that it would be interesting to look at NAS patent committee decision making from a problem-solving perspective. This led me in turn to related literature on reasoning (primarily from law and philosophy) and decision making (primarily from economics and political science), which in turn led me to the methods I used. So you see that, from the start, my historical questions were grounded in an interdisciplinary approach. It's not that I restricted my historical account to its cognitive aspects; it's that I particularly attended to them, as a kind of additional layer, so that I could better understand the how and why of what happened over a nearly 50-year period of dynamic change in the university's role in scientific research that was greatly influenced by external economic and political pressures.

I believe this layering on of cognitive framing and analysis allowed me to credibly portray the institutionalization of university patenting as an agenda-driven problem-solving process (shown in a time- and event-related map, Figure 8.7), and to support an argument that it was essentially "novice" in construction and solution according to cognitive theory—and why it succeeded nevertheless. Moreover, and consistent with my initial goals, I not only addressed the critiques that neo-institutional theory insufficiently addresses people and process, including cognitive process, but also was able to offer some grounded theoretical conclusions from my combination of traditional and cognitive history. These conclusions relate to the sizable role of individual or small-group agency in large-scale policy and institutional change; the intentional, strategic use of language; institutional change and isomorphism as communicative processes (*communicative isomorphism*) that resemble what today we would call viral marketing; and the *relay effect* across both institutions and time of *organizational mantras* that shape institutional logics of action, often in the absence of, or contrary to, evidence, and come to define the accepted thinking on a subject. Finally, cognitive history allowed me to posit a cycle of relations within and between universities and industry as moving through stages of cooperation, co-optation, competition, and around again. It is cooperation with industry that first co-opted universities into commercial interest-sharing; then ultimately led to competition *with* industry and *between* universities; and has now, I believe, reached a point where there may be a return to cooperation, perhaps across universities and industries, even nations. But that's just a theory; I will need to do more history to know.

CONCLUDING REMARKS AND REMAINING QUESTIONS

Quantification in history can take many forms. Traditional methods are based on data that are numeric in their original form. They include simple counts, descriptive statistics, survey results from oral histories that are an interesting twist on a traditional method, and regression or other methods of prediction/causality; examples of the latter on education topics are sparse and confined primarily to policy and labor history. A more recent form of quantification in history, illustrated with my own approach that I call cognitive history, converts text from primary sources into numerical data that can then be treated in a traditional manner: counts, descriptive statistics, regression.

All forms have potential, as well as limitations, for advancing understanding of the history of higher education. Judged by the standards considered in this chapter, economy and effectiveness as a form of historian's parsimony, quantification is not a substitute for the in-depth historical narrative constructed from primary sources. Rather, it is a complement that allows some aspect of the whole to be represented in a manner intended to be either more efficient, or more credible and persuasive, than the narrative alone. Counts and descriptive statistics best meet these criteria; those derived from cognitive history are especially useful for understanding process and agency in institutional change. Regression may be *less* economical and effective considered in context of the whole, as its sources have generally undergone substantial manipulation and derivation, which serves as qualifiers to any model outputs. For this reason, regression in history is valuable for generating questions and specific insights into source data, and perhaps for

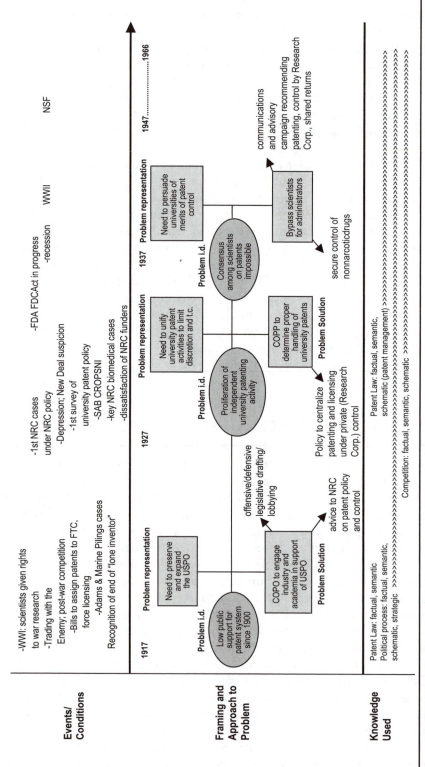

Figure 8.7 NAS/NRC Patent Committees: Problem Representation and Solution in Context

Source: Jane Robbins, "Solving the Patent Problem" (Ph.D. diss., University of Pennsylvania, 2004), 400.

confirming broad, top-level trends. But because of the simplifications required to perform the analysis and achieve results that are considered satisfactory to the researcher, and the ease with which such simplifications can be diverted to purposes other than those for which they may have been intended, discrete regression results should be viewed with caution, particularly as a basis for policy or institutional decision making.

For me, the greatest benefit of quantification is its ability to visually represent the text, and the greater depth of understanding or persuasion that it offers; in this sense, I like the confirmatory or triangulating potential of quantification of historical data. And I like *reading* empirical analyses as another source of ideas and way of thinking about issues, even when I can challenge the design. Many of my own questions concern the specific nature of relationships or impacts of differences among groups or time frames—questions that lend themselves to regression. As a historian, I want to use whatever is available to me to better understand and communicate the historical record, without sacrificing its depth and breadth. This means, with caution.

Therein lies the continuing paradox of history. Whereas the assumption that quantitative methods are more precise and rigorous than nonquantitative methods has made inroads into the history of higher education, taken 'to extremes they may present a danger to both the historical record and to organizational and policy decision making. Done with skill and discipline, the historical narrative based on primary sources offers the more comprehensive, complete, and precise avenue to understanding the past and integrating its social, political, and economic influences into a meaningful whole. Quantification is the cherry that rests on this foundation.

Yet, this chapter is simply the beginning of a conversation, the raising of the conundrum of the proper role or contribution of quantification in history. This question is part of the larger—and perennial—question: What is history? If history is investigative as well as narrative story-telling, what kinds of investigative methods are applicable?[23]

QUESTIONS FOR DISCUSSION

1. Does the association of quantitative data and methods with history threaten history's reputation for careful, thorough analysis grounded in primary documents, or does it offer the potential to enhance both the discipline and its outputs?
2. Is the quantification of history a sign of the growing trend toward interdisciplinarity, or is it a sign of increasing disregard for the humanities? Should historians and social scientists collaborate to achieve the best of both worlds?
3. Are the terms efficiency and effectiveness used in this chapter appropriate measures for historical work?
4. In the field of higher education history, where many historical questions are organizational or policy questions, what methods beyond the traditional narrative have the greatest potential to influence decision makers? Why?
5. Are quantitative methods "history," or are they rather "methods that use historical data for an object other than history"?
6. Empirical methods such as regression claim to look at long time frames and draw aggregate results and patterns, whereas history tends to take smaller, more manageable bites because of the labor involved. Could the kind of broad, "aggregate" benefits of empirical research be achieved by taking a "project" approach to the history of higher education: dividing a large historical question among many

historians, each working on a part or period of a single question, which would then be purposefully sewn together?

NOTES

1. Richard E. Neustadt and Ernest R. May, *Thinking in Time: The Uses of History for Decision Makers* (New York: The Free Press, 1986).
2. Richard J. Shavelson and Lisa Towne, eds., *Scientific Research in Education* (Washington, DC: Committee on Scientific Principles for Educational Research. National Research Council, National Academy Press, 2002).
3. Sumantra Ghoshal, "Bad Management Theories Are Destroying Good Management Practices," *Academy of Management Learning & Education* 4, no. 1 (March 2005): 75–91.
4. Warren G. Bennis and James O'Toole, "How Business Schools Lost Their Way," *Harvard Business Review Online*, 1 May 2005, http://harvardbusinessonline.hbsp.harvard.edu/b02/en/hbr/hbrsa/current/0505/article/R0505F.jhtml. Retrieved 4/28/05.
5. Imre Lakatos and Alan Musgrave, *Criticism and the Growth of Knowledge* (Cambridge: Cambridge University Press, 1970).
6. Roger Geiger, "Culture, Careers, Knowledge, and Money: Change in American Higher Education Since 1980," Keynote Address to *Deutsche Gesellschaft für Amerikastudien* (Jena, Germany, 2009).
7. The HERS dataset is available from the Inter-University Consortium for Political and Social Science (ICPSR) at http://www.icpsr.umich.edu/ File name: HERS Alumnae Survey.
8. Barbara W. Tuchman, *Practicing History: Selected Essays* (New York: Ballantine Books, 1981).
9. Claudia Goldin and Lawrence F. Katz, *The Race Between Education and Technology* (Cambridge, MA: Harvard University Press, 2008). See their Figure 8.3, p. 300, minus its notes.
10. Concerns related to traditional forms of regression also apply to other methods used to study large sets of data. One is event history, a form of time-series analysis also known as survival analysis that seeks to estimate changes over time. Despite its promising moniker, it too has problems with choice of period and lack of comparability of data from different periods, and what is called left- or right-censoring—arbitrary cut-off points that may render generalizations from the data suspect (historians face a similar challenge, although less so).
11. Barbara W. Tuchman, *Practicing History: Selected Essays* (New York: Ballantine Books, 1981).
12. Reinhard Bendix, *Social Science and the Distrust of Reason*, University of California Publications in Sociology and Social Institutions (Berkeley: University of California Press, 1951).
13. Andrew H. Van de Ven and Timothy J. Hargrave, "Social, Technical, and Institutional Change: A Literature Review and Synthesis," in *Handbook of Organizational Change and Innovation*, ed. M. S. Poole and A. H. Van de Ven (New York: Oxford University Press, 2004), 259–303; Warren G. Bennis and James O'Toole, "How Business Schools Lost Their Way," *Harvard Business Review Online*, 1 May 2005, http://harvardbusinessonline.hbsp.harvard.edu/b02/en/hbr/hbrsa/current/0505/article/R0505F.jhtml. Retrieved 4/28/05; Rob Raynard and Ray Crozier, "Cognitive Process Models and Explanations of Decision Making," in *Decision Making: Cognitive Models and Explanations*, Rob Raynard, Ray W. Crozier, and Ola Svenson (London: Routledge, 1997), 5–20; William M. Goldstein and Elke U. Weber, "Content and Discontent: Indications and Implications of Domain Specificity in Preferential Decision Making," in *Research on Judgment and Decision Making: Currents, Connections, and Controversies*, ed. W. M Goldstein and R. M. Hogarth (Cambridge, UK: Cambridge University Press, 1997).
14. Marc Bloch, *The Historian's Craft: Reflections on the Nature and Uses of History and the Techniques and Methods of Those Who Use It*, trans. Peter Putnam (New York: Vintage Books/Random House, 1953).
15. Philip Selznick, *The Organizational Weapon: A Study of Bolshevik Strategy and Tactics*, The Rand Series (New York: McGraw-Hill Book Company, 1952).
16. David G. Winter, "Content Analysis of Archival Materials, Personal Documents, and Everyday Verbal Productions," in *Motivation and Personality: Handbook of Thematic Content Analysis*, ed. Charles P. Smith, with John Atkinson (Cambridge: Cambridge University Press, 1992), 401–18.
17. Jane Robbins, "Solving the Patent Problem: Cognition, Communication, and the National Academy of Sciences in the Evolution of University Patent Policy, 1917–1966" (Ph.D. diss., Philadelphia, PA: University of Pennsylvania, 2004), 452 pp; Jane Robbins, "Shaping Patent Policy: The National Research Council and the Universities from World War I to the 1960s," *Perspectives on the History of Higher Education* 25 (2006): 89–122.
18. M. P. Golding, *Legal Reasoning* (Peterborough, ONT: Broadview Press, 2001); R. D. Rieke and M. O. Sillars, *Argumentation and Critical Decision Making, 4th edition* (NY: Longman/Addison Wesley Longman, 1997).

19. Philip E. Tetlock, "Cognitive Style and Political Ideology," *Journal of Personality and Social Psychology* 45 (1983a): 118–26; Philip E. Tetlock, "Accountability and Complexity of Thought," *Journal of Personality and Social Psychology* 45, no. 1 (1983b): 74–83.

20. Clark Kerr, *The Uses of the University, with a "Postscript–1972"* (Cambridge, MA: Harvard University Press, 1972); James B. Conant, "Tercentenary Oration of the President, Sept. 18, 1936," in *What is a University?* (Boston: Associated Harvard Clubs, 1938).

21. Jane Robbins, "Toward a Theory of the University: Mapping the American Research University in Space and Time," *American Journal of Education* 114 (February 2008): 243–72 plus online supplement.

22. Linda Eisenmann, "Integrating Disciplinary Perspectives Into Higher Education Research: The Example of History," *Journal of Higher Education* 75, no. 1 (January/February 2004): 7–2; Ruben Donato and Marvin Lazerson, "New Directions in American Educational History: Problems and Prospects," *Educational Researcher*, November 2000, 1–12.

23. Leon H. Goldstein, *Historical Knowing* (Austin and London: University of Texas Press, 1976).

9

LIFE HISTORY AND VOICE

On Standpoints and Reflexivity

William G. Tierney

The past was little more than a dream and its force in the world greatly exaggerated. For the world was made new each day and it was only men's clinging to its vanished husks that could make of that world one husk more.

Cormac McCarthy, *The Crossing*

ON BECOMING A LIFE HISTORIAN

I am a junior majoring in English at Tufts University. In the dead of winter I sit in the poet Denise Levertov's office. Our knees are touching and I can hear the radiator hiss as she reads Walt Whitman. I have an independent study with her on Whitman and every late Tuesday afternoon we drink tea and talk poetry. She asks me questions about Whitman and directs me to read a passage from *Song of Myself*. "I am the poet of the Body and I am the poet of the Soul," I intone, "The pleasures of heaven are with me and the pains of hell are with me." I rush to the end and put the book down. She leans forward and brushes my chin with her hand. "Listen to the words," she says. "What is he trying to say?" We sit in silence and I hear the radiator.

I have arrived in Tahala, Morocco after six weeks of Peace Corps language training. My house has no running water, sporadic electricity and a mob of children waiting outside my door to hear me mangle my beginner's Arabic. I am as lonely as I have ever been in my young life and consider going home. I hear a knock on the door and hesitate; I fear it is the children trying to torment me. I open the metal door to find the man who will become my language tutor. He takes my hand and we walk up to the olive grove above town. I speak slowly and he nods as if I am fluent. "What do you want to say?" he asks. "What are you trying to say?"

My friend has left me alone with her father in the living room of the family's log frame house. They have lived all of their lives on this reservation, in this same home. I look outside and wonder if the snow will start to fall and if I should start for home. The old man sees me looking out the window and intuits my question. "You're wondering if it will snow. It won't. Not until late tonight. You'll be home by then." He sips his coffee. "Don't be in such a hurry," he says. I settle into the chair.

Even though I have turned up the heat in our living room, my friend has the blue blanket pulled up to his shoulders as he lies on the faded gray rattan couch. We both know he is dying of AIDS. I am working with him on his life history. He laughs when I repeat something he has said and I make a mistake. "Listen to my words carefully, Bill. Use my words with care." I close my eyes and try to capture the rhythm of his language as he speaks. His right foot falls to the floor and the blanket slides off his shoulders. We pull the blanket back up and pick up where we left off.

My young friend sees me drive up and he yawns as he puts his seat belt on and I pull away. I am helping him with his college essay. He was very nervous when I first met him; he could not stop shaking, but now he is more comfortable as his thin fingers drum against the dashboard. We talk about our first meeting and I ask him why he was nervous. He shrugs and shakes his head. I say, "It's because I'm white. A white guy." He laughs and nods his head. He steals a look at me and says, "Yes, white. And old." I playfully hit him on the arm and he smiles back at me. He sinks down into the seat as we drive past Echo Park.

WHAT ARE WE TRYING TO ACCOMPLISH?

Over the last decade we have seen an increase in calls for research that uses quantitative measures such as randomized experiments to advance an understanding of education.[1] Many of the demands for such research hinge on the ability of the experiment to be valid and reliable. Large-scale surveys that extend across school districts or university systems are thought to lend strength to our understanding of how better to inform educational policy. Many of the rationales for such research make good sense. Does the preparation of a teacher by a School of Education and the certification by the state improve teacher performance? Do college preparation programs make a difference in increasing access for the poorest students in our country? Are remedial courses successful in universities? The answers to such questions, if rightly phrased and rigorously studied, have the potential of providing considerable insight, and more importantly, improving public policy and educational performance.

Whether one actually can answer such questions with a particular methodology is not my purpose here. I also am not interested in raising concerns about the strengths and weaknesses of the underlying epistemological and theoretical assumptions posed by those who propose such studies. Although such questions are important and in part help frame how we do research in the early 21st century, a related question pertains to methods that do not fall within the scientific paradigm. Rather than try to make a qualitative method more quantitative, what we need to do is think about how a particular qualitative method might be improved based on its own epistemological underpinnings. Accordingly, I am concerned with one qualitative method—life history—and consider what its purpose and role is in the 21st century. What are we trying to accomplish when we say we do a life history? What is the relationship of the researcher to the subject of life histories? And who is the audience who will read such a text? The answers to these questions depend upon which framework one chooses to employ when undertaking life history.

THE USES OF LIFE HISTORY

A life history differs from a singular interview or an oral history primarily through its focus and coverage. An interview, for example, may be one or two interviews with a person about a particular topic. An oral history may be about a particular topic with several individuals. A life history, however, is a "full-scale autobiographical account that allows interviewees to relate their entire life, from childhood to the present."[2] Although a life history is an "n" of 1, obviously, some will suggest that we might use a life history as a *portal.* Linde has described this process in the following manner: "The portal approach attempts to use the life history to learn about some reality external to the story, which the life history is presumed to mirror."[3] The life history, then, is an entryway into, and representative of, a culture. I have never attempted a life history exclusively from this perspective, although I assume that individuals may read life histories of mine in this manner. In effect, we reduce how people live, act, and interpret the world to the individual whose life history has been recorded. We learn about a social group through the portal of one individual, or we learn about how a group makes sense of something—such as applying to college—by way of the life history of a potential college applicant. Kristin Haglund has pointed out how such a method is useful for understanding health-related issues pertaining to adolescents; Peter Davis has made the same point with regard to understanding poverty dynamics because of the ability to unearth poverty and spatial dynamics through life histories.[4]

A second approach, championed by Clifford Geertz, is what I shall call the "*process* approach."[5] Process focuses on trying to interpret narrative. Rather than assuming that a life history is a mini-version of a culture, the life history becomes as individualized as a poem. A life history from this perspective can no more stand for anything than a poem by Emily Dickinson stands for all poems, or all poems by women, or all poems from the 19th century, and the like. The process approach struggles to understand the individual life history just as we might read *Leaves of Grass* to understand what Whitman meant. "What is he trying to say?" my English teacher asked me about Whitman in the opening paragraph. The use of life history when the process approach is employed is to gain an in-depth understanding of a life, and perhaps, the underlying structures or categories of lives. A life history I conducted of a young Malaysian Muslim derived from this perspective.[6]

Inevitably, the role of the life historian comes into play. There is not a definitive reading of a life history any more than there is a definitive reading of Walt Whitman. The life historian's interpretation is critical. Because interpretation matters, the life historian needs to focus on the manner in which he gathers, analyzes, and especially writes down, data. My previous sentence, for example, utilized the gendered pronoun he. The use of "he" paints a picture in the reader's head of the life historian as a male whereas the life historian might be a female. The point is not so much that there is a correct use of language, but that language is highly charged and undoubtedly going to be interpreted—by the person whose life history we collect, by the life historian, and by the reader. Process, then, forces us to move from the "all the world in a teacup" sort of stance of the portal, to an individualized approach. We also recognize that a life history is not collected in isolation. Contexts matter—of the individual, of the historian, and of the reader. We can read Whitman and Dickinson and see if they share any underlying relationships because of time, nuance, view of the world, and the like. Thus, we use the process approach in context rather than simply as an abstracted or decontextualized story that has no interest other than in the telling.

The third approach to life history is more introspective and focuses intensively on the relationship between the informant and the life historian. More commonly known as *cultural biography*, this approach is particularly concerned with the situated-ness of the interviewer and the sort of relationship that gets developed during the course of the data-gathering. In some respects, this form of life history is less interested in the specifics of a person's life and more concerned with how the aspects of that life come to get unearthed, created, and interpreted by the individual who is conducting the life history.

These three approaches share commonalities although they are quite different in epistemological assumptions. Each life history focuses on an individual, and the data that get developed are primarily about aspects of that person's life. The individual who collects the data is one person, rather than a team of individuals. The collection of the data occurs over an extended period of time and the primary methodological tool is the interview. No life historian makes claims to generalizability and terms such as validity and reliability are not employed.

The differences are as significant as the similarities. Cultural biographies may extend over a significant amount of time—perhaps years—whereas traditional portal or process life histories are usually considerably shorter. A portal approach will work from a protocol and deviate from it as different points arise. A process approach concentrates on language and its semiotic meanings whereas the more traditional life historian is likely to assume that correct interpretations exist. Cultural biographies do not really have protocols but instead have general themes that are expected to emerge and develop over time. As I will elaborate on below, because each form of life history has different epistemological assumptions, the stance one takes with the informant, and how one thinks of him- or herself varies significantly as well. Of consequence, what the findings are, and how they are to be used, will differ.

LIFE HISTORY'S FINDINGS

The portal approach to life history offers findings that ostensibly can be used to explicate particular aspects of a culture. Paul Radin's classic life history of *Crashing Thunder*, for example, told us something about the social workings of the Winnebago through the eyes of a middle-aged man.[7] Similarly, Oscar Lewis's *Children of Sanchez* helped coin the phrase "culture of poverty" because of the data gathered from his work.[8] Although the researchers are studious in not trying to generalize or claim that such work fits all people, the work makes claims to understanding such that the reader gains a window into the life processes of a particular people or problem.

The process approach is more circumspect with regard to findings, and its proponents are by no means in search of deep structures or pervasive meanings. However, just as a poet studies a poem not only to try to understand the meaning of the text, the assumption is that a life history's worth goes beyond merely the text. Indeed, one question that we need to ask as readers and as authors is "why is this text worth reading?" Those who subscribe to the portal approach assume that the text affords an understanding of something more than merely the individual under investigation. A process-oriented approach will claim that the meaning itself is critically important, which is why the focus is frequently as much on how one constructs the text as what the author says. But in addition to the beauty of the text, the assumption is that the text tells us something about underlying processes. If the life history focuses on how an individual experiences school, for example, presumably different categories will arise from the data. The point is not that because the interviewee experiences teacher–student relationships in a particular way that all students experience relationships in such a manner. Rather, the assumption is that the categories that have been developed deserve investigation and elaboration. The young fellow who said he was initially nervous around me not only because I was White, but because I was old, for example, has a particular interpretation of school—it is boring. The point is surely not that I should assume that all students think of school as work, but instead, seek to consider how others define school. Thus, the worth of the reading of such a text is that it presumably challenges the reader to reflect on similar ideas and concepts, and stimulates a desire to see how such findings fit or do not with related forms of reality.

The cultural biography takes such a point one step further. The reader may not learn as much about the individual as one might in a traditional life history. However, given the manner in which the text is constructed, reflexivity is essential. The author raises questions about how he or she has come to meet the person under investigation and while we will learn about the interviewee, the text turns on the relationship of the two. How the text gets constructed becomes paramount, and the reader is supposed to turn inward and reflect on his or her own relationship with similar individuals and topics.

My Moroccan teacher asked me, "What do you want to say? What are you trying to say?" The answer from a portal proponent would be, "I want to convey how someone lives a life and what that tells us about the culture in which he or she is embedded." Such a response would likely contrast with a process-related individual's desire who might say: "How I interpret these events is important. I want to see if I can understand what someone is saying and then provide a provisional meaning to them, embedded in contexts that the reader is likely to understand." "It's paramount that the reader understand the relationship I developed with the person I worked with," the cultural biographer will say, "This text is really co-developed insofar as it arose out of the interactions she and I had. I hope what I say forces the reader to think about his or her own life."

THE SUBJECTS OF LIFE HISTORIES

I have used the word "subject" purposefully insofar as those who employ a cultural biography are likely to reject even the term, which has the ring of objectivity. Who are the people we interview? An "informant" is someone who provides data that we subsequently write up with a degree of distance and certainty about the meaning of the text. From this perspective the subject is someone who has data that are presumably of worth for providing insight into the larger culture. The research subject, while certainly treated with care and concern, is not unlike a subject in an experiment.

My friend who was dying of AIDS said, "Listen to my words carefully. Use my words with care." Such a comment speaks to what the individual desires when we listen, but this "subject" is again redefined. The portal perspective will agree that the subject's words need to be listened to carefully because he or she offers meaning that will be greater than simply the words. The process-oriented approach, however, begins with acknowledging the import of such a statement and its conditionality. The listener can neither ascribe larger meanings to someone's words nor will such words be understood with meaning. Indeed, words need to be listened to carefully because of their conditionality.

The cultural biographer moves one step further. The subject is likely to be a friend, certainly not merely an informant, and hence the use of the term "subject" appears off-putting and inappropriate. Rather than seek distance, the author/researcher needs closeness, even intimacy. The "data" that the person has are not necessarily of import for anything greater than the context in which they derive—out of interviews and interactions with the author. The cultural biographer is focused on the moment with the individual rather than a larger picture or an underlying text. Whereas a process approach assumes that once the data are spoken their meanings become important because they are to be interpreted, the cultural biographer looks on the import of those data not because they are narrative but rather because of what they say of the dynamic relationship between speaker and listener.

Again, some commonalities exist with life histories across traditions. More often than not famous people or leaders of a group are eschewed in favor of more commonplace individuals. To be sure, prominent individuals may be the subjects of a biography, but they generally are not the subjects of life histories. Conversely, common individuals, frequently from subjugated groups, may voice their own "testimonio" rather than have an interlocutor devise a life history.[9] Life histories, then, are penned by an individual who is not the subject of the text about someone who is not famous. James Muchmore utilized a portal approach to understand teacher thinking of a person who might fit the description of a "typical" teacher.[10] Vincent Crapanzano's *The Fifth World of Forster Bennett*, tells the story of a Navajo man and Ruth Behar's *Translated Woman* draws on a woman who is Mexican.[11] Neither person is a hero nor a villain and both authors subscribed to a process-focus for life history. Gelya Frank's *Venus on Wheels* chronicles the life of Diane DeVries, an extraordinary woman because of her multiple disabilities, but not someone who everyone knows or who will go down in history for a particular achievement.[12] However, one of the underlying assumptions, of course, is that ordinary people have extraordinary stories to tell. Why they are extraordinary differs depending upon the stance one assumes, but the life historian believes that the words are of worth to the reader.

THE READERS OF LIFE HISTORIES

Who the reader is for a life history is also similar and different based on the three perspectives. My young friend who is going to college has a story to tell to people who are interested in the lives of the young and the challenges they face if the text is read as a traditional life history. The young Malaysian Muslim I worked with offers us insight into how a working-class individual makes sense of his life in the early 21st century; issues of race, class, and gender come to life through his words. Those who subscribe to processes will try to compare and contrast the underlying meanings of the story and see what fits with other such narratives. A cultural biographer will want to read of the relationship that I have developed with the young man and how that shaped the story.

Life histories tend to be more readable than other forms of research because they involve the story of a life from one or another perspective. The telling of the story evolves over time and the narrative structure often has a dynamic arch that typical research does not. "Don't be in such a hurry" my Native American friend's father chided me; he had stories to tell and they were not meant to be summarized merely in a paragraph or two. The result is that the potential for life history is significantly different from typical forms of research. While I do not quarrel here with the argument that quantitative measures of research have the potential to generalize in ways that life histories never can, I also recognize the power of life history. A story well told can reach readers well beyond the rarefied air of the academy, and has the ability to provoke action. Regardless of the stance of the life historian, the potential exists to create a sense of care and concern in a reader about a particular life that often cannot be done with standard research.

WHAT ARE THE CHALLENGES?

Discussions of methodology frequently revolve around the training one receives in courses. When we interview candidates for a faculty position and he or she says that they can teach this or that methodology course we generally want to know who they have trained with, if they have taken special courses offered by a particular organization such as the Educational Testing Service or the American Educational Research Association, and if they have published work in refereed journals and presented at juried conferences. Increasingly we are also concerned about an individual's technological capability. What sort of software do you use? How do you go about utilizing the internet to conduct literature reviews? Do you keep a blog or read blogs about your particular area of inquiry?

When we review articles for journals or read dissertation proposals we also look for the methodological flaws of the author. If someone says he or she has conducted a life history, for example, and I then read that the person interviewed someone for two hours, I am likely to be critical. A life history may be hard to define, but virtually everyone will agree that two hours is insufficient to conduct a life history. If I am reading a life history I may not be concerned about validity and reliability, but I will want to know how the author has analyzed the text and how I am to judge if the text is trustworthy.

All of these and related issues are of critical import but I wish to turn here to issues that often do not get addressed and most likely are as important in determining if the life history is to be successful. I am not suggesting an "either–or" approach where if a life historian concentrates on these issues then the ones I have just mentioned are irrelevant. However, I wish to suggest that too often we obsess about issues such as data analysis and trustworthiness to the exclusion of other matters. Our concern is likely that we want to appear as scientific as possible and even if we cannot ape the scientific paradigm we can at least try to have trustworthy data—and that is fine and good. But what is not fine and good is if we overlook what I have found are essential components of conducting a life history but often go undiscussed.

CROSSING BORDERS

A norm in conducting a life history is that the person to be interviewed will be different in some manner from the life historian.[13] My friend with AIDS was also Native American; I neither had AIDS nor am I Native American.[14] I also have done a cultural biography of a Black teenager, but I am not Black nor an adolescent.[15] I currently have two graduate students who are conducting life histories of homeless youth; the population is composed of men and women, gay, straight, and transgender, Black, Hispanic and White. All of them, of course, are homeless. My students are not homeless; they are both men, both straight, and one is White and the other is Black.

In each of these examples the author has had to deal with difference. I know individuals who might not be so adept at crossing borders of identity.[16] Working with homeless youth demands spending time in locales far different from someone who interviews faculty on a university campus for a study. When I undertook my work with the man who had AIDS the stigma attached to the disease was significant and he was not out either to his family or to most of his co-workers. To interview someone thirty years younger or older than you also demands the ability to, if not lessen differences, at least acknowledge them in a manner that makes the individual feel comfortable.

My assumption, then, is that even though we will never be able to understand the "other" entirely, attempts at meaning can help us cross borders of identity—race, class, gender, and the like. Life history helps this border crossing insofar as the extended amount of time the researcher is going to spend with someone suggests that some, if not most, of the meetings are going to be informal and in settings quite different from structured sites. The data to be gathered are also likely to be of a personal nature such that the person needs to feel comfortable disclosing information. My friend commanded me to "listen to my words carefully" because he knew I was different from him. I did not grow up poor on an Indian reservation and he was adamant that I not portray him in a particular way. My young friend reminded me that I was not only racially different from him but also different by a generation (or two).

These borders are not easy to transgress but they are essential if one is to be able to reach the point where we worry about data analysis, trustworthiness, and the like. The challenge for me is that I do not believe one can teach these sorts of skills in a manner akin to how we teach students in our methods classes. Life's experiences have prepared me for crossing borders. Two years in a mountain town in the Peace Corps where I was constantly different from everyone else demanded of me to think about difference. Yet such a statement assumes that all Peace Corps volunteers might be adept life historians and that is surely not the case. Again, working on a Native American reservation where the bulk of my friends were American Indian fostered introspection. Being gay at a time when one's sexual orientation was grounds for dismissal in certain states and countries also has contributed to my understanding of what I need to do to cross borders. But all of these experiences are mine—they are what have enabled me at least to try to listen to an individual's words and make sense of them from his or her perspective rather than my own. My experiences, however, are not to be thought of as ingredients for a life history recipe, as if all budding cultural biographers have to do this or that activity. But if someone is going to undertake a life history I know that he or she needs to have thought about these issues and hopefully had experiences where they have had to cross borders of their own.

EMPATHY, PATIENCE, AND COURAGE

The ability to cross borders suggests that the person is comfortable dealing with difference. A related point is that the individual will be able to empathize with whomever he or she is interviewing. Empathy does not necessarily demand agreement. Empathy is the ability to understand how the person has come to think and act the way he or she has. Judgment on whether the person is good or bad is of less importance than having the capacity to understand the other's state of mind. Indeed, compassion is not even necessary, for in some instances we will interview someone who may have committed horrible acts. When there is compassion there is a desire to see the person improve or be better off tomorrow than today. Empathy concerns the ability to see how someone has reached a particular conclusion. Somewhat tautologically, I have found that if one has not crossed borders in some fashion then empathy is that much more difficult.

Patience refers to what my friend's father told me: "don't be in such a hurry." Life histories are inevitably a significant amount of time that will most likely not be efficient. I have conducted interviews and case studies on college and university campuses that have been remarkably well executed. One week in advance of my visit I have given my research design to my institutional contact; I have asked for 45 minute interviews and a 15-minute break in between. I have started at 8 AM and concluded at 5 with a focus group dinner. In the course of 3 days I may have done 30 individual interviews and had 3 focus groups of 5 individuals each. The schedule may be exhausting, but it is efficient.

Life history is the opposite. I have met with people on their time and talked with them when they wanted to talk. Sometimes their conversations have extended well beyond what we initially thought would be the time for the interview. I have received calls in the middle of the night where someone may have been in crisis or needed my advice or help, but I also have received late night phone calls simply to talk. I have scheduled times when the person for one reason or another says, "I don't feel like talking today." The result is that if one is going to do a life history then they need to have patience, and I must admit, it is not a virtue that comes in abundance for me. I remind myself, however, that I am getting someone else's words and stories, and to be able to listen is a privilege that requires me to focus on the person's temporal and emotional needs, not mine.

Courage comes in many forms. I am not speaking of the courage a soldier may have when facing the enemy or the courage showed by cancer patients as they struggle with chemotherapy. Such forms of courage have to do with either physical perseverance or mental and emotional maturity dealing with an external threat. My friend with AIDS was courageous in the manner in which he faced his disease.

The courage of the life historian might be akin to the courage of the poet. When we listen to the stories of others and we are not judgmental and we are able to empathize, one result is that we are likely to become more reflective and introspective. The ability to think about one's self in this manner requires a degree of courage. The life historian ends up asking questions not only of the other, but also of him- or herself. Such questions have forced me at times to confront aspects of my life or my beliefs that are not always pleasant and may make me nervous. A life history is an emotional process that requires engagement by two individuals—not simply one. Such an engagement is uniquely different from other methodologies and requires the life historian to be able to raise questions in a way that go far beyond a typical protocol.

HUMAN "SUBJECTS" AND ETHICS

Although training exists with regard to how to navigate one's research project through an institutional review board (IRB), larger issues come into play with regard to life histories. On the one hand, some in the federal government have sought in their own way to demean oral and life history research by claiming it is not research so that it need not go through IRB. On the other hand, the sort of data that can be gathered while conducting a life history have the potential to be quite significant in an individual's life and, of consequence, are among the most important sort of data that need to be dealt with in a caring manner.

The individual with AIDS whose life history I worked on needed assurances about confidentiality and security that went well beyond masking his name. He did not, at first, want me to contact anyone in his family or very many people with whom he worked. When we met I needed to be creative in my responses with individuals when they asked what we were doing. And the review of his life also brought up an array of emotional issues that I needed to be prepared to deal with in a sensitive manner as we proceeded. More often than not when I do interviews for a case study the relationship with the interviewee ends when the interview concludes. With my friend who had AIDS, however, he had a desire, a need, to talk frequently after our sessions. An ethic of care assumes that the life historian in such a situation accommodates the individual in ways that an interviewer frequently does not need to consider.

I also have done a cultural biography of a young man who was undocumented.[17] He came to the United States when he was an infant from Mexico with his parents. At first, he was extremely reluctant to disclose information that might make his or his family's position in the United States any more precarious than it already was. Over time, as I gained his confidence, we moved to a different level of concern. I learned about the violence in his family and his problematic relationship with his father. The questions I asked raised issues for him that he had thought about but never verbalized to anyone before.

I do not want to give the impression that all life histories deal with traumatic issues such as terminal illness or family violence. But when one encounters someone over a significant amount of time in a setting that suggests serious issues need to be discussed, more often than not, the result is that sensitive topics will arise. Although the concerns of confidentiality and the admonition to "do no harm" are useful guides for institutional review boards, the sort of issues one encounters in life histories also demand the life historian to think about the ethics of the undertaking. Life historians become engaged with individuals in a manner different from the norm, and of consequence, need to think about how they deal not simply with the data, but with what the data raise in their interviewees. As I noted above, the result is that my relationship with my interviewees tends to be much more far-ranging than with those whom I interview for an hour and never speak with again.

DEDICATION TO THE CRAFT

One aspect of graduate work that we do not focus on very much is writing. Again, we demand that students take a significant number of courses in one or another methodology. The normal complaint is that they need to take more methods courses, that they have only scratched the methodological surface. And again, I agree. For those who do life history, however, writing is paramount. How we translate what we have heard to the written word is not simply a matter of transcription or narrative structure. Unlike the other points raised in this section writing can be taught. Unfortunately, we usually do not teach it. We assume that students learn to write by osmosis, or we believe that our comments at the end of a text suffice for improvement.

Good writing demands at least three undertakings. First, students need to read good writing. I know that a great deal of ink space and bandwidth have been spent trying to define what good writing is, but I am less concerned with what budding life historians offer as their exemplars par excellence of good writing. I am more concerned that they read broadly and determine for themselves what they like or do not like about a particular text. And to read broadly means that students need to read fiction. Most academic scholarship that I have read over the years is poorly written and boring to read. The findings may be superb and the research design elegant, but the vast majority of academic scholarship that we have students read will not pass muster by most anyone as good writing. For a life history to succeed, however, the text needs to be compelling.

The other two tasks for good writing have to do with the writing itself. Good writers sweat over a sentence; they worry about how to quote and whether the scene they portray paints a picture in as vibrant hues as they desire. The implication is that life historians need to have their work read and critiqued not only to ensure that it is methodologically sound, but also to see if it is elegantly written. And that suggests that the text will be written numerous times, and in that rewriting, the author needs to think about what words mean, how they will be read, and what he or she actually wants to say.

ON STANDPOINTS AND REFLEXIVITY

I have worked from the assumption that life histories are different from traditional methodologies and that even what we mean by life history is up for grabs. More traditional notions of life history subscribe to the text as an entryway for viewing and understanding another culture. A rising concern over the last generation has been how to interpret life histories; we have seen studies that utilize the work of Clifford Geertz in trying to come to terms with the processes of a life history. More recently cultural biography has risen in importance and the relationship between the life historian and the person whose life history is being recorded has become of interest. I suggested that these three variations of life history share similarities but also have differences.

I then posited that although various topics that one learns in methodological courses are fine and good, there is another set of issues that one needs to know about in order to be a successful life historian. One needs to come to terms with difference and figure out how to honor those with whom one works on a life history. Insofar as a life history is a joint undertaking, the life historian needs not only to try to understand the individual whose life is being recorded, but also be self-introspective. The life history ends up only as good as it is written, so a focus on writing becomes central.

I began this chapter with vignettes from various parts of my life. My point was not to suggest that these vignettes synthesize what it takes to do life history. Rather, a life historian is one who is always becoming. The experiences of one's life help us to think about how to work in ethical ways with those who are different from us, which in turn enables us to think about our own situations. It is out of these interactions, I suppose, that one reaches some sort of communion with the other, however fleeting.

QUESTIONS FOR DISCUSSION

1. The author outlines three approaches to life history? What are they and how do they differ?

2. Do you think it is possible for a heterosexual to do a life history of a gay man? How about an upper-class White person doing a life history of a poor Native American? Or a graduate student doing a life history of an emeritus professor? What criteria do you choose when you say someone is qualified or not qualified to do a life history?

3. How can someone acquire skills to do a life history of someone radically different from him- or herself? What is your standpoint?

4. The author mentions "empathy, patience and courage" as critical to being able to do a life history? Do you agree that these are important?

5. If writing is important to conducting a good life history, provide an example of a book, short story or essay that you think exemplifies good writing and tell us why you liked it.

NOTES

1. Robert E. Slavin, "Evidence-based Education Policies: Transforming Educational Practice and Research," *Educational Researcher* 31 (2002): 15–21.
2. Donald Ritchie, *Doing Oral History: A Practical Guide* (New York: Oxford University Press, 2003).
3. Charlotte Linde, *Life Stories: The Creation of Coherence* (New York: Oxford University Press, 1993).
4. Kristin Haglund, "Conducting Life History Research with Adolescents," *Qualitative Health Research* 14 (2004): 1309–1319. Peter Davis, "Poverty in Time: Exploring Poverty Dynamics from Life History Interviews in Bangladesh" (Paper presented at the CPRC Workshop on Concepts and Methods for Analyzing Poverty Dynamics and Chronic Poverty, Manchester, UK, October 2006).
5. Clifford Geertz, *Local Knowledge* (New York: Basic Books, 1983).
6. William G. Tierney, "Globalization and Life History Research: Fragments of a Life Foretold," *Qualitative Studies in Education*: in press.
7. Paul Radin, "The Autobiography of a Winnebago Indian," *American Archaeology and Ethnology* 16 (1920): 381–473.
8. Oscar Lewis, *The Children of Sanchez: Autobiography of a Mexican Family* (New York: Vintage, 1961).
9. William G. Tierney, "Beyond Translation: Truth and Rigoberta Menchu," *Qualitative Studies in Education*, 13 (2000): 115–129.
10. James A. Muchmore, "Methods and Ethics in a Life History Study of Teacher Thinking," *The Qualitative Report* 7 (December 2002): http://www.nova.edu/ssss/QR/QR7-4/muchmore.html.
11. Vincent Crapanzano, *The Fifth World of Forster Bennett* (New York: Viking, 1972). Ruth Behar, *Translated Woman* (Boston: Beacon, 1993).
12. Gelya Frank, *Venus on Wheels: Two Decades of Dialogue on Disability, Biography, and Being Female in America* (Berkeley: University of California Press, 2000).
13. Vincent Crapanzano, *The Fifth World of Forster Bennett* (1972).
14. William G. Tierney, "Self and Identity in a Postmodern World: A Life Story," in *Naming Silenced Lives: Personal Narratives and the Process of Educational Change*, ed. D. McLaughlin and W.G. Tierney (New York: Routledge, 1993), 119–134.
15. William G. Tierney, "Mushutu and Juan: A Tale of Two Students," in *Urban High School Students and the Challenge of Access: Many Routes, Difficult Paths*, ed. W.G. Tierney and J.E. Colyar (New York: Peter Lang, 2006), 13–36.
16. Ruth Behar, *Translated Woman* (1993). Daniel McLaughlin and W.G. Tierney, eds., *Naming Silenced Lives: Personal Narratives and the Process of Educational Change* (New York: Routledge).
17. Tierney, "Mushutu and Juan: A Tale of Two Students," 13–36.

Section III
Critical Examinations of Special Issues

10

"POOR" RESEARCH

Historiographical Challenges When Socio-Economic Status is the Unit of Analysis

Jana Nidiffer

Historians of higher education approach their discipline from numerous perspectives. The extant literature contains a great deal of information about how various institutions were founded, funded, or managed. Historians have also concentrated on how the curriculum evolved and the religious and intellectual foment in which colleges and universities worked. Another long-standing tradition in the field is the study of the life and work of central actors in the enterprise such as faculty members or presidents and other key administrators. Perhaps more recently, scholarship has centered on the symbiosis of higher education and the larger society, especially with regard to higher education's role in what I might label the "military-industrial-academic complex," to paraphrase President Eisenhower. Of equal significance, albeit with a much shorter tradition, is the question of who had access to colleges and universities and the concomitant implications for the social and economic status of those groups admitted.

The "who had access?" question has produced an explosion of research in the last 25 years or so. Particular attention has been paid to access based on race, especially the struggle of African Americans for integration, parity, and social justice in higher education. The issue of gender and the experience of women have also received considerable scholarly notice. In addition, historians have studied access based on religious affiliations other than Protestant and, to a lesser extent, access based on a student's ability to pay.

All of the above groups are important historically and remain significant in contemporary society. In fact, the President's Commission on Higher Education (the "Truman Report") of 1947 identified five significant deterrents to completing a college degree: race; gender; religion; geography; and socio-economic background.[1] Religious beliefs and geography no longer present substantial barriers to access to the same degree as observed by scholars on the Commission. Race, gender, and socio-economic status (SES) still remain significant.

Gender and race as categories of analysis have interesting parallels: both women and people of color were implicitly and explicitly denied access from the earliest forms of US higher education; both groups began their struggle in the 19th century by fighting for admission to existing institutions and simultaneously founding colleges to serve their group exclusively; both suffered from deeply held prejudices that asserted that neither women nor African Americans were intellectually capable of a college education; both groups won legal and policy battles for admission, but must deal with the lingering manifestations of prejudice in the form of sexism and racism in contemporary academia; and both groups have made extraordinary strides. They enter the 21st century with a level of access and accomplishment that the earliest pioneers could scarcely have dreamed. Women undergraduates, for example, outnumber their male peers and, as of this writing, women serve as presidents of half of the prestigious "Ivy League" universities. This is not to say that gender inequity no longer exists. In most roles in academe—for example tenured, full professors—women's experience can still be described as "the higher, the fewer," but the gains of the last three decades are undeniable.

The situation of access based on socio-economic status (SES) is a very different story. Today, SES is the best predictor of who will *not* go to college.[2] Ironically, "the poor" were the one demographic group that American higher education pledged to serve from the founding of Harvard in 1636. In a missive entitled *Harvard's First Fruits*, written to entice backers in England to support fledging Harvard College by sending money, goods, or their sons, the writers declared their mission to educate "the poor, but hopeful scholars whose parents are not able to comfortably maintain them."[3] Perhaps because reaching out to the poor was one of the original purposes of higher education, such a commitment has taken on almost a mythical quality, integrally tied to notions of American democracy. This correlation was made obvious by some of the titles of early histories of higher education such as: *Democracy's College; Colleges for Our Land and Time: The Land-Grant Idea in American Education;* and *The State Universities and Democracy.*[4]

Thus, it is important for scholars to place an analytical lens on how this story unfolded; from pledging to serve the poor, to barely reaching the poor. This essay concentrates on answering this question specifically for the 19th through early 20th centuries because it was during this period of growth that the myth of American higher education serving the poor was born and then later extolled by historians. It is also during this long era that archival and demographic records are the least precise and require the most detective efforts to interpret.

THE SCHOLARSHIP ON HIGHER EDUCATION AND THE POOR

In a 1999 *History of Education Quarterly* article, I suggested the extant literature on higher education and the poor could be described by a typology analogous to Peggy McIntosh's method of categorizing scholarship on women.[5] Organizing the literature in this manner continues to be a useful heuristic. Only scholarship in the latter categories deals with the two primary historiographic challenges and the principal contribution of this work: defining what is meant by "poor" and then identifying which students can be described as "poor." The significance of the work is the exploration of what access denied based on a student's poverty means to the larger social commitment of higher education.

I labeled the five categories of my typology: *Traditional/Omission; Increased Inclusion; Center of Analysis; Issue Specific;* and *Broader Social Analysis.*[6] These categories do not follow a rigid linear progression, although there is a sense of sequence with the *Traditional/*

Omission works frequently being the oldest and the more recent histories reflecting the latter categories.

Scholarship that falls in the *Traditional* group often provides an almost romanticized view of the topic where, for example, the Morrill Act colleges of the latter 19th century are ballyhooed as "Democracy's Colleges" because they served the poor. Such an example is Frederick Rudolph's *The American Colleges and University: A History*. As the label implies, work in the *Omission* category fails to address the topic at all.

Work in the second category, *More Inclusion*, incorporates some analysis of the higher education of poor although it is not the primary theme. Such literature follows Geraldine Clifford's exhortation to include the people overlooked in previous educational histories.[7] Clifford was speaking to the experiences of women, but the historical inclusion of those from the lower classes follows the same logic. In Joseph Kett's *The Pursuit of Knowledge Under Difficulties: From Self-Improvement to Adult Education in America, 1750–1990*, the subject is various forms of "non-traditional" education (meaning outside of established institutions and not for purposes of a degree). Within his discussion are educational pursuits by those who could not afford to attend traditional colleges, but such people were not the primary focus of the book.

Scholarship where SES is at the *Center of Analysis* begins to define what is meant by "poor" or the various synonyms that appear in primary documents such as "paupers," "working classes," "lower classes" or even "laborers." *Issue Specific* studies comprise the multiple, in-depth, focused, and even narrow micro-studies that form the building blocks necessary to fashion a comprehensive historical treatment of higher education and the poor. For example, studies of low SES students in land-grant colleges, historically Black colleges and universities, urban universities that serve recent immigrants, and even some prestigious institutions begin to paint a larger portrait of those students' experiences nationally. In *Paupers and Scholars: The Transformation of Student Life in Nineteenth-Century New England*, David Allmendinger begins to describe what he meant by "paupers" although his definitions have been subsequently challenged. Sherry Gorelick's *City College and the Jewish Poor: Education in New York, 1880–1924* takes a very specific look at the immigrant poor during a defined time period.

Finally, literature that provides a *Broader Social Analysis* moves toward a "critical theory" or "class analysis" approach. Such work is analogous to studies by feminist scholars who have moved beyond reconstructing women's experiences merely as "add-ons" to the main narrative and instead write history where women and, perhaps more significantly, the construction of gender (and how the male higher education establishment responded to both) were viewed as a dynamic force for change, not a by-product or incidental occurrence. Two such examples are David O. Levine's *The American College and the Culture of Aspiration, 1915–1940* and Clyde W. Barrow's *Universities and the Capitalist State: Corporate Liberalism and the Reconstruction of American Higher Education, 1894–1928*. Barrow's work is especially interesting with respect to his discussion of the connections between higher education and the labor market.

THE HISTORIOGRAPHICAL CHALLENGES OF STUDYING THE POOR

The most significant challenge to studying the experiences of low SES students in higher education is defining the word "poor" and its various synonyms. The second issue is identifying students who fall into the category of "poor" once the definition is determined.

What Is Meant by "Poor"?

An important consideration in this work is to proceed with caution if relying on the language of most primary documents, especially those of the 19th and early 20th centuries. Two conditions make such documents difficult to interpret. The first is the interchangeable use of possibly related terms such as "poor," "industrial classes," and even "sons of farmers" without any precision whatsoever. The second concern is "poor" compared to whom?

The "poor compared to whom?" question is difficult to answer because the frame of reference of the speaker (in the primary document under analysis) is difficult to deduce. In other words, was the speaker noting that students at his (the speakers were usually male) college were "poor" compared to his own economic circumstances? Or, were students poor compared to actual or perceived impressions of "rich" students at, typically, the elite institutions of the East Coast? Or to national or regional estimates of "average" income? The speakers in these documents were commenting on the SES of students in the absence of any official standard of what constituted poverty. In fact, it was not until the 1960s that the federal government established poverty thresholds (later the poverty line) and all who fell below were considered poor. The 19th century had no such benchmark.

Because there were no federal guidelines on what was meant by "poor," the work of a handful of late 19th-century social scientists provides some insight into 19th-century attitudes and perceptions. Henry Mayhew's *London Labour and the London Poor*, published in England in 1849 but equally influential in the U.S., was one of the first books on poverty from a sociological, data-driven, and less judgmental perspective.[8] This was a dramatic change from theologically inspired texts that discussed the "deserving" and "undeserving" poor—ideas brought to the Colonies based on Elizabethan Poor Laws.[9] Mayhew's work was followed by other sociologically based work that consisted of documenting the conditions of extreme poverty, which has been credited with being the intellectual foundation of modern social work.[10] A notable American example is Jacob Riis' study of New York City, *How the Other Half Lives*, published by Charles Scribner's Sons in 1890. In 1891–1893 *Scribner's Magazine* also published exposés of New York and other major cities.[11] Most of these publications concentrated on White and ethnic/immigrant groups, primarily of Western and Eastern European backgrounds. There was very little attention paid to African Americans living in poverty in Northern urban or Southern rural areas. The early work of W.E.B. Du Bois provided one of the first examples when he documented African American poverty in Philadelphia at the turn of the 20th century.[12]

What Mayhew, Riis, Du Bois, and others had in common was the tendency to concentrate on the "very poor." In 1889, Charles Booth, author of *Life and Labour of the People in London*, formally divided the poor into two sub-groups. He described those below the aristocracy and peerage as the "comfortable" class; below them were the "poor" and the "very poor." Robert Hunter then published *Poverty* in 1904 with an explicit mission of defining the term.[13] For Hunter, working men (and families who had at least one wage earner) were poor or just "getting by," and always precariously on the brink of pauperism. But, the "poor" were not yet in need of relief. Being "very poor" was equivalent to pauperism—people living in almshouses, the destitute, the ill, the disabled, and the socially unwanted for whom accepting charity and relief was necessary.

Modern social scientists have corroborated the observations of Booth and Hunter. In the 1990s, Economist Gordon M. Fisher systematically researched 19th-century efforts in the U.S. and abroad to define poverty and establish a "poverty threshold" or "poverty line" as discussed earlier. Like Himmelfarb, he credits Booth's work to a great degree, and also notes other examples where poverty was equivalent to pauperism or receiving relief, but there was often a group who, although poor, were slightly better off than the paupers.[14] Since the mid-20th century, it has been common for the distribution of income in the U.S. to be divided into quartiles and the lowest quartile comprises those who live below the poverty line. However, in terms of discussing who among the lowest quartile of SES attains a college degree, it is still useful to divide the lowest group into two sub-groups. Historian Michael Katz refers to the poorer of the two sub-groups as the "underclass," and there is considerable evidence that such individuals rarely make it to higher education.[15] However, as mentioned above, in both the 19th century and today, students from the top half of the lowest quartile—which I have labeled the "penultimate class"—are somewhat more likely than their underclass peers to attend college.[16]

Absent a concrete standard, however, Americans probably at least understood who fell below the middle class. Historian Burton Bledstein argued that by the 1830–40s "middle class" had an explicit identity and therefore those who were above and below this standard were recognizable to their contemporaries.[17] As the 19th century wore on, middle-class status became increasingly associated with certain occupations to the point that the phrase "professional class" was used almost synonymously with "middle class."[18] Bledstein's assertion is useful to a point but presents a particular problem when doing research on colleges residing in areas of the country that remained primarily agricultural throughout the 19th century. As certain occupations became identified as professions conferring middle-class status, farmers and other agricultural workers remained outside of that connotation. The notion that farmers' families were automatically thought of as poor was probably driven by East Coast-centric, industrial-generated notions of wealth during the latter half of the 19th century, but such a generalization —like most generalizations—was not true in all cases.

An example from the University of Michigan is illustrative. President James Angell conducted a survey in 1886 responding to criticism that the University was "aristocratic."[19] Angell was especially sensitive to this critique because he viewed the University as accessible to all members of the state. In fact, he would say in 1887, "the founders organized it on the plan of bringing education within the reach of the poor . . . The whole policy of the administration of this University has been to make life here simple and inexpensive . . . we are proud of the fact, [that Michigan is] the University of the poor."[20]

Angell's survey revealed the following distribution among 1,406 student respondents in terms of their fathers' occupations: farmers, 502; merchants, 171; lawyers, 93; physicians, 83; lumbermen, 65; mechanics, 54; manufacturers, 52; clergymen, 51; real estate and insurance agents, 33; bankers and brokers, 28 and teachers, 26; contractors and builders, 17; salesmen, clerks, and bookkeepers, 17; druggists and chemists, 16; tailors, 15; dealers in livestock, 14; millers, 14; commercial travelers, 14; dentists, 12; common laborers, 8; and other, 162. For Angell, this data demonstrated that the "poor" were attending the University because he conflated physical laborers with those from a "humble" background. "Most persons will be surprised to see how greatly the number of farmer's [*sic*] children exceeds every other class. If we assume that the farmers gain their living by manual toil, and add to them the other classes who unquestionably support themselves by physical labor, I estimate that the fathers of 45 per cent [*sic*] of the students who reported may properly be considered as thus gaining their livelihood."[21] In a 2004 article co-authored with Jeffrey Bouman for the *American Education Research Journal*, we demonstrated that, when using other means to determine who was really poor, very few Michigan students actually hailed from the lowest income strata.[22]

Historian Gertrude Himmelfarb furthers Bledstein's argument that middle-class status (and thus who fell below) was recognizable.[23] Just because historians cannot define terms precisely, Himmelfarb asserts, they should not assume that the people who lived with and used such terms did not have clear meanings for themselves. Therefore, historians may (and perhaps should) use definitions as understood by the subjects of the study. In her work, Himmelfarb demonstrates how clearly members of England's Victorian middle class understood the meaning of "respectability"—and therefore its opposite—although contemporary scholars have difficulty operationalizing that term.

However, Himmelfarb's assertion brings up the dilemma of presentism. If a contemporary understanding of poverty asserts that the poor are those who fall in the lowest quartile of national income distribution, should that standard be used when writing history? Or, as she suggests, should historians rely on the understandings of those under study? I would argue that educational historians do both. It is historically accurate and necessary to understand the perspectives of the actors whom historians are researching. On the other hand, contrasting the historical perspective with a contemporary understanding is also important. As mentioned earlier, the belief that higher education served and continues to serve the poor is not fully accurate and such inaccuracy, even to the point of myth, may contribute to a policy reluctance to increase access for such students. Historians can demonstrate that it is more correct to say that higher education has rarely been accessible to the very poor, but sometimes open to those who fall just below the middle class.

As mentioned earlier, college and university primary documents can be quite imprecise in their language of how many students were actually poor. For example, at the University of Michigan, President James Angell made a common error. As was the case with the middle class, membership in the "industrial classes" became associated with occupational choice, almost regardless of income. As a result, Angell argued that because the University enrolled students whose fathers were physical laborers, Michigan could remain the "University of the poor." Some of the students mentioned by Angell were middle class based on income estimates, and some came from the "penultimate class," but few if any were among the "very poor."[24]

Because of such ambiguity, it is necessary to find a method to evaluate independently the entering SES level of students using various means of triangulation. A wonderful example is J. Gregory Behle and William Edgar Maxwell's 1998 article, "The Social Origins of Students at the Illinois Industrial University, 1868–1894."[25] The authors explore the SES backgrounds of students in the early years of what became the University of Illinois. A founding voice at the University was Jonathan Baldwin Turner, an early champion of higher education for the industrial professions (agriculture, engineering, etc.) whose ideas found expression in the Morrill Act of 1862. Baldwin and others touted the fact that the University of Illinois provided an education for the "Industrial Classes." Such rhetoric later served to perpetuate the "democracy myth" that American higher education was open to anyone, including the poor. Behle and Maxwell collected students' fathers' names from admission data and were able to use U.S. Census data to determine average family income. Using the work of economic historians, they then compared the college students' incomes to the rest of the population of the state. Interestingly, they found that several such students came from families whose incomes were in the middle—not lower—ranges for Illinois in that era.

Researching the University of Michigan during roughly the same era that Behle and Maxwell studied the University of Illinois, my co-author and I had to use less straight-forward means to come to a similar conclusion. Because the University of Michigan archives did not have admissions data that included fathers' names and we found no economic history that provided income patterns, we took a different approach in signifying that the University became harder to attend by poor students as early as the 1880s. We demonstrated the rising cost of attendance, the higher cost of living in Ann Arbor, and the University's failure to compensate these increases with a systematic approach to financial aid combined to make Ann Arbor less affordable to the poor.

Using registrar and treasurer records and very early histories of the institution, it was possible to show that from 1849 to 1899, the average fees rose from approximately $14 to $54 per year, or somewhere between a three- and four-fold increase over fifty years.[26] To gauge the gravity of such a price increase, we compared it to other costs of the era. In a slight publication from 1920 by W. Randolph Burgess, we found data on price increases for certain goods in an "average market basket" during approximately the same 50-year period.[27] According to Burgess, the prices of flour, sugar, calico, and oil actually fell. While fresh beef, milk, potatoes, blankets, and shoes increased in price, none of them ever doubled. By comparison, attending college became more expensive. We were also able to demonstrate that living in Ann Arbor became more expensive using primary data provided by a 19th-century faculty member who compiled a four-volume encyclopedic survey of the University and secondary data of more modern historians of 19th-century Ann Arbor.[28]

One modern concern for low-SES students is that the amount the institution states a full year of college will cost can be misleading. A low estimate on the part of the institution may result in the financial aid formula providing low-income students less money than they really need and requiring them to work more and more hours to earn money. Research at the University of Michigan indicated that the University probably underestimated expenses over and above the matriculation and tuition fees for incoming students in the 19th century as well.

The University's catalog stated that such additional expenses of attending rose a mere $38 between 1871 ($362) and 1909 ($400). But data from a survey of graduating seniors and a few surviving student account books revealed that the University's estimates were consistently low. A survey was administered to 67 graduating seniors in 1874 that asked the question, "Amount spent on your college education?" The students reported an average of $483 per year, $113 above the catalog estimate.[29] In fact, as early as mid-century, students recorded their disagreement with University estimates of the cost of living at college. H.B. Nichols wrote his father in 1850 outlining his expenses: "So you see it is all a humbug for the catalogue to say the charges will range from $5.00 to $7.50 per year, as it will not be less than $15.00 to each student, or $30.00 to each room and if a student rooms alone his charges will be $21.00 per year!"[30]

Several detailed account books from Angell's era have survived.[31] In these the students noted, often to the penny, the price of what they purchased. The University expenses stated in the catalog were said to be "average" expenses, so we used account books from "average" students to the best that we could determine. We did not use an account book if there was evidence of extravagant or luxury purchases such as travel, expensive clothes, or servants assuming such students were well heeled. We then tried to determine the relative cost of the items the students did purchase—paper, pens, ink, room, board, common taxes for building damages, other food, laundry, shoe repair, medicine, and especially books. To the extent possible, the prices that students noted in their accounts were compared to the actual costs of goods in Ann Arbor at the time. At random intervals, the student newspapers, and especially their advertisements, were consulted for the prices of local goods of interest to students.[32] Although prices in ads were more common after the 1880s, it did appear that these students were not buying "top of the line" merchandise, which encouraged the speculation that they were not among the wealthiest students. For example, fountain pens were advertised for $1.50, but two students noted that they paid 70¢ and 90¢ for theirs. These students sometimes mentioned "amusements" or "entertainments" in their budgets, typically spending between 25¢ and 45¢. In the newspapers, most events on campus offered tickets at three prices, usually at 25, 50, and 75¢. Several mentioned buying tablets of paper for a nickel, and one store announced that tablets were 5, 10, or 15¢. Although no student mentioned buying new shoes, frequently advertised as $6–7 for men, two noted the cost of shoe repair.

In each of the seven account books examined, students' expenditures totaled more than the catalog estimate of the year they attended and kept records. Thus, the student account books and survey responses suggest that the actual cost of living in Ann Arbor was higher than the estimate published in the university catalog, making it less affordable.

How Do You Identify which Particular Students Were, in Fact, Poor?

Determining the demographic characteristics of college students from archival records can be a challenge. However, determining a student's entering SES is probably the most difficult because unlike a student's race or gender—which is unwavering throughout the college experience and in all alumni records—a student's SES is the one characteristic that a college education is designed to alter. Gender is perhaps the easiest to ascertain because throughout much of the 19th century, many institutions remained single-sex. In coeducational schools, students' first names typically allow historians to make assumptions about gender with confidence. In addition, by the latter part of the 19th century and throughout the 20th, many colleges had yearbooks or other publications with photographs. Race is less easily determined by names (and sometimes even the Black and White photos that may be available) but because the percentage of African American students in predominantly White colleges was so appallingly small in the 19th century, the presence of such students is sometimes noted elsewhere. For example, institutional histories may mention the enrollment of African American or International ("foreign") students because they stood out on these homogenous campuses.

Other important sources of demographic data are admission, graduation and alumni records. In my experience, official graduation or alumni records have rarely helped determine a student's entering SES level. However, some alumni associations began collecting biographical or anecdotal information on graduates, often in the form of autobiographical paragraphs submitted by alumni for special anniversaries such as

10th, 25th, or even 50th year reunions. Occasionally, a student's background can be confirmed by these documents.

Admissions data may have the most information on students, but seem the least likely to exist in archives. One archivist noted that at the college for which she worked, the specific admissions forms used in the late 19th century were thrown away the year the admitted students graduated. Perhaps other institutions had a similar sense that such information was not worth keeping. If available, however, such data can be found almost anywhere, in the records of the president, the board of trustees, the registrar, or filed among the collections of other administrative offices. In addition, there is little continuity in what information was collected on admissions cards or forms and how it was recorded either within an institution across time, or across various institutions. However, when such information is available, it is remarkable to note what was used to determine admission. In addition to academic data (e.g. entrance examination scores, proof of secondary school attendance, name of recommender, etc.) colleges sometimes noted a student's home address; religion (usually coded with a C for Catholic, J for Jewish, and sometimes a P for Protestant; even if "P" was the presumed religion, some institutions noted specific denominations within Protestantism); race (African Americans were noted with N for Negro or even C for "Colored"); and gender (usually F for female; M was the assumed default). For determining a student's SES level, the most useful data are the father's name, occupation, and/or family income. The father's name and home address facilitates using U.S. Census data which can provide occupation and/or income. However determined, occupation and income, when combined with sound economic histories of the region, allow inferences to be made about which students came from families living below "average" income levels.

Other data that can be helpful is financial aid information, although again such information is sometimes hard to find or evaluate. Some institutions keep data on which students were awarded scholarships, and some also noted on what criteria the award was based. However deduced, once specific names are gleaned from any of the above methods, alumni records, necrotic files, and other archival sources might contain additional information to corroborate the student's entering SES level.

SIGNIFICANCE

Today, the poor aren't making it to college, even the so-called "working poor."[33] In a recent white paper for the Institute for Higher Education Policy, the authors note:

> Despite working long hours to provide for their families, their incomes still teeter on the brink of poverty. They understand that enrolling in college and earning a degree will help them improve their skills and increase their earnings potential. However, given their work and other responsibilities, it is difficult for them to enroll full time, thus making it harder for them to receive financial aid and complete the classes necessary for a degree.[34]

Such facts of life make attending college a trial, but even the *perception* that college might be too expensive affects low-income students disproportionately. Research has shown that the mere assumption by low-SES families that they cannot afford to send their children to college discourages them from even applying.[35] When poverty is compounded by other factors such as race or immigrant status, the chances of completing a higher education degree is increasingly unlikely. Yet, there is an enduring strain of national discourse that purports an American system of higher education that is "open to all" and perhaps even a lingering belief of the U.S. as a "classless" society, or at least a class-permeable society. As recently as July 2008, researchers from the Center for American Progress began their analysis of limited mobility based on wealth as well as income by invoking the "American Dream." They stated, "conventional wisdom considers the United States to be a land of equal opportunity where the possibility for upward economic mobility is limitless. With hard work, everyone has a chance to move from rags to riches in a generation."[36]

While it is true that the U.S. has an extraordinary percentage of adults with some post-secondary education, there is a disconnect between such rhetoric and a policy commitment to make college realistically affordable.[37] President Kennedy once said, "the great enemy of the truth is very often not the lie—deliberate, contrived, and dishonest—but the myth—persistent, persuasive, and unrealistic."[38] The work of all historians who strive to tell the whole, messy, complicated, glorious, and flawed story of American higher education should discuss how promises made—such as "everyone" can go to college—are part of our democratic mythology but not always kept. Such history is not revisionist, dispiriting, or even unpatriotic as has been charged. Instead it is work that cares deeply about how higher education might live up to the promises made and contribute to a national dialogue about making college truly accessible.

Despite the challenges, the history of higher education to the poor is worthwhile and do-able. Methodologically, triangulation is key. Admissions data, financial aid records, local and regional economic histories, and census data are some of the official sources to which other primary documents can be prepared. Presidential speeches and correspondence, student letters and diaries, and even college newspaper accounts can paint compelling portraits of life on campus and whether such experiences were available to low-SES students.

QUESTIONS FOR DISCUSSION

1. What evidence exists from primary documents regarding the "democratization" ideology of higher education? Examples might include college mission statements, presidential speeches, legislation such as the Morrill Act, important reports such as the Truman Commission, etc.
2. Using the work of local or regional economic historians, locate data that provide some sense of a "middle income" range for a particular era. What institutional archival evidence would you look for to determine if a student's family income fell below that level?
3. Race is often a powerful determinant of socio-economic status (SES) in the U.S. How would you approach the question of whether poor African American students were able to attend a particular college or university depending on whether you were discussing an integrated but primarily White institution (PWI) or an historically Black college or university (HBCU)?
4. Why does access to higher education for low-income students matter?

NOTES

1. President's Commission on Higher Education, *Higher Education for American Democracy*, Vol. II (New York: Harper and Brothers, 1947), 29.

2. In a March 2003 Century Foundation white paper, "Socioeconomic Status, Race/Ethnicity, and Selective College Admissions," authors Anthony P. Carnevale, vice president for assessments, equity, and careers at Educational Testing Service, and Stephen J. Rose, a senior research economist with ORC Macro International, stated that there is even less socio-economic diversity than racial diversity in elite higher education. Using longitudinal data from the National Center for Education Statistics and the High School and Beyond studies, they concluded, "Access to selective colleges is highly skewed by race and ethnicity, although not as much as by SES," p. 10. Although highlighting the effect of SES at selective institutions, they noted that, in general, enrollment rates for lower-SES students are below those rates for African American or Hispanic students. See also, Thomas Mortenson, "Educational Opportunity by Family Income," *Educational OPPORTUNITY*, No. 86, August, 1999, and Thomas Mortenson, "Educational Attainment of Young Adults, 1940–1995," *Educational OPPORTUNITY*, No. 56, February, 1997.

3. Samuel Eliot Morison, *Three Centuries of Harvard, 1636–1936* (Cambridge: Harvard University Press, 1936), 102.

4. Earle Dudley Ross, *Democracy's College* (Ames, IA: Iowa State College Press, 1942); Edward Danforth Eddy, Jr. *Colleges for Our Land and Time: The Land-Grant Idea in American Education* (New York: Harper & Brothers, 1956); and Allan Nevins, *The State Universities and Democracy* (Urbana: University of Illinois Press, 1972).

5. Jana Nidiffer, "Poor Historiography: Challenges and Dilemmas in Exploring the History of the 'Poorest' in American Higher Education," *History of Education Quarterly*, 39 (3), Autumn, 1999, 321–336. My scheme does not duplicate but was clearly influenced by Peggy McIntosh's stages on the development of women's history. See Peggy McIntosh, "Interactive Phases of Curricular Revision: A Feminist Perspective." Working Paper #124, Wellesley College Center for Research on Women, Wellesley, MA, October 1983. In my scheme of the representative categories of women's higher educational history, the following may serve as examples for clarification to readers familiar with the field: *Traditional/Omission*, where little, if anything is mentioned about women—e.g. Laurence R. Veysey, *The Emergence of the American University* (Chicago: University of Chicago Press, 1965); *More Inclusion*, where women warrant some inclusion, but are not the main thrust of the argument—e.g. Helen Lefkowitz Horowitz, *Campus Life: Undergraduate Cultures from the End of the Eighteenth Century to the Present* (New York: Alfred A. Knopf, 1987); *Center of Analysis*, where women are the focus of the study and the treatment is generally broad—e.g. Barbara Miller Solomon, *In the Company of Educated Women* (New Haven: Yale University Press, 1985); *Issue Specific*, a specific issue, type, or concern of women's higher educational history is given a full analysis—e.g. Margaret W. Rossiter, *Women Scientists in America: Struggles and Strategies to 1940* (Baltimore: Johns Hopkins University Press, 1982); and *Broader Social Analysis*, where larger social, intellectual, psychological, or political forces are examined as the underlying theme—e.g. Rosalind Rosenberg, *Beyond Separate Spheres: The Intellectual Roots of Modern Feminism* (New Haven: Yale University Press, 1982).

6. The full citations for the texts mentioned in my typology are: Frederick Rudolph, *The American Colleges and University: A History* (New York: Vintage Books, 1962); Joseph Kett, *The Pursuit of Knowledge Under Difficulties: From Self-Improvement to Adult Education in America, 1750–1990* (Stanford, CA: Stanford University Press, 1994); David Allmendinger, *Paupers and Scholars: The Transformation of Student Life in Nineteenth-Century New England* (New York: St. Martin's Press, 1975); Sherry Gorelick, *City College and the Jewish Poor: Education in New York, 1880–1924* (New York: Schocken Books, 1982); David O. Levine, *The American College and the Culture of Aspiration, 1915–1940* (Ithaca, NY: Cornell University Press, 1987); and Clyde W. Barrow, *Universities and the Capitalist State: Corporate Liberalism and the Reconstruction of American Higher Education, 1894–1928* (Madison: University of Wisconsin Press, 1990).

7. Geraldine Joncich Clifford, "Saints Sinners, and People: A Position Paper on the Historiography of American Education," *History of Education Quarterly* 15 (2), 257–273.

8. Henry Mayhew, *London Labour and the London Poor; Cyclopedia of the Condition and Earnings of Those That Will Work, Those That Cannot Work, and Those That Will Not Work* (London: Griffin, Bohn, and Company, 1861).

9. See Michael B. Katz, *Improving Poor People: The Welfare State, the "Underclass," and Urban Schools as History* (Princeton, NJ: Princeton University Press, 1995); and Theda Skocpol, *Protecting Soldiers and Mothers: The Political Origins of Social Policy in the United States* (Cambridge: Harvard University Press, 1992).

10. See especially, Roy Lubove, *The Professional Altruist: The Emergence of Social Work as a Career, 1880–1930* (New York: Athenaeum, 1977).

11. In 1895, Charles Scribner's Sons published these essays as a book, *The Poor in Great Cities.*
12. See W.E.B. Du Bois, *The Philadelphia Negro: A Social Study* (Philadelphia: Published for the University, 1899).
13. Robert Hunter, *Poverty* (New York: The Macmillan Company, 1904).
14. See Gordon M. Fisher "The Development and History of the Poverty Thresholds," *Social-Security-Bulletin,* 55(4), Winter 1992, 3–14, and "From Hunter to Orshansky: An Overview of (Unofficial) Poverty Lines in the United States from 1904 to 1965" *Poverty Measurement Working Papers* (Washington, DC: U.S. Census Bureau, 1997).
15. Michael Katz, *Improving Poor People: The Welfare State, the "Underclass," and Urban Schools as History* (Princeton, N.J.: Princeton University Press, 1995).
16. Nidiffer, "Poor Historiography: The 'Poorest' in American Higher Education."
17. Bledstein devotes considerable energy to establishing this point. He notes early uses by Alexis de Toqueville, for example, and Webster's first entry in his dictionary for the "middling class," but he bases his conclusion primarily on four shifts in the U.S. economy that began around the 1830s. See, *The Culture of Professionalism: The Middle Class and the Development of Higher Education in America* (New York: W. W. Norton, 1976), 14–18.
18. This is the essence of Bledstein's primary thesis and because higher education became the gatekeeper to such professions, it emerged as the principle gatekeeper to middle-class status.
19. James B. Angell, "President's Report," in the *Proceedings of the Board of Regents* (Ann Arbor: University of Michigan Press, 1887), 162–163.
20. James B. Angell, *Commemorative Address* (Ann Arbor: University of Michigan Press, 1887), 95.
21. James B. Angell, "President's Report," in the *Proceedings of the Board of Regents* (Ann Arbor: University of Michigan Press, 1887), 163.
22. Jana Nidiffer and Jeffrey P. Bouman, "'The University of the Poor': The University of Michigan's Transition from Admitting Impoverished Students to Studying Poverty, 1870–1910," *American Educational Research Journal* 41 (1), Spring, 2004, 35–67.
23. See, Gertrude Himmelfarb, *Poverty and Compassion: The Moral Imagination of the Late Victorians* (New York: Vintage Books, 1991), especially chapter 1.
24. Nidiffer and Bouman, "'The University of the Poor'."
25. Gregory J. Behle and William Edgar Maxwell, "The Social Origins of Students at the Illinois Industrial University, 1868–1894," *History of Higher Education Annual* (1998) 18: 93–110.
26. A full discussion of our process is in Nidiffer and Bouman, "'The University of the Poor.'" Some of the sources we used were: Andrew Ten Brook, "The Rise of our University," X, *The Chronicle,* v. 1, n. xviii, June 11, 1870. Wilfred B. Shaw, *A Short History of the University of Michigan* (Ann Arbor: University of Michigan Press, 1937), 151. Treasurer Records, University of Michigan, 1839–1920. Bentley Historical Library, University of Michigan, Ann Arbor (Hereafter: BHL).
27. W. Randolph Burgess, *Trends in School Costs* (New York: The Russell Sage Foundation, 1920).
28. Shaw, *University of Michigan: An Encyclopedic Survey, 1761–1765.* Orlando Worth Stephenson, Ann Arbor: *The First Hundred Years* (Ann Arbor, MI: Chamber of Commerce, 1927). This was also corroborated in Jonathan Marwil, *The History of Ann Arbor* (Ann Arbor: University of Michigan Press, 1991). Marwil uses Chamber of Commerce minutes, and in addition, he consulted the financial records of several local businesses, and the local newspapers to make his assessment of Ann Arbor's general prosperity. Ann Arbor historian Jonathan Marwil depicted the town as generally prosperous, even weathering the economic downturns of the 1870s and the mid-1890s well.
29. Survey, Class of 1874. Bentley Historical Library, University of Michigan, Ann Arbor, MI.
30. As cited in Wilfred B. Shaw, *The University of Michigan* (New York: Harcourt, Brace and Howe, 1920), 174.
31. At the Bentley Historical Library, University of Michigan, Ann Arbor, the following student account books for the period of our study are available: Arthur Lyon Cross papers, 1897–1940; Winfred Foster Whitcomb papers, 1896–1925; H. Winnett Orr papers, 1892–1949; Ione Haydon papers, 1892–1948; Mabelle Agnes Gilbert papers, 1889–1914; Mark S. Knapp papers, 1887–1948; George Owen Squier papers, 1883–1934.
32. The newspapers were: *The Chronicle* (published from 1868 to 1890) and the *University of Michigan Daily* (published from 1890–1903) available at the Bentley Historical Library.
33. This phenomenon is not abating, even at institutions that have the fiscal capacity to fund needy students fully. See Karen Fischer, "Wealthy Colleges Show Drop in Enrollments of Needy Students," *Chronicle of Higher Education,* 24 April 2008. Retrieved 4/26/08 at http://chronicle.com/free/2008/04/2604n.htm.
34. Courtney McSwain and Ryan Davis, "College Access for the Working Poor: Overcoming Burdens to Succeed in Higher Education," Washington, DC: Institute for Higher Education Policy, July 2007, p. 8.

35. There are multiple examples of work in the vein, but perhaps the most recent is Alex Usher, "A Little Knowledge Is A Dangerous Thing: How Perceptions of Costs and Benefits Affect Access to Education" Stafford, VA: Education Policy Institute, Canadian Education Report Series, July 2005.

36. Dalton Conley and Rebecca Glauber, "Wealth Mobility and Volatility in Black and White," Washington, DC: Center for American Progress, July 2008.

37. For a discussion on what is considered in public policy debates, see Gary Orfield, "Public Policy and College Opportunity," *American Journal of Education*, Vol. 98, No. 4, Changing Patterns of Opportunity in Higher Education (August 1990), 317–350.

38. Commencement address, Yale University, New Haven, Connecticut, June 11, 1962.

11

WHERE IS YOUR "HOME"?

Writing the History of Asian Americans in Higher Education

Sharon S. Lee

WHERE I ENTER: PERSONAL STRUGGLES TO FIND A HOME

Opening Scenes: I am born and raised in a predominantly White suburb of Cleveland, Ohio, the second child of Korean immigrant parents.

Elementary School: "Ching chong, ching chong!" "Chinese, Japanese!" Kids pull their eyes down and laugh at me. "Can you see out of your eyes? Are you related to Bruce Lee? Do you know kung fu?" I get so tired of the questions, I lie and say that Bruce Lee is my uncle. I warn kids that I will use my martial arts moves if they don't leave me alone.

"Are you Chinese or Japanese?" I do not know how to respond. I ask my parents, who explain I am Korean. But I don't know what that is, since aren't I American? I eat Korean food, go to a Korean church (the only time I am surrounded by Korean faces once a week) and only know a few phrases in hangul.

High school: I hate my face, stature, and hair. I want to be blond, blue-eyed, tall. I watch other Korean American girls go to Korea for the summer, returning with eyelid surgery to make their eyes appear fuller, more Caucasian. I am painfully aware of external forces pushing me to be something I am not, overlooking my complex identities.

College: I am overwhelmed at the numerous activities for Asian American students; I feel uncomfortable and try to belong. I envy the Korean Americans I meet from California. They show me their high school yearbooks that have huge Asian American social clubs, they grow up with a more confident sense of their heritage and identity. While I am uncertain about joining a social or political Asian American movement, I find solace in reading. I begin to slowly research and learn about the histories of Asians in the United States. For the first time I learn about the internment of Japanese Americans. I feel cheated, lied to, misled by my American history textbooks that conveniently omitted this racist episode of our nation's past. I am angry that I never learned my own family's history. I am empowered by this new education. I find a home in Asian American Studies, even though it does not exist as an official curriculum at my small liberal arts college. Instead, students teach each other, and I learn on my own.

Post-college: I move to Los Angeles' Koreatown for a year, working in the community. I am excited at first, eager to finally find my "home" in idealized California, where Asians abound and my complexities can exist in peace. I am crushed when I feel the same level of judgment from the community there—to be "more Korean," to learn the language, attend a Korean church, find a Korean husband. When I do not deliver, I am dismissed as stranger from Ohio, somehow intrinsically "not Korean." I return to the Midwest.

Grad School, Attempt #1: I enter a prestigious doctoral program in U.S. history. I am eager to return to scholarly pursuits of Korean immigration history. My colleagues intimidate me, most of them White students from Ivy League schools. I am paired with an advisor who does not think much of Asian American history (he says so publicly in various venues) but tolerates my research and tolerates me. I lose my voice and leave the program, as many students of color do.

My home in Asian American Studies: By good fortune, I find a job working as a university administrator for Asian American Studies programs. By working with a diverse range of faculty, staff, and students, I see the complexities of Asian American experiences alongside our similarities. The language in which to critique institutional oppression and racism refreshes me. I see commonalities with other ethnic studies units and with women's studies seeking to become part of an institution that is suspicious of our scholarship. With some trepidation, I return to graduate school to research and improve the experiences of Asian American college students, this time in a program that supports and recognizes my work and my being.

Finding a Home: A Note About "Home"

I include the preamble because I believe it is important to reveal and to reflect upon our points of origin as scholars. Who we are and what we experience (especially aspects of our identities that are affected by power dynamics—gender, race, class) reflect how we see life, what issues jump out at us, what we seek to do with our work. While historians have long sought for an ideal of objectivity,[1] I believe that scholarship is never truly objective. It is more important to recognize and be upfront about our positions than to cover up our ever-present biases.[2]

I am a second-generation Korean American woman from the Midwest. Caught between generations and communities, I have never felt truly whole in any one place in my life. Ostracized by mainstream communities and media images, I have always been aware of my other-ness and of being racialized as an Asian woman, whether that means expectations to be a model student, quiet, submissive, to be continually from some Asian country and unable to speak English or fully be American, or to be exotic (I am none of these expectations). At the same time, I have felt ostracized by Korean immigrant communities' expectations—to speak Korean, follow gendered patterns of behavior, attend a Korean church, marry a Korean husband and produce Korean babies (if you haven't guessed by now, I have not, nor do I plan to do any of the above). Because I have faced judgment and rejection from multiple spaces, I identify with the political movement of Asian American Studies—I am a racialized, gendered individual who resists oppressive expectations, barriers, and messages that rob me of my individuality.

Because of the disempowering effect of stereotypes and broad categories, I seek to show the more nuanced complexities of any social phenomenon, in this case, the experiences of Asian American college students. Historical research is essential to this endeavor because many media (mis)representations abound of this population, namely that Asian Americans are a high-achieving model minority group that makes no trouble and has no problem accessing or excelling in higher education. Yet, history shows us that this has not always been the case. Racial barriers kept Asians from entering the United States and blocked them from access to higher education.[3] Many prestigious universities denied admission to Japanese Americans resettling from internment camps because of issues of "national security."[4] By recognizing this history, we see that it is only through shifting discourses, locations, sites, and periods that the image of Asian American students has radically changed, thus begging the question: how did this happen? By recognizing these shifts, we can also see that the current state of Asian American educational "success" is not something intrinsic or unique to this community. Concomitantly, what has not changed? Negative campus climate, questions of admissions quotas against Asian Americans, and a sense of an "Asian invasion" of competitive schools reflect continuing discussions of Asians as interlopers on the U.S. landscape.[5] How do these enduring representations vary, change, reappear, ebb, and flow throughout historical periods and sites?

The goal of this chapter is to raise some questions regarding "home" for a scholar embarking on historical scholarship of Asian American college students.[6] I use the metaphor of home because it symbolizes this constant search for a space where one can relax, be at peace, and exist in full complexity and nuance—something that is often a luxury and not a given for marginalized persons. As a new scholar researching the history of Asian American college students, I struggle with locating my home for sources, methodology, and disciplinary department. When I was invited to write this chapter, I hesitated—unsure of what I could contribute, as I feel I have struggled much of my life to find my home and to understand what it exactly is that my scholarship does. Yet, I hope that my struggles ultimately reflect what this process is about, that it is messy and uncertain. While by no means do I claim to know where the ideal home is (or if one even exists), I hope to raise questions and offer some road maps that I have found along the way. At the same time, I believe that one's home is of one's choosing and creation. The last thing I want to do is to be yet another didactic force telling others seeking to do this work who they should be and how they should do this history. Home is constructed . . . so where we hang our hats is ultimately where we decide.

Welcome to the "Neighborhood": The Landscape of Asian American Educational Historiography

Those seeking a home in Asian American educational historiography may feel alone. It's not a big surprise but, as Eileen Tamura points out, the landscape of Asian American educational history is sparse.[7] Ruben Donato and Marvin Lazerson also identify this work as understudied. They write of the field,

> Although changing, most historians of education typically conceive of "minority" educational histories very narrowly so as to include only the schooling of African Americans; they write and teach the histories of people of color primarily within a Black/White context. Few history of American education courses and too few scholarly writings discuss the experiences of Asian Americans, Native Americans, or Latinos."[8]

Welcome to a neighborhood that, while it may not necessarily evict or reject you, may not understand your work.

What we do know is, as the literature on K-12 educational histories reveals, like other non-White groups in the United States, Asian immigrants encountered barriers to equal education.[9] Depending on locale, Asians could be defined as "White" or "Black" and mandated to attend segregated schools. Valerie Pang, Peter Kiang, and Yoon Pak describe how the 1885 Supreme Court cases *Tape v. Hurley* and *Aoki v. Deane* as well as the 1927 *Gong Lum v. Rice* case involved Chinese and Japanese immigrants challenging policies that denied their American-born children access to White schools.[10] A special issue on Asian American educational history by the *History of Education Quarterly* also features new work that documents the educational experiences of Japanese and Chinese Americans in Hawai'i, Mississippi, and abroad.[11]

The history of Asian and Asian American access to higher education is also a new development. Institutions of higher education varied in their level of access to Asian immigrants. Barbara Posadas and Roland Guyotte document the case of Filipino pensionados, students sponsored by the Philippine government to obtain an American education for future government positions upon their return. Between 1903 and 1907, the Philippine government sponsored about 200 men and a dozen women to attend colleges in the United States.[12] In Midwestern cities such as Chicago, Filipino students formed associations for support and cultural fellowship, as many eventually settled in the United States.

During the height of early Asian immigration to the United States in the mid-nineteenth and early years of the twentieth century, most Asians attending colleges and universities were international students. The second generation, American-born Asian population was small in number; thus, their admission to prestigious schools on the East Coast did not pose a visible threat or at the least facilitated beneficence. Marcia Graham Synnott writes of the early twentieth century: "The admission of Chinese and Japanese to Harvard did not arouse fear of a yellow peril, because the percentage of American-born Orientals [*sic*] living in the eastern United States was very small and because almost all of these students were foreign-nationals. Instead the education of Orientals [*sic*] appealed to American altruism and belief in the 'White man's burden.'"[13]

California, home to more Asian immigrants during this time, struggled with anti-Asian sentiment and access. The University of California held a commitment to admit students who reflected the diversity of the state; however, the state struggled with a history of segregation and discrimination against Asians, such as in the case of alien land laws barring Japanese immigrants from land ownership. Still, John Aubrey Douglass notes that the University of California never adopted racial or ethnic exclusions or formal quotas.[14] Rather, minority students' numbers remained low due to state laws that excluded Chinese and Japanese from public schools—in 1874, the state Supreme Court ruled that segregation of schools for Black children violated the Thirteenth and Fourteenth amendments but made no similar provisions for Chinese and Japanese children. Restrictive zoning laws also segregated Blacks, Asians, and Latinos into certain neighborhoods, leading to segregated schools.

One area of historical research focusing on Asian American experiences in higher education has been the experiences of incarcerated Japanese Americans during World War II who were able to leave internment camps to attend colleges in the nation's interior.[15] Allan Austin documents how these students were pioneers in Japanese American resettlement. Among this group, 4,000 Nisei enrolled in over 600 colleges and universities, through the assistance of the National Japanese American Student Relocation Council, which functioned from 1942 to 1946.[16] Still, despite these efforts, most large, prestigious universities were not open to them; even for schools who admitted these students, most set quotas to limit their numbers due to concerns about a racial backlash. Thus, access to prestigious research universities was still hampered for Japanese Americans during World War II.

When entering the neighborhood then, any historical work on Asian American educational history will be fairly new. This means at least two things. The good news is that whatever one writes on the topic will be a much needed contribution. There is a lot of new ground to uncover, creating numerous opportunities and sites of research. The bad news is that there are few road maps, few directions, and often times too few mentors to assist in this work. The journey may be solitary and require looking for models of scholarship from other areas (African American educational history, women's history) that can inspire, as well from generous scholars who might not be completely knowledgeable on Asian American issues but whose support is critical.

WHERE IS YOUR "HOME" FOR SOURCES? A BRIEF NOTE ON REGION

With a general sense of the educational historiography, one can begin to assess where one's "home" can be for sources. In whatever region one starts, it is critical to have an understanding of Asian immigration and history at this site and what forces shape the demographic emergence of U.S.-born generations and their access to equitable education.

Immigration legislation affected Asian immigration to the United States. Most notably, anti-Asian legislation began to block the entry of Asians (Chinese, Japanese, Koreans, Asian Indians, and Filipinos) in the late nineteenth and early twentieth centuries. Immigration from Asia would not open up again until the 1965 Immigration Act abolished national origins quotas. Thus, one elementary periodization of Asian American history can be drawn around pre- and post-1965 immigration.

A pre-1965 history favors sites such as Hawai'i and California, given the longer histories of Asian immigration and longer generational tracks there, with an American-born population emerging earlier. Still, immigration laws blocked the entry of Asian women, particularly for Chinese and Filipino immigrants in the late nineteenth century, thus affecting the development of U.S.-born generations.[17] Even for groups from which a second generation could emerge (e.g. Japanese Americans), it was not always the case that this U.S.-born generation could gain much access to education, and these barriers need to be documented.

While Hawai'i and California are obvious sites for sources, there are other areas that need examination and may serve as a home of sources. Chinatowns on the east coast, most notably New York, have a long history.[18] The South, with its history of Chinese immigration, is often an overlooked area.[19] The Midwest is also a prime site for historical research and has become my current home for sources: Asian immigrants' settlement in Chicago has a long history and implications for their later American-born children's experiences at state universities. Chicago has been home to a history of

Filipino pensionados and Chinese immigrants since the 1880s.[20] In addition, as Japanese internment camps began to close after World War II, nearly 30,000 Japanese Americans began their resettlement in the windy city.[21]

Thus, there are many possible regional sites for educational historians to examine the experiences of Asian American college students, following immigration and generational trajectories. By grounding one's work along these histories, potential leads may emerge to begin looking for sources, through university archives and community organizations.

WHERE IS YOUR DISCIPLINARY HOME? OTHERWISE KNOWN AS ARE YOU A "REAL" HISTORIAN?

I feel I am forever trying to define my work and trying to think about what kind of academic department would house me, as I imagine and prepare for the job market. Do I want to be in a traditional history department? A college of education? Asian American or Ethnic Studies? In each space, I feel the risk of marginalization and suspicion, as educational historians face in history departments (is she a real historian?) and in colleges of education (what does history have to do with preparing teachers or addressing current educational policies?). In addition, the history of higher education has been viewed as marginalized in the broader field of educational history.[22] Asian American Studies has not been a place widely known to center educational scholarship either, along with other social science research.[23] I know I am in for a struggle wherever I go.

Educational historians have expressed frustration of being disregarded as not "real" or "serious" historians because they study schools/colleges or because they are affiliated with Schools of Education instead of traditional history departments. Personal stories were shared in abundance on a recent H-Education list-serve discussion, with scholars describing how an affiliation with a college of education can elicit discrediting at historical associations.[24] Some reasons for this were offered, including the sense that education is a lesser prestigious "applied" science. Jonathan Zimmerman writes, "There is a prima facie assumption—or, if you prefer, a stereotype—that ed school professors lack intellectual rigor and accomplishment."[25]

This snobbery (for lack of a better word) of what makes a good historian has plagued me, and I believe this self-doubt comes partly from a lack of explicit curricular training but also from the marginalized nature of Asian American history. My path as a developing historian has been filled with doubt. Part of this comes from the fact that my undergraduate institution did not require a course on methodology or theory for history majors, so when I began my M.A. program in U.S. history, I did not really know quite what I did or how I did it. It just felt intuitive—read, read, read, and write with lots of sources and context. My unsupportive M.A. experience did not do much for a sense that my scholarship was worthy or well done.

My current doctoral program has helped prepare me in a much better way to approach issues of methodology as well as providing a stronger support in Asian American issues, with specific courses and seminars that help me to read historical works with an eye towards interpretation. Reading works this way has helped me pinpoint what it is about them that I admire as well as to realize when a work feels unsubstantiated. Yet, even in these classes, the mystery of "what does a historian do" still lingers. What is good historical methodology? What is the place of theory? There is a wide range of opinions on these matters.

My own methodological claim to being a historian has been revealed to me in subtle ways. Encouraged importantly by amazing mentors in my program, I have been told that my work *is* historical because of my methodology, even though it crosses into the 1980s and 1990s (a note on recency of my work next). It is historical because of the numerous sources I use (policy reports, oral transcripts from court proceedings, legal documents, newspaper articles) and because of the way I contextualize my work. I began to see this in other methodology courses I took. My history courses and oral history courses felt like home in many ways—in the types of secondary works we read, the questions that were asked, the uses of theory that, while varied, did not force an imposed interpretation beyond what the sources showed.

In the midst of my search for my methodological identity, I took other courses. In qualitative methods, I began coding oral history interviews I had done for my dissertation. I offered codes for six interviews to my professor, to which she remarked at the volume of data I had collected already and urged me to start writing up my data chapter. I was stunned—six interviews? Six interviews provided me with six individual perspectives and interpretations, but just one source to interpret, among many others I had yet to collect including archival materials, historiography of the time period I was examining, and additional oral histories as well. Thus, I have found qualitative methodology to be more like visiting a friend than finding a home. I like that friend and have things in common with her, but it is not a kinship.

In another course on cultural studies, I submitted a draft of a chapter of my dissertation, documenting the rise of Asian American student services at a Midwestern university and the discursive challenges of student activists. My professor urged me to employ a Gramscian theoretical interpretation of my work. While I also like visiting cultural studies, the level of theorizing feels uncomfortable to me. In a seminar on historical methods, we discussed the uses of theory. As Martha Howell and Walter Prevenier outline, though the use of theory has varied in the historical field over time, many historians distrust theory due to a suspicion of crafting a teleology or a causal theory that may lack nuance.[26] While we approach any topic with a set of questions and ideas, that seminar taught me the importance of being open to what is found (and not found) in the sources and to craft interpretations carefully.

While visiting my friends of qualitative methods and cultural studies, I have learned important methods and theoretical frameworks that I do employ, yet in an odd way I found myself identifying as a historian because of what I did *not* identify with in these spaces. This is not to say that one should not consider multiple methodologies or intersections of intellectual spaces, in fact the opposite—since I have felt that these forays make me a better scholar. Rather, I believe I am finally able to claim that I am a historian because of my methodological foci on sources, context, and interpretation. It does not matter that the work is in or on education.

WHERE IS YOUR DISCIPLINARY HOME PART II: WHERE DO EDUCATIONAL HISTORIANS FIT IN SCHOOLS OF EDUCATION?

Another challenge exists in colleges of education, in particular the meeting of historical perspective and present-day concerns, an issue that would make some historians cringe with fears of presentism. Being housed in a school of education does necessitate some analysis of history with present-day issues, which presents a tension. As Donato and Lazerson note, few historians think in terms of "educational lessons," and a focus on current-day policies can reduce rigorous, complex, and nuanced historical interpretation to simplistic bullet points.[27] I have certainly felt this struggle, as I am constantly trying to explain that Asian American students are diverse, complicated, messy—far beyond a stereotype of a "model minority." Yet, even after presenting this material, I am still asked reductive questions as to what are the top three policy recommendations for this group?

At the same time, historical analysis provides an important perspective to understanding current-day issues. Zimmerman supports the idea that history *should* inform public policy and that we are all invested in studying the past to see how it can inform our understanding of the present. The danger of presentism comes, however, when present-day agendas and questions drive the search for historical data to justify a foregone conclusion.[28]

One benefit of colleges of education, as David Labaree pointed out in the H-Education list-serve discussion, is the space for interdisciplinarity and multiple conversations that it provides. The statistical reality is that more historians of education do live in schools of education.[29] Such an affiliation may come with a sense of lower "status" than history departments but can also offer sites to build a more flexible academic identity rather than be tied to one disciplinary lens. Linda Eisenmann also noted the potential good that such conversations will have on scholarship of higher education, rather than a watering down of a disciplinary historical approach, stating that historians "must welcome and converse with other scholars—even those not trained in history—who apply elements of historical analysis to contemporary concerns. This approach never diminishes disciplinary inquiry but gains the added strength of extending the increasingly vital field of higher education research."[30] Thus, colleges of education may provide important sites of connection between historical research and our understanding of current educational issues, as long as current agendas do not mold the questions asked or detract from what the sources show.

ARE YOU A REAL HISTORIAN IF YOUR WORK IS TOO RECENT? STUDYING HISTORY IN THE POST-WORLD WAR II ERA

The recency of my work examining Asian Americans in higher education in the post-1960s era has proven to be a prickly problem. For scholars who seek to study Asian American issues, many historical questions arise after 1965, due to immigration changes. Hence, this recency poses common challenges.

What is history? While some people have told me that history is history if it happened yesterday, others have told me history is not history unless we have some perspective on it, normally thirty years to reflect and fully understand its significance. Part of this perspective-taking is a source matter, when records and archives are sealed until a certain time in protection of an individual's reputation. I agree with this need for historical perspective that comes with the passing of time—for instance, I do not think that we can even begin to fully understand the significance of the events of September 11, 2001 for quite some time, since the implications of what followed are still playing out. However, given this lens, then what does this mean for someone who studies Asian American history in a recent era?

I have learned of the problems of my topic at the History of Education Society (HES) meetings. At my first HES meeting, a respected educational historian told me that if I were her student, she would advise me not to extend my work past 1970. At my second HES meeting, I presented my work on a panel of scholars that did work on the 1970s, to which the chair joked that he was pleased that the 1970s were now being considered "history". W. Bruce Leslie points out the challenges to writing a recent history: "Most of us are more comfortable writing after the dust has settled. After all, the unique intellectual contribution of historians is observing change over time with perspective. Something in the range of a half-century is a normal comfort range; and archival rules reflect and enforce that distance."[31] Hence, there is a clear message—my work would not be taken as history if it crossed a certain date, and I should wait time out.

However, the periodization of Asian American history, especially in light of 1965 immigration legislation, means that any analysis of second generation, US-born Asians will not come until the 1970s, 1980s, and 1990s. Demographically in higher education, Asian American presence explodes during this time. Don Nakanishi cites that between 1970 and 1980, Asian Americans had increased from 1.5 million to 3.5 million, making them America's fastest growing group at that time.[32] The children of post-1965 Asian immigrants did not reach college age until the 1970s through 1990s. Thus, often times this is where a historical analysis begins.

Therefore, it is important that historical research involve a post-1965 lens for Asian Americans. There are also important reasons to begin to write a recent history, as Leslie points out. For one, sources may be fleeting if not documented now. Often administrators' personal papers are taken with them and not deposited in an archive. Finding sources when you can is critical for future historical work. Oral history is another important way to capture people's memories and perspectives. Though historical interpretation may be preliminary, there is comfort in knowing that additional interpretations will follow, with greater insight as time passes.

SOME POTENTIAL SITES FOR BUILDING A HOME IN ASIAN AMERICAN HIGHER EDUCATION HISTORY

While everyone's home is different, I offer here some sites of possible homes that have given me comfort and guidance in my work on post-1965 Asian American college students. As I straddle the lines of history and policy, I borrow from frameworks that incorporate history as an essential component.

This first is a framework for campus climate. Sylvia Hurtado, Jeffrey Milem, Alma Clayton-Pedersen, and Walter Allen argue that campus climate is produced within larger institutional and environmental contexts such as government policies (e.g., financial aid, affirmative action) and socio-historical forces that propel policy change.[33] Within an institution, this framework highlights four interconnected dimensions in which to assess racial climate: an institution's history, structural diversity (numerical representation in student body and faculty), psychological climate (student perceptions of group relations), and behavioral climate (how groups actually interact).

In higher education policies, an overreliance on structural diversity alone (statistical representation, fueled by ideological representation and stereotypes of Asian American students as model minorities) provides a rationale for the exclusion of Asian American students from minority student services or admissions considerations. Yet, Hurtado et al. examine the history of an institution as well as its psychological and behavioral dimensions. Historical and qualitative data reveal a much more complicated picture. A university's history provides an important context from which to understand the evolution of its diversity policies.

The second framework is Critical Race Theory (CRT) and specifically "AsianCrit," which emerged in the late 1970s. Critical race theorists recognize that racism is pervasive and permanent in U.S. society and embraces a contextual/historical analysis of the law.[34] CRT also centers the experiential voices and counter-narratives of people of color. Thus, CRT allows me to address current-day experiences of Asian American students with a larger historical framework to show a history of Asian American struggle for equitable access to education.

Oral history methods are also an important part of my research, as many of my sources are still living. While this poses new ethical dilemmas and struggles with Institutional Review Boards on how to identify my sources (a requisite in historical research) and protect their interests, it also introduces a more fluid type of methodology to historical work. While some may question the flaws of memory, I see oral history as useful in the endless process of constructing meaning. Alessandro Portelli articulated that the perceived weaknesses of oral history (its subjectivity, its influence of the interviewer, the credibility of memory) are actually its strengths. While oral sources can provide important leads (to be verified by other sources) on historical facts, they say more about meaning than events; Portelli writes that, "Oral sources tell us not just what people did but what they wanted to do, what they believed they were doing, and what they now think they did."[35] Oral sources have a different type of credibility; they merge a process of constant meaning making that involves the past and present. And he asserts that no source is entirely objective, it is oral history's subjectivity that is important. Thus, it provides one way to reveal how Asian American alumni recall their experiences in college within a larger understanding of how issues such as race, class, and gender affect them in the present. I have enjoyed rich conversations with alumni who are mildly embarrassed at the letters and reports they wrote in their college activist days yet also pensive about seeing the larger significance of these efforts today. And while they often caution me about stating what they recall as fact, their memories and impressions of their experiences are rich contributions to constructing a sense of a certain time and space, offering both important starting points for additional archival work as well as sources that reveal the humanity behind the historical paper trail of reports, memos, and newspaper headlines.

CONCLUSION

I hope that this chapter has identified some challenges (and opportunities!) in researching the educational histories of Asian American college students. While the struggle for "homes" along multiple dimensions may always exist, there are also sites of collaboration and innovation. As I noted above, one's home is ultimately where one decides. In the H-Education list-serve discussion, it was clear that this search is not always dire. Mona Gleason wrote, "Increasingly, I'm of the mind that we must create our own homes—not because they don't already exist in some form or another but because there are so many more opportunities if we use our knowledges creatively and usefully."[36] In addition, Stephanie Y. Evans described how her appointments in Black studies and women's studies meant that she often faces pressure to align herself in one way. However, she remarked that having to live in a specific space was not necessary. "Rigorous interdisciplinary research requires identifying clear disciplinary roots. But that does not mean one has to live in mainstream professional spaces, which are often quite scary."[37] As the boundaries of historical research open up with new theories, methodologies, and ideas, a collaborative approach can help us rethink our research questions and teaching.

As I continue to work through my doctoral program, I have tried to put the strategic questions of how to position myself for a future job on the back burner. When I asked a friend how to align myself amidst all these struggles to find an academic "home," he shared some sage advice: to research and write about what you love to do, not what you think potential search committees will want you to do. Basically, build the home you love instead of compromising your comfort to live somewhere else. I respect his advice because he has done just this, becoming a prolific writer whose own academic career has taken many twists and turns, including positions at a small liberal arts college, as the founder of a national educational center, a specialist at a national education association, and now a tenured faculty member at a research university. His own path to tenure was circuitous and non-traditional, yet his consistently strong scholarship and his clear passion for his work surely led him there.

Such passion sustains many scholars' work on marginalized groups, including myself. As I shared in the beginning of this essay, my own roots and search for "home" are greatly informed by a sense of living in between spaces in the hopes that new venues can be created. It is not easy work, but it is important. A historical analysis provides an important contribution to understanding a history of racialization and racism against Asian Americans in higher education, which challenges present day ahistorical notions of Asian American educational access. By examining the local, historical, and complex contexts of these images alongside the voices and experiences of Asian American students themselves, a greater, nuanced interpretation of Asian American students can emerge, helping these students themselves feel more at "home" in the academy.

QUESTIONS FOR DISCUSSION

1. How do you navigate finding a "home" in your own research?
2. Does the author's identity as an Asian American woman advantage or disadvantage her in researching Asian American educational history? How so?
3. Why is studying the history of Asian Americans in higher education important? Why has it been marginalized/invisible in the field of higher educational history?
4. Respond to the discussion about the methodological challenges of studying recent events as a historian. What is the historian's role and responsibility in interpreting the past, if the "past" is relatively recent?
5. Imagine the "ideal" types of sources for studying the history of Asian American college students. Now, what alternative sources could you turn to, if those ideal sources do not exist?

NOTES

1. Peter Novick outlines the development of the ideal of objectivity among professional historians in the United States. Peter Novick, *That Noble Dream: The "Objectivity Question" and the American History Profession* (Cambridge: Cambridge University Press, 1988).

2. As Howell and Prevenier state, "If we can understand or at least acknowledge our ideological position, we can also write histories that self-consciously display those limitations to our readers. We can thus implicate our audiences in the histories we write, making them see *how we see* as well as what we see." Martha Howell and Walter Prevenier, *From Reliable Sources: An Introduction To Historical Methods* (Ithaca, NY: Cornell University Press, 2001), 148.

3. For instance, William Wei notes that due to laws that restricted Asian immigration to the United States in the late nineteenth and early twentieth centuries (and especially those banning the entry of Asian women), a second generation was slow to grow. Coupled with segregation in schooling and housing, Asian American college enrollments did not increase until after World War II. William Wei, *The Asian American Movement* (Philadelphia: Temple University Press, 1993), 2.

4. Allan Austin, *From Concentration Camp to Campus: Japanese American Students and World War II* (Urbana: University of Illinois Press, 2004).

5. For a good overview of the Asian admissions quota controversy, see Dana Takagi, *The Retreat From Race: Asian American Admissions and Racial Politics* (New Brunswick, NJ: Rutgers University Press, 1992). Recent media headlines and campus satires reveal a sense of over-competitive Asian students "taking over schools"; Suein Hwang, "The New White Flight," *The Wall Street Journal*, November 19, 2005, p. A1. For a critique of campus satires on Asian American students, see Sharon S. Lee, "Satire as Racial Backlash Against Asian Americans," *Inside Higher Ed*, February 28, 2008, http://insidehighered.com/views/2008/02/28/lee.

6. When I speak of Asian American students, I am focusing primarily on the experiences of Asians in the United States, not international Asian students. However, the racially constructed category of "Asian American" is complex and involves a variety of immigration trajectories; thus, others take a more transnational/diasporic perspective. I believe that multiple frameworks are needed to conceptualize Asian/Asian American experiences, and to capture their full complexities. At the same time, scholars should be explicit in how they are defining this group.

7. For instance, in a review of the number of essays and book reviews published by the *History of Education Quarterly* from 1990 to 1999, she found only one essay and one book review on Asian Americans (both published by herself or on her work). Eileen Tamura, "Asian Americans in the History of Education: An Historiographical Essay," *History of Education Quarterly* 41 (2001), 58–71.

8. Ruben Donato and Marvin Lazerson, "New Directions in American Educational History: Problems and Prospects," *Educational Researcher* 29 (2000), 8.

9. Charles M. Wollenberg, "'Yellow Peril' in the Schools (I and II)," in *The Asian American Educational Experience: A Source Book for Teachers and Students*, ed. Don T. Nakanishi and Tina Yamano Nishida (New York: Routledge, 1995), 3–29. Also see Meyer Weinberg, *Asian-American Education: Historical Background and Current Realities* (Mahwah, NJ: Lawrence Erlbaum Associates, Publishers, 1997). In the interest of space, I do not deeply explore Asian American K-12 educational historiography here. A good place to start is Tamura, "Asian Americans in the History of Education," 58–71.

10. Valerie Ooka Pang, Peter Kiang, and Yoon Pak, "Asian Pacific American Students: Challenging a Biased Educational System" in *Handbook of Research on Multicultural Education, Second Edition*, ed. James A. Banks and Cherry A. McGee Banks (San Francisco, CA: Jossey-Bass, 2004), 542–563.

11. "A Special Issue on Asian American Educational History," ed. Eileen Tamura, *History of Education Quarterly*, 43 (2003).

12. Barbara M. Posadas and Roland Guyotte, "Unintentional Immigrants: Chicago's Filipino Foreign Students Become Settlers, 1900–1941," *Journal of American Ethnic History* 9 (1990), 28.

13. Marcia Graham Synnott, *The Half-Opened Door: Discrimination and Admissions at Harvard, Yale, and Princeton, 1900–1970* (Westport, CT: Greenwood Press, 1979), 53.

14. John Aubrey Douglass, *The Conditions for Admission: Access, Equity, and the Social Contract of Public Universities* (Stanford, CA: Stanford University Press, 2007), 61.

15. See Austin, *From Concentration Camp to Campus* and Gary Okhiro, *Storied Lives: Japanese American Students and World War II* (Seattle: University of Washington Press, 1999).

16. Austin, *From Concentration Camp to Campus*, 1.

17. Sucheng Chan, *Asian Americans: An Interpretive History* (Boston: Twayne Publishers, 1991).

18. Peter Kwong, *The New Chinatown, Revised Edition* (New York: Hill and Wang, 1996).

19. Sieglinde Lim de Sanchez, "Crafting A Delta Chinese Community: Education and Acculturation in Twentieth-Century Southern Baptist Mission Schools," *History of Education Quarterly* 43 (2003), 74–90.

20. Susan Moy, "The Chinese in Chicago: The First One Hundred Years," in *Ethnic Chicago: A Multicultural Portrait*, ed. Melvin G. Holli and Peter d'A. Jones (Grand Rapids, MI: William B. Eerdmans Publishing Company, 1995), 378–408.

21. Masako Osako, "Japanese Americans: Melting into the All-American Pot," in *Ethnic Chicago: A Multicultural Portrait*, ed. Holli and Jones, 423.

22. Ruben Donato and Marvin Lazerson, "New Directions in American Educational History: Problems and Prospects," *Educational Researcher* 29 (2000), 10.

23. This is not a pointed critique of the field per se, but an observation. In recent years, the Association for Asian American Studies has not showcased many education papers/panels.

24. H-Education, "Where do Historians of Education Live? Disciplines and Interdisciplines in the Academy," http://www.h-net.org/~educ/H-Education-interdisciplinary-discussion.htm (accessed August 9, 2008).

25. "Interchange: History in the Professional Schools," *The Journal of American History* 92 (September 2005), 573.

26. Howell and Prevenier, *From Reliable Sources.*

27. Donato and Lazerson, "New Directions in American Educational History," 9.

28. "Interchange, History in the Professional Schools," 560.

29. Rury notes that of the 130 participants in the 2004 HES meeting 68% were in schools or colleges of education, and less than 20% were housed in history departments. John L. Rury, "The Curious State of the History of Education: A Parallel Perspective," *History of Education Quarterly* 46 (2006), 590.

30. Linda Eisenmann, "Integrating Disciplinary Perspectives into Higher Education Research," *The Journal of Higher Education* 75 (2004), 18.

31. "Symposium Report: Exploring our Professional Backyards: Toward Writing Recent History of American Colleges and Universities," *History of Higher Education Annual* 20 (2000), 83.

32. Don T. Nakanishi, "A Quota on Excellence? The Asian American Admissions Debate," *Change,* (1989), 38–47.

33. Sylvia Hurtado, Jeffrey Milem, Alma Clayton-Pedersen, and Walter Allen, *Enacting Diverse Learning Environments: Improving the Climate for Racial/ Ethnic Diversity in Higher Education.* ASHE-ERIC Higher Education Report, 26(8), Washington, DC: The George Washington University, Graduate School of Education and Human Development, 1999.

34. Adrienne Dixson and Ceclia Rousseau, eds., *Critical Race Theory in Education: All God's Children Got a Song* (New York: Routledge, 2006).

35. Alessandro Portelli, "What Makes Oral History Different," in *The Oral History Reader, Second Edition,* ed. Robert Perks and Alistair Thomson (New York: Routledge, 1998), 36.

36. H-Education, "Where do Historians of Education Live?"

37. H-Education, "Where do Historians of Education Live?"

12

BEYOND BLACK AND WHITE

Researching the History of Latinos in American Higher Education

Christopher Tudico

One population noticeably absent from the expansive literature on the history of higher education is Latinos.[1] This, despite the fact that Latinos have participated in American higher education since shortly after the Treaty of Guadalupe Hidalgo of 1848—just about 160 years. Often overlooked are the sons and daughters of Mexican American landowners, called *Californios*, being among the first to matriculate at institutions such as Santa Clara and the University of California at Berkeley in the mid 19th century. Often ignored is the founding of la Universidad de Puerto Rico in 1903, or that several hundred Puerto Rican students attended college on the mainland at schools ranging from Tuskegee to Cornell in the first decade of the 20th century.[2] Often forgotten is the Mexican American Movement (MAM)—a student-led organization that published their own newsletter, *The Mexican Voice*, in order to promote the value of higher education among the larger Mexican American community of southern California from 1934 to roughly 1950. Remarkably, each of these rich stories has yet to take their rightful place within the greater literature of the history of higher education.

In this chapter, I will provide a short historiography of Latinos in the history of higher education. But more importantly, I will address the challenges and rewards of researching a largely unwritten history. This chapter will be largely autobiographical, as I will rely upon my own experiences as a young scholar to give the reader a sense of how I "do" research on a largely unexplored topic within the field of the history of higher education. I trust the story of how and why I have come to conduct research on Mexican Americans in higher education will be able to inform other scholars; some of whom I hope will join me in uncovering the much larger history of Latinos in higher education, so that this diverse population is overlooked no longer.

I have been interested in the study of history for as long as I remember. When I was a young boy, while my friends collected comic books, I read books about the Civil War. In the fall of 1990, not quite 12 years old, I watched each installment of Ken Burns's documentary, *The Civil War*, on PBS. Along with my dad, I was one of the 40 million viewers to watch the initial broadcast (a pre-teen like myself was likely not the target demographic). I still vividly remember historian Shelby Foote's slow Southern drawl as he described the strategy and leadership of Ulysses S. Grant and Robert E. Lee leading the Union and Confederate armies. I was mesmerized. For me, history had very much come to life before my eyes. Similarly, I often shunned the reincarnations of adolescent book series like *The Bobbsey Twins* and *The Hardy Boys* for historical fiction. My favorite book till this day (other than *The Count of Monte Cristo*) is *Rifles for Watie*, a coming of age tale of a Union soldier from Kansas during the Civil War.[3] I still read it at least once a year.

I arrived at graduate school a number of years later still harboring a deep appreciation of history. The very first class I enrolled in, History of American Higher Education, was the perfect fit for me—a union between my two chief interests, history and higher education. After picking up my rather hefty bulk pack (which I still have, thankfully), I immediately immersed myself in the literature. I read the works of prominent historians of education such as James D. Anderson, Roger Geiger, Julie Rueben, and John Thelin. When the class ended, I continued reading, becoming more and informed about the history of higher education. The following semester, now admitted to a Ph.D. program in higher education, I began to give a great deal of thought to how historians of higher education actually conduct research. In the meantime, I picked the brain of my advisor, and she passed along the required reading of any serious would-be historian: Martha C. Howell and Walter Prevenier's *From Reliable Sources* and Peter Novick's *That Noble Dream.*[4]

As I moved along in my course of study as a graduate student, I became aware that many historians of higher education often maintained focus and emphasis on elite and traditional institutions, as well as the elite students who attended them. In my view, a major influence on the research agendas of historians of higher education has been Hispanophobia, defined as the "historical profession's neglect or outright bias concerning the history of the largely Roman Catholic Spanish peoples and institutions."[5] I believe the primary symptom of this particular strain of Hispanophobia has been the long-standing omission of Latinos from the literature of the history of higher education.[6] For instance, in 1965, when Laurence Veysey published his highly influential *The Emergence of the American University*, the bulk of the volume was littered with the names of institutions such as Harvard, Columbia, Johns Hopkins, Stanford, Chicago, Michigan, and the University of California at Berkeley.[7] Veysey's fascination with the history of elite universities, like other historians after him, obscures the stories of countless educational institutions (and the students who enroll at them) in the United States—the majority of which are neither universities nor elite.

Two of the most popular monographs on the history of higher education are Frederick Rudolph's classic *The American College and University: A History*, written in 1962, and John Thelin's more recent *A History of American Higher Education*, completed in 2004.[8] According to Thelin, "Rudolph's work devotes most of its attention to established colleges and universities."[9] In contrast, I believe Thelin's work is far more inclusive. In the introduction, he informs the reader how his account of the history of American higher education attempts to include new analysis of the "historical significance of other understudied institutions, such as community colleges, women's colleges, and the historically Black campuses."[10] He largely succeeds. Even so, when I read the monograph, I noticed that Thelin only mentioned Latinos indirectly. One line during the last chapter of his work links Latinos to the growing diversity in contemporary American higher education.[11] In Thelin's defense, his work is "admittedly selective."[12]

Still, while he makes a very valid point by claiming "no author can succeed at narrating a wholly comprehensive chronology of American higher education in a single, concise volume," I believe the reader should still question whether one line is enough to encapsulate the entire Latino experience in American higher education, a people who have enrolled in one American college or another for approximately the last 160 years.[13]

In the only journal exclusively dedicated to the study of history of higher education, *Perspectives on the History of Higher Education* (formerly known as *The History of Higher Education Annual*), no articles on Latinos have been published in its more than twenty-five years of being in print. A second journal, *The History of Education Quarterly*, has provided a broader forum for scholarship since 1961. Yet, like *Perspectives*, *The History of Education Quarterly* has not featured articles on the Latino experience in American higher education. Likewise, the editors of the *ASHE Reader Series on the History of Higher Education* are handicapped by research produced within our own field, for they struggle to include articles beyond the Black/White paradigm since few exist, often relying upon a handful of influential pieces such as Michael Olivas's "Indian, Chicano, and Puerto Rican Colleges" and Bobby Wright's "'For the Children of the Infidels'?: American Indian Education in the Colonial Colleges."[14] Both Wright and Olivas's invaluable research pushed the study of the history of higher education forward, but those author's works largely stand alone. In a sense, the primary and most apparent symptom of the Hispanophobia that currently afflicts historians of higher education is the omission of the Latino experience from peer-reviewed journals. These resources are generally recognized as forums for new research and scholarly discussion. Without the publication of articles in journals like *Perspectives on the History of Higher Education* and *The History of Education Quarterly*, the study of the history of Latinos higher education will remain on the fringe of scholarly inquiry.

As a result of the aforementioned state of literature within the history of higher education, I largely picked my research topic based on what was "missing" from current scholarship within the field. I sought to know why Latinos were largely omitted from the history of higher education. Surely members of the Latino community had attended college at one time or another. I concluded the following: when educational historians discuss the challenges and opportunities of conducting research on race within our field, they often do so through the lens of the Black/White binary. And while in many ways I think the study of the Black/White dichotomy informs our understanding of how race is constructed in the United States, I believe the Black/White paradigm cannot serve as the only lens of inquiry employed by historians of higher education. Primarily focusing on histories bound within the Black/White binary ignores the past participation of Asian Americans, American Indians, and Latinos in American higher education. In light of the above, I narrowed my research interests to the history of the Mexican American experience in higher education. I did so in order to demonstrate how exploring a particular topic can challenge traditional views of what scholars consider worthy of study, and expand the general public's understanding of a largely ignored people.

Historians of education, both young and old, can attest to the rewards as well as the challenges of conducting "new" research on a topic. Trailblazing in a field is an exhilarating feeling—knowing with certainty that you are about to fill a gap in the literature. But the very opportunity to conduct innovative research on a "new" topic such as the history of Latinos in higher education is also an inherent challenge. Where does one actually begin to do research? For me, the sense of not knowing where to start research on Mexican Americans in the history of higher education was a helpless feeling. Compounding my frustration, traditional archives of primary sources were not readily available to me. My experience beginning to search for sources can be contrasted with a scholar who sets out to conduct research on the history of Blacks and higher education in the South. For that researcher, structures such as the Freedmen's Bureau, religious missionary and philanthropic organizations (like the American Baptist Home Mission Society and the General Electric Board), and Black colleges themselves all leave a litany of primary sources for scholars in the present day to guide their study. A similar paper trail for Mexican Americans in higher education was not readily available to me or anyone else, as a structured system of higher education akin to Black colleges did not occur for Latinos within the United States (Puerto Rico excluded) until the latter quarter of the 20th century. Hispanic Serving Institutions (HSIs) are very much a new invention.[15]

For all intents and purposes, I could not rely on literature within the field of the history of higher education to garner additional understanding about the topic I chose to research for my Ph.D. Still, I had a hunch that the absence of Mexican Americans in journals and broad historical monographs by Rudolph and Thelin did not necessarily mean members of the Mexican American or broader Latino community avoided attending college. Rather, for a more lengthy historical account of Mexican American participation in higher education in the United States, I looked outside the field of the history of higher education and read monographs and journal articles within the discipline of American history itself.

Unlike historians of higher education, our colleagues within the field of American history are no longer afflicted with an acute case of Hispanophobia. At the outset of the 20th century, scholars of American history took pains to avoid research on the Mexican American experience in the United States. But once the history of the West became a viable strand of inquiry within the larger field of American history, a door opened for scholars like Carlos E. Castañeda and George I. Sánchez to document the stories of Mexican Americans in the West and Southwest.[16] Their efforts, in turn, laid the foundation for a new generation of Chicano scholars to emerge, including historian and activist Rodolfo "Rudy" Acuña.[17] In the last two decades, historians have produced a wide variety of scholarship, from David G. Gutiérrez's intriguing account of Mexican immigration and the politics of identity in *Walls and Mirrors* to Linda Gordon's *The Great Arizona Orphan Abduction*, a narrative of the racism exhibited in a 1904 White vigilante uprising against the Mexican American foster parents of White children.[18]

Within the field of American history, I located a handful of secondary sources that greatly aided my research of Mexican Americans in higher education. A few journal articles offered a snapshot of the Mexican American experience in higher education missing from *Perspectives on the History of Higher Education* and *The History of Education Quarterly*. Collectively, the authors of the articles focused on the enrollment of Mexican Americans at Californian colleges and universities from 1851 to roughly 1876. In the first article of note, "Hispanic Californians and Catholic Higher Education: The Diary of Jesús María Estudillo, 1857–1864," historian Gerald McKevitt chronicles the collegiate experience of a wealthy young Mexican American gentleman, Jesús María Estudillo, who enrolled at Santa Clara College.[19] During this time period, following the Treaty of Guadalupe Hidalgo, the grand majority of Mexican Americans were *mestizo*, or of mixed patronage between Spanish and Indian ancestry.[20] A small number of

Mexican Americans, including Estudillo, were predominantly the descendants of Spaniards. They called themselves *Californios*. After locating and reading the diary for myself at the University of California at Berkeley's Bancroft Library, I thought Estudillo's story was of such vital importance to the history of higher education that I decided to focus on the diary in the first half of my dissertation. Estudillo's experience at Santa Clara sheds light on not only the lives of Mexican Americans, but greater Californian society as well. In effect, Estudillo now bookends my chronicle of the Mexican American experience in Californian higher education.

Two other scholars, David J. León and Dan McNeil, worked together on two articles: "The Fifth Class: A 19th Century Forerunner of Affirmative Action," and "A Precursor to Affirmative Action: Californios and the Mexicans in the University of California, 1870–72."[21] In each article, León and McNeil examine how approximately two dozen Mexicans and *Californios* were among those who enrolled at the University of California at Berkeley in a college preparatory program known as the Fifth Class from 1870 to 1872. The Fifth Class provided a high school education that aided students in their preparation for the university entrance examination. What is provocative about León and McNeil's two articles is how the authors draw a link between the Fifth Class and the contemporary construct of affirmative action. After reading their work, and visiting the University of California at Berkeley's Special Collections to familiarize myself with the primary sources noted by the authors, I arrived at a different interpretation of the significance of the Fifth Class. In my view, León and McNeil's main argument is not entirely convincing. The Fifth Class, ultimately, was not an affirmative action program, but rather an initiative designed to attract students from all backgrounds to the young state institution. Looking beyond León and McNeil's conclusion is a story that is far more significant. The University of California at Berkeley's Fifth Class documents another instance of Mexican Americans who attended college alongside of Whites, and provides further evidence that a blossoming state system of higher education existed in California alongside parochial colleges like Santa Clara in the mid 19th century.

As a graduate student, I have supplemented my course load in the graduate school of education by enrolling in several classes and seminars in the college's history department. In one such course taught by historian Michael Katz, I read George G. Sánchez's monograph, *Becoming Mexican American: Ethnicity, Culture and Identity in Chicano Los Angeles, 1900–1945.*[22] In his work, Sánchez offers the reader a sophisticated view of the Mexican American experience, chronicling the story of immigrants and their quest to forge a Mexican American identity in early 20th century Los Angeles. Throughout his work, Sánchez examines the fluidity of the borderlands between the United States and Mexico, and offers a rich and complex description of Mexican immigrants moving back and forth across the border in order to have a better life. Sánchez's last chapter, "The Rise of the Second Generation," introduced me to the protagonists of the second half of my dissertation: the college students who founded the Mexican American Movement.[23] A trip or two later to the Library of Congress to read MAM's newsletter, *The Mexican Voice*, and I began to appreciate how MAM's members formed the organization and published their own newspaper in order to promote the value of higher education among the larger Mexican American community of southern California. In the inaugural issue of *The Mexican Voice*, one contributor to the newsletter penned the following:

Education is the only tool which will raise our influence, command the respect of the rich class, and enable us to mingle in their social, political and religious life . . . today a college education is *absolutely necessary* for us to succeed in the professional world . . . Education means a complete knowledge of yourself, a good knowledge of your fellowmen and a thorough knowledge of the world in which you live. . . . If our opinion is to be had, respected, our income raised, happiness increased, we must compete! *EDUCATION is our only weapon!*[24]

One incarnation or another of MAM lasted from 1934 to approximately 1950. Some time later, I read revisionist Chicano scholar Carlos Muñoz, Jr.'s *Youth, Identity, Power,* and contrasted his argument that MAM was predominantly an assimilationist organization with my own point of view as a historian of higher education, namely that the members of MAM did not abandon their roots in becoming Mexican American—a delineation I believe Muñoz, Jr. comes down on both sides on.[25]

Over the course of the last two years, I have been able to start to piece together a cohesive narrative of the Mexican American experience in Californian higher education from 1848 to 1945. While Whites curtailed the citizenship of the majority of Mexican Americans, *Californios* such as Jesús María Estudillo flourished in mid 19th century California. The opportunity to go to school of any kind, let alone college, was far beyond the realm of possibility for the grand majority of Mexican Americans (or anyone else) who called California their home.[26] But as the story of Estudillo and the Fifth Class corroborates, the most privileged sons and daughters of wealthy Mexican American landholders attended college, some 100 years before Mexican American professors, students, and activists pushed for and established the first Department of Chicano Studies at California State University at Los Angeles in 1968.

However, the combination of Whites pushing Mexican Americans off their land, *Californios* losing their wealth and power through continued emigration to the West, and the legal immigration of approximately 678,000 Mexicans to the United States transformed the face of Californian society, and indirectly, who participated in higher education by the turn of the century.[27] As a result, the Mexican Americans attending college by 1934 were the sons and daughters of immigrants, not necessarily wealthy landowners. This phenomenon signified an important transformation in the role higher education played for Mexican Americans who aspired to go to college. The Mexican American students who organized MAM and published *The Mexican Voice* did not attend college to assure their place in high society like the wealthy *Californios* did a half a century earlier, but rather to obtain an education in order to uplift themselves and their community.

As I mature, I feel more comfortable assessing the value of the primary sources I have found. I can compare and contrast my interpretation of the past with that of others. Using the story of Estudillo and MAM as a springboard, I have been able locate a number of other sources that not only continue to guide my current study, but give me ideas about conducting new strands of research in the future. My study of Mexican American college students in early California is not complete, but rather just beginning.

Researching the history of the Mexican American experience in higher education is my attempt at pushing back against the Black/White binary as well as my way of declaring that the history of Latinos in American higher education is indeed worthy of further study. Higher education, has, and always will be, a microcosm of American society. Documentation of the enrollment of Jesús María Estudillo and the students of MAM in college can not only can add significantly to our knowledge of higher education, but also to our understanding of race, ethnicity, citizenship, and class in the American West. Those Mexican Americans were extraordinary, but I know they were not alone. Their experiences in higher education represent only a couple strokes of a much, much broader landscape. Numerous other stories of Latinos participating in higher education need to be studied—histories still unwritten. What were the experiences of Mexican Americans who attended colleges and universities in states besides California, for instance, in Arizona, Colorado, New Mexico, and Texas? Who were the Puerto Ricans that attended college on the mainland during the first decade of the 20th century? Did others from the Latino Diaspora matriculate at American colleges and universities prior to El Movimiento of the 1960s? These stories, the history of Latinos in higher education, must be researched. They cannot be forgotten.

At heart, I am that boy who read *Rifles for Watie*; I am still keenly interested in history. If you have read this entire chapter, I hope you may have an interest in the history of higher education, much like I do. If you have come this far, I urge you to come a bit further. If you have not yet already, I hope you join me in researching and writing the rich history of the Latino experience in American higher education.

QUESTIONS FOR DISCUSSION

1. What other resources would contribute to the history of Latinos in higher education? Where should scholars look to uncover this history?
2. Have other racial and ethnic groups been left out of the history of higher education? Why? And How?
3. What are the ramifications of being left out of historical discussions and in effect, left out of history?

NOTES

1. In this chapter, I use the term Latino as opposed to Hispanic—a government-regulated term coined for use in conducting The United States census.
2. Carlos Rodríguez-Fraticelli, *Education and Imperialism: The Puerto Rican Experience in Higher Education, 1898–1986* (New York: Centro de Estudios Puertorriqueños Working Papers Series, 1986).
3. Harold Keith, *Rifles for Watie* (New York: Harper & Row, Publishers, Inc., 1987).
4. Martha C. Howell and Walter Prevenier, *From Reliable Sources: An Introduction to Historical Methods* (Ithaca, NY: Cornell University Press, 2001); Peter Novick, *That Noble Dream: The "Objectivity Question" and the American Historical Profession* (Cambridge and New York: Cambridge University Press, 1988).
5. Victoria-María MacDonald, "Hispanic, Latino, Chicano, or 'Other'?: Deconstructing the Relationship between Historians and Hispanic-American Educational History," *History of Education Quarterly* 41, no. 3 (Fall 2001): 367. MacDonald, a historian of education, borrowed this term from David J. Weber in her historiography (K-12) of Latino educational history. See David J. Weber, "The Spanish Legacy in North America and the Historical Imagination," *Western Historical Quarterly* 23 (February 1992): 4–24.
6. Victoria-María MacDonald is immune from the Hispanophobia that afflicts historians of higher education. MacDonald broadly examines the history of Latino education in the United States, and is the only researcher that has authored an overview of the history of Latinos in American higher education. See Victoria-María MacDonald and Teresa García, "Historical Perspectives on Latino Access to Higher Education, 1848–1990," in *The Majority in the Minority: Expanding the Representation of Latina/o Faculty, Administrators and Students in Higher Education*, eds. Jeanette Castellanos and Lee Jones (Sterling, VA: Stylus Publishing, 2003), 15–43.
7. Laurence Veysey, *The Emergence of the American University* (Chicago: The University of Chicago Press, 1965).

8. Frederick Rudolph, *The American College and University: A History* (1962; reprinted Athens: University of Georgia Press, 1990); John Thelin, *A History of American Higher Education* (Baltimore, MD: Johns Hopkins University Press, 2004).

9. Ibid., xx.

10. Ibid.

11. Ibid., 349.

12. Ibid., xxii.

13. Ibid.

14. Lester F. Goodchild and Harold S. Wechsler, eds., *ASHE Reader Series on the History of Higher Education*, 2nd ed. (Old Tappan, NJ: Pearson Custom Publishing, 1997); Lester F. Goodchild, Harold S. Wechsler, and Linda Eisenmann, eds., *ASHE Reader Series on the History of Higher Education*, 3rd ed. (Old Tappan, NJ: Pearson Custom Publishing, 2007).

15. The development of most HSIs has taken place within the last four decades. They were not formally recognized by the federal government until the reauthorization of the Higher Education Act in 1992. See Margarita Benítez, "Hispanic-Serving Institutions: Challenges and Opportunities," *New Directions for Higher Education* 1998, no. 102 (1998): 57–68; and Berta Vigil Laden, "Hispanic-Serving Institutions: Myths and Realities," *Peabody Journal of Education* 76, no. 1 (2001): 73–92.

16. The evolution and growth of subfields within the discipline of American history provided an opening for scholars to break free from the symptoms of Hispanophobia and conduct more thorough research on the Latino experience, including Mexican Americans. For a more lengthy discussion, see MacDonald, "Hispanic, Latino, Chicano, or Other," 372–374; Wilbur R. Jacobs, *On Turner's Trail: 100 Years of Writing Western History* (Lawrence: University Press of Kansas, 1994); Gerald D. Nash, *Creating the West: Historical Interpretations 1890–1990* (Albuquerque: University of New Mexico Press, 1991); Russell M. Magnaghi, *Herbert E. Bolton and the Historiography of the Americas* (Westport, CT: Greenwood Press, 1998); David J. Weber, "John Francis Bannon and the Historiography of the Spanish Borderlands: Retrospect and Prospect," in *Establishing Exceptionalism: Historiography and the Colonial Americas*, ed. Amy Turner Bushnell, vol. 5 of *An Expanding World: The European Impact on World History* (Brookfield, VT: Variorum, 1995): 297–330; Mario T. García, "Carlos E. Castaneda and the Search for History," chap. 9, and "George I. Sánchez and the Forgotten People," chap. 10 in *Mexican Americans: Leadership, Ideology, & Identity, 1930–1960* (New Haven, CT: Yale University Press, 1989), 231–272; and Carlos K. Blanton, "George I. Sánchez, Ideology, and Whiteness in the Making of the Mexican American Civil Rights Movement, 1930–1960," *The Journal of Southern History* 72, no. 3 (2006): 569–604.

17. See Rodolfo Acuña, *Occupied America: A History of Chicanos*, 3d ed. (New York: Harper Collins, 1988).

18. David G. Gutiérrez, *Walls and Mirrors: Mexican Americans, Mexican Immigrants, and the Politics of Ethnicity* (Berkeley, CA: University of California Press, 1995); Linda Gordon, *The Great Arizona Orphan Abduction* (Cambridge, MA: Harvard University Press, 1999).

19. Gerald McKevitt. "Hispanic Californios and Catholic Higher Education: The Diary of Jesús María Estudillo, 1857–1864," *California History* 69, no. 4 (1990): 320–331, 401–403.

20. See Martha Menchaca, *Recovering History Constructing Race: The Indian, Black, and White Roots of Mexican Americans* (Austin, TX: The University of Texas Press, 2001), 216–218. The United States Congress gave state legislators the right to define the citizenship status of Mexican Americans. In California, the state constitution of 1849 granted only Whites full citizenship—American males and "White" Mexican men were given the right of suffrage; *mestizos* were ineligible to vote and gradually stripped of most of their political rights. See also Evelyn Nakano Glenn, *Unequal Freedom: How Race and Gender Shaped American Citizenship and Labor* (Cambridge, MA: Harvard University Press, 2002), 146–147.

21. David J. León and Dan McNeil, "The Fifth Class: A 19th Century Forerunner of Affirmative Action," *California History*, 64, no. 1 (1985): 52–57; David J. León and Dan McNeil, "A Precursor to Affirmative Action: Californios and Mexicans in the University of California, 1870–72," *Perspectives in Mexican American Studies* 3 (1992): 179–206. More recently, León forgoes a discussion of comparing the Fifth Class with modern affirmative action programs, but rather focuses on the story of one individual, Manuel Corella, who the author states was the first Mexican American student and teacher at Cal Berkeley. See also David J. León, "Manuel M. Corella: The Broken Trajectory of the First Latino Student and Teacher at the University of California, 1869–74," *Aztlán* 26, no. 1 (2001): 171–79.

22. George J. Sánchez, *Becoming Mexican American: Ethnicity, Culture and Identity in Chicano Los Angeles, 1900–1945* (New York and Oxford: Oxford University Press, 1993).

23. Ibid., 253–269.

24. José Rodríguez, "The Value of Education," *The Mexican Voice* (July 1938), 7.

25. Carlos Muñoz, Jr., *Youth, Identity, Power: The Chicano Movement*, Revised and Expanded Edition (London: Verso Press, 2007), 44–58.

26. MacDonald and García, "Historical Perspectives," 19; and Roger Geiger, "New Themes in the History of Nineteenth-century Colleges," in *The American College in the Nineteenth Century*, ed. Roger Geiger (Nashville, TN: Vanderbilt University Press, 2000), 1–36. The possession of a college degree or even any semblance of a collegiate experience in mid 19th century America was rare for anyone regardless of race, gender, or class. College graduates represented only around one percent of the male workforce on the eve of the Civil War.
27. Rogelio Saenz, *Latinos and the Changing Face of America* (New York: Russell Sage Foundation and Population Reference Bureau, 2004), 2.

13

WRITING THROUGH THE PAST

Federal Higher Education Policy

Philo Hutcheson

Writing history is not the simple act of listing names, dates, and places. For centuries historians have grappled with how to interpret the past, how to understand human lives when the historians themselves were not alive, have no direct experience with the events of the time, and must determine what sources provide what kind of meaning for those people and events. I'll take this opportunity to survey some key events in the history of federal higher education policy, with my interpretation of those works and discussion of the challenges and opportunities in writing historically about federal policy. Foremost among those challenges is one that historians face in their efforts to re-create the past: presentism. In addition, many who read histories of higher education may not realize that historical study employs a number of conceptual approaches and sub-disciplines, such as political history, cultural history, intellectual history, etc., and I see the choice of sub-discipline as an opportunity. I will address both of those characteristics of historical study, presentism and sub-disciplines, in this chapter.

Presentism is the historical error of unknowingly, or more disconcerting, unthinkingly applying conditions of the present to the past, and thereby creating an interpretation that speaks little to the experiences, beliefs, and thoughts of those who are the subject of the historical inquiry, but in fact offers a picture of what happened in the past as if it were the present. For example, historians of higher education as well as historians of education continue to grapple with the question of when the civil rights movement started. While it is easy enough to identify the years when the Civil Rights Movement began (note the difference in case), sometime in the late 1950s or early 1960s, and most certainly after the 1954 and 1955 *Brown v. Board of Education* decisions, it is far more difficult to know when the movement toward civil rights, especially for African Americans, began even in general terms. Relevant to higher education, the Legal Defense Fund of the National Association for the Advancement of Colored People (NAACP) began a planned attack on professional and graduate schools in the 1930s because its leaders knew that states would be unlikely to want to fund separate but equal schools at that level, in view of the cost of those programs.[1] (*Nota bene*: historians read footnotes and endnotes because they often include discussion, important but not central to the topic.

Footnotes are much better than endnotes because they appear on the page where the citation occurs, but presses prefer endnotes, for reasons unknown to me. I hope dear reader that you will mark the page where my endnotes begin and indulge me, if not yourself, in reading the notes.) Hence, it is reasonable to conclude that a key condition of the civil rights movement began in that decade, although whether or not that marked the beginning of the civil rights movement remains subject to question. (In fact, the term "civil rights" appeared as early as the middle of the 1800s in the United States, obviously complicating the question of origin.)[2] Regardless of the year or years of origin of the civil rights movement, historians of higher education take great care not to assume that the battles for voting rights or access to integrated schools or the professions (including the professoriate) marked by demonstrations, marches, and enthusiastic speeches are the conditions of the movement. So, for example, historians of higher education do not assume that the battle for desegregation of Southern higher education began with the highly visible, and courageous, acts of such students as James Meredith at the University of Mississippi or Charlayne Hunter Gault and Hamilton Homes at the University of Georgia, the first African Americans to personally attempt to enter those institutions' White hallowed halls of academe. Rather, Legal Defense Fund activities in the 1930s indicate a commitment to civil rights, reaffirmed in the 1940s when President Truman's Committee on Civil Rights highlighted the term itself, that attempted to desegregate professional schools in states such as Missouri (a former slave state) and Oklahoma.

History is composed of a variety of sub-disciplines, each with typical questions and means of investigation. In the case of federal policy, it is perhaps easiest to draw upon political history to tell the story of policy decisions. The focus in political history draws upon elected actors, government officials, interest groups, the policy development process, legislative and executive acts, and their consequences. More specifically, the history of higher education policy has tended toward political analysis, recounting the political forces at work (or not at work) in the development of legislation and administrative implementation. Often, in fact, such a historical approach is embedded within a perspective resting more on political science or political sociology than history.[3] Political history offers analyses of political events, movements, and political philosophies. As one historian argues, "political history deals with the development and impact of governmental institutions, along with the proximate influences on their actions."[4] There is a grand tradition of political history, a history that in fact most of us learned in school as we learned to recount such diverse historical facts as the Emancipation Proclamation and Pearl Harbor. Thus, Hugh Davis Graham's substantial work, *An Uncertain Triumph: Federal Education Policy in the Kennedy and Johnson Years*, accurately portrays the ebb and flow of political actors in the development of key federal education acts in the 1960s by examining the elected and appointed federal officials engaged in education debates as well as the several key interest groups such as the National Education Association and the Roman Catholics.[5] Despite that grand tradition, readers of histories of higher education ought to keep in mind that the authors, often without any direct statement, write within specific analytical frameworks.

For the remainder of this chapter, I examine some commonly considered landmark federal activities in higher education policy, first addressing presentism and then second addressing two sub-disciplines of history, political history and intellectual history. There are many strong works in the history of federal higher education policy that could well be substantial subjects for this discussion of sub-disciplines, but here I will take the authorial privilege of discussing my work on the 1947 President's Commission on Higher Education.

PRESENTISM, PRESENT, AND PAST

At the core of the challenge to avoid presentism for anyone examining the history of federal higher education policy is how much the federal government now means to higher education. Even a casual observer of federal higher education policy today would likely be overwhelmed by the complexities of engagement between the federal government and institutions of higher education, as well their associations. As a telling example, the intricacies of federal research funds for college and university professors, with such notions as overhead costs and Institutional Review Boards and ethical conduct, is most certainly a set of conditions that began in the early 1950s with the development of the National Science Foundation and accelerated in the late 1950s under the aegis of the 1958 National Defense Education Act. During the 1960s the federal government increasingly funded research beyond the approximately 20 elite research universities that had dominated the federal research scene, resulting in remarkable levels of funded federal research.[6] Thus, it is most curious, and a demand to separate as best as possible from presentism, to read the works of a variety of scholars and policymakers advocating a huge federal commitment to financing higher education in the late 1940s, most of whom asserted without hesitation or qualification that the federal government had indeed shown through New Deal legislation and activity, as well as through the G.I. Bill, that it would allow colleges and universities nearly full autonomy even while providing large amounts of money.[7] That is, as is likely the case for most historians, one of those moments when I stop and smile; perhaps, then, it is not the business of historians to predict the future because we ought to know so well the flawed predictions of the past. Today, of course, federal regulation of higher education occurs daily, if not more often, in the offices of administrators and professors alike.

Equally subject to presentism would be the concept of affirmative action, a federal mandate, to ensure that previous acts of discrimination and exclusion do not continue to form processes of selection into, for example, the workforce. Affirmative action is most certainly a contemporary concept (for historians, I venture to claim that the 1960s and thereafter are, indeed, contemporary, if only, sigh, because many of us tend to remember the 1960s and thereafter). As much as institutions of higher education attend or fail to attend to affirmative action in hiring policies and processes, there is no cogent historical comparison between those policies and processes and the acts of colleges and universities as recently as the 1950s. In fact, this issue is further complicated by an easy assumption that is, frankly, wrong. Racial and ethnic minorities of the past may or may not be minorities in the present. The meanings of race and ethnicity have changed over time, so concerns about affirmative action and race and ethnicity ought to be in the context of race and ethnicity definitions at the time under examination. By and large historians of higher education stop discussing affirmative action when they write back into the 1960s. Hence historians regularly, although rarely explicitly, consider the problems of presentism.

Despite the avoidance of the explicit, the historian as individual must address his or her own place in the present, if only to know how it might have an impact on writing through the past. For example, I am nearing the end of a history of the 1947 President's Commission on Higher Education, following years of research, presentations, some articles, and distracting although important demands. I will return to the topic of that work later in this chapter, but for now I want to address my experience with presentism in developing my understanding of the context for the Commission. As I have argued in presentation and publication, two powerful forces were extant when the Commission met and wrote its report: civil rights and national defense. As I noted above, we know that the civil rights movement was well underway in the 1930s, and obviously, in 1947, the nation was flush with its victory in World War II. It appears then, that I have found an invaluable context, with both contradictions and similarities, perhaps all best captured in the notion of the Double V, Victory in World War II, Victory in Civil Rights, a slogan first articulated in a letter to the editor of a Black newspaper, the *Pittsburgh Courier*, in 1942.[8] Nevertheless, I was troubled by this conclusion, and looked inward for resolution. I reasoned that, in the words of an early draft of the preface, "civil rights and national defense provided imperatives for the commitment to higher education." I have stayed with that conclusion, but in a subsequent draft introduction for a submission to a university press, I offered the following:

> These issues have long held my interest. In a conference session review of my first book, *A Professional Professoriate*, a colleague noted that I opened the book with a preface informed by my voice but then quickly moved to a dispassionate and far less engaging tone in the first chapter. I took that assessment to heart for a variety of reasons, not the least of which is that voice is part of my evaluation for students' grades. More important, my foray into an examination of the professoriate was a choice of passion as well as reason, and I fear that first-book anxieties caused me to restrain my voice. Whatever the anxieties of a second book, I know that this work is informed by my passion, by my comprehension of civil rights and national defense. In personal terms, I still remember accompanying my mother to the Washington, D.C. offices of the Southern Leadership Conference to help stuff envelopes for some large event I only dimly understood at age 11, the historic 1963 March on Washington. We were in the Washington area because my father had his first assignment at the Pentagon at that time; my childhood was the life of an Army brat.

I thought I had conquered presentism by bringing to the forefront for the reader the importance of my experience and my careful reflection upon that experience. Perhaps not surprisingly, the press's external reviewer (someone clearly with substantial historical perspective, in view of her or his comments), while praising the work overall, singled out that passage and indicated that it did not fit into the articulate way that I had presented my interpretation of the President's Commission. I wrote in response:

> Simply put, I will edit to a far briefer set of statements my attempt to establish voice; the reviewer's comments are an appropriate reminder that how I establish voice might be better done as more of a private, internal conversation than one shared with readers of the book.

Hence, it is important to remember in reading historical texts that historians take for granted the challenge of presentism, that how I write into the past is presumed to be subject to thoughtful consideration of who I am, and how I have become who I am, but with no need to state it directly. (In this regard, the common trope of personal discussion in qualitative research highlights one of many distinctions between historical inquiry and the various forms of qualitative inquiry. The major among these distinctions, as Clif Conrad once noted, is simple: Historians look into the past.) In subsequent editions of the introduction, I deleted that passage, and in fact, it was difficult to retrieve it despite the huge number of files I have for the book; I indeed buried Caesar.

What, then, does federal higher education policy look like in historical terms with explicit consideration of presentism? What changes can historians identify that differentiate the present from the past, and equally important, what similarities are there to the present? Presentism matters not only because it separates the attempted historical interpretation from the events and people of the time but also because it can serve as a thoughtful aid to what we have sustained over the decades or centuries.

A common device in historical inquiry is to determine the beginning and begin the narrative with that time period. Many a historian has been grateful that a major event, such as the Revolutionary War, provides an easy marking point, and that is the case in this situation. While the early leaders of the Republic were enthusiastic about the need for education, if only to create citizens in a nation decidedly unique, with little recent political heritage to draw upon, their ideas were more notable than their actual outcomes. Many of those leaders focused on the need to provide higher education in the United States rather than expecting that college-bound students would go to Europe or elsewhere for their education. Thus, one of the more curious stories of federal higher education policy is that of the national university.

A major challenge facing the new Republic after the Revolutionary War was the education of its citizens and leaders in the context of a democracy—and returning to my theme of presentism, readers must understand, or recall, that in the late 1700s, the idea of a democracy was so antithetical to the traditions of Europe that the United States was looked upon as an experiment likely to fail. The nation was hardly the robust global actor that it is today. Political leaders of the time, including Thomas Jefferson and Benjamin Rush, advocated for higher learning that would benefit and sustain the new nation. In fact, the first seven United States presidents at one point or another supported the idea of a national university, even to the extent that George Washington deeded land on the Potomac for such an institution. Thus, in one very real sense, we can look at the idea of the national university as a curious example of the need to educate for the new Republic, to ensure that citizens and leaders would not be tempted to go overseas; even given the nine colonial colleges as well as the burgeoning number of state universities and private colleges that appeared in the late 1700s and early 1800s, the nation's leaders were very worried about losing people to European notions of life as taught by European universities. Yet the idea of a national university is more than long gone, as David Madsen indeed argues; those arguments persisted into the post-World War II era, although not articulated by the presidents of the nation.[9] From a presentist perspective, a reader might think that the idea, although perhaps interesting, is just as dead as the early United States presidents. But, a dominant theme in studies of the history of United States education is the powerful and sustained goal of Americanization. By the early 1800s, national and state political leaders were deeply worried that the increasing number of immigrants would threaten the foundation of society, with their strange languages and strange customs (such as, for example, Catholicism). They argued for, and by and large schools implemented, programs of Americanization that ranged from readers that used the moral codes of Protestantism to the elements of organizational discipline such as regular attendance and civility in order to make sure that all members of the United States society were good citizens and leaders, and the lower class and immigrants were compliant citizens and workers. So the national university has implications beyond a failed notion of educating citizens and leaders; it is also a fine example of the particularistic way in which we have defined being a good citizen or a good leader, structured in terms of class and imbued with specific moral and organizational behaviors. And for the present? The next time you drive by a school sign with a character education word neatly posted on it, just think, "Gee, and we almost had a national university, where all of the nation's college students could learn to be a good citizen or leader."

Despite the story of the national university, the federal government generally eschewed any direct involvement with higher education until the Civil War. Other than the establishment of the United States Military Academy in 1802 and the United States Naval Academy in 1845, the federal government operated not unlike the English system, where the discussion of scientific principles and experiments tended to be within scientific societies rather than at English universities, especially Oxford. A highly important exception here is Scottish higher education where there were many talented and well-educated scholars in a variety of fields, from philosophy—such as John Locke, one of the most important Enlightenment philosophers—to medicine, such as Benjamin Rush, signer of the Declaration of Independence and prolific advocate of schools in the early Republic. Federal involvement with matters pertaining to higher education, such as the developing study in the sciences as we know them today (biology, chemistry, geology, and physics, for example), typically existed within agencies or special projects such as the Lewis and Clark expedition to explore the far West in the early 1800s.[10] So it is difficult to trace federal interest in the practical matters of the nation until the Morrill Land Grant Act of 1862, which seemingly defined the modern curriculum and institutionalized it.

The Morrill Land Grant Act of 1862 is never overlooked in histories of United States higher education. It articulated the need for useful college-level study in the agricultural and mechanical arts, as well as military instruction (that area has been routinely overlooked).[11] And, as one scholar pointed out years ago, these institutions were hardly important, nor even robust, throughout most of the nineteenth century. As he argues, it would be (but often has been) a worst case of presentism to understand the 1862 Morrill Land Grant Act from the present status of so many large and prestigious state universities.[12] Yet, the issue of liberal arts, which are indeed explicitly mentioned in the Act, is far more complex than pointing at large state universities today and highlighting their scientific and technological work while deriding the uselessness of the liberal arts. Presentism can easily lead us to the latter conclusion, and often leads professors to enter into sincere defenses of the usefulness of the liberal arts. Those who major in engineering or business indeed have a useful education that can be put to immediate application, while those who major in French and English as I did are only equipped to read wine labels in two languages. Such a presentist dichotomy ignores the role of the liberal arts not simply in preparation for professional and graduate school, a highly useful preparation in the eye of probably the vast majority of professional and graduate school faculty members, but more important for the sake of this argument, in terms of the historic role of the liberal arts. First, within the United States in the 1800s, while the liberal arts—or more accurately, a classical curriculum, since the domination of the disciplines and their concomitant aspects in the liberal arts (i.e., biology, English, sociology) did not occur until the late 1800s and early 1900s—were indeed the dominant curriculum of the time, college graduates were a unique part of the population and therefore a more valuable commodity, to use a highly utilitarian term, than the population at large. Finding a job may not have always been easy for college graduates, but they had a special preparation. Furthermore, careers and professions were far more fluid at that time, with apprenticeships rather than professional schools providing most of the professional preparation. Indeed, professional preparation was in such an ambiguous form that in 1851 the Indiana state legislature passed a law that anyone who was a citizen of the state could practice law.[13] Second, in the Middle Ages where we can discern the origins of the liberal arts, the *ars liberalis* and the nearly infamous *trivium* (grammar, rhetoric, and logic) and *quadrivium* (arithmetic, geometry, music, and astronomy), the first degree offered by the northern European universities was the *licentia docendi*, the license to teach, a decidedly practical degree. Hence the issue of a practical curriculum in historical terms is complicated by both a presentist view not only in the present but also in the past; leading figures such as Benjamin Franklin most certainly preferred a practical curriculum, in the context of the apparently limited usefulness of the classical curriculum, no doubt based more on the presentist perception of the classical curriculum rather than the outcomes for graduates of that curriculum.

Presentism, then, is complicated. It falls upon the historian, but the historian generally resists much discussion of it. It operates within our own present, and somewhat awkwardly, in the present of those in the past. If I am thoughtful, or lucky enough to be thoughtful in writing a historical analysis, I try to ask myself if people really thought and behaved that way back then.

FEDERAL HIGHER EDUCATION POLICY: POLITICAL HISTORY? INTELLECTUAL HISTORY?

As I noted earlier, political history is the dominant approach to understanding the history of federal higher education policy, which in many ways makes sense. After all, educational policy at any level derives from government acts. Nevertheless, I cannot resist challenging that idea, if only because one subject, the 1947 President's Commission on Higher Education, resists such political analysis in view of its impact. The Commission is one of the most widely cited reports on higher education in the United States, perhaps the most cited. Many observers of the federal higher education policy scene have assigned primary cause for such developments as the incredible growth of community colleges and the huge funding of federal grants for college students starting with the 1965 Higher Education Act to the 1947 Commission.[14] Oddly, however, as an independent scholar, Robert Pedersen, pointed out to me in an e-mail years ago, both of those events occurred 15 to 20 years after the Commission report, a long time indeed for a report to have an impact. In fact, I can assert with great confidence that most of the central actors in the development of the Commission, its writing, and its dissemination, were dead by the mid-1960s. I have come to the conclusion that I need to interpret the Commission and its report, *Higher Education for American Democracy*, in terms of intellectual history.

What, then, is intellectual history? Admittedly, it has its own challenges; as Peter Novick noted in his remarkable work, *That Noble Dream*, writing intellectual history is like "'nailing jelly to the wall'" according to, ironically, a "crusty political historian."[15] Intellectual history is the history of ideas and may not even have an ebb and flow—which may provide one reason why Veysey's *The Emergence of the American University* is such a dense volume, attempting to explain how the ideas of utility, research, and liberal culture rested side by side in the same institution while each reflected more or less elements of discipline and piety.[16] Of particular interest to intellectual historians is text. In the words of Dominick LaCapra, "Texts are both historical events in their own right and a crucial basis for our inferential reconstruction of other events; the problem of how to read and interpret them should be considered vital for the historian."[17] Intellectual history is one attempt to locate the text:

> Any assumption that one context or set of contexts is particularly significant (or "essential") must be made explicit and argumentatively defended, for it is contestable. Moreover, one crucial question is precisely how texts come to terms with the various contexts bearing on them. Even stereotypical, formulaic, vulgarizing texts (such as political propaganda, commercial advertising, and pulp literature) do not simply reflect or illustrate a context but reproduce it with typically legitimating ideological effects.[18]

How then are we to understand federal higher education policy as intellectual history? A first step would be to address key underlying ideas about education, and I posit that we have long understood education as serving two purposes: as an enactment of an inalienable right (for participation in basic civic, political, and economic opportunities, albeit moderated as I argued in the discussion on presentism by a variety of factors including class and race and ethnicity) and as a good (for the achievement of civic, political, and economic opportunities).[19] Thus beyond political history, the recounting of previous successful and failed attempts to enact legislation or establish executive orders, one coherent meaning of policy as intellectual history would examine what arguments political actors present about the distribution of rights and goods, based in great part on the philosophical and historical conditions of their time, and to what degree they attempt to put those arguments into political action. Ideas are represented as underlying and shaping the ways in which political actors decide which policies are most appropriate at the time. At this point it is necessary to distinguish between ideas and ideologies, in part because ideologies too readily fall into the domain of political history. More important, ideologies form a particular construct in intellectual history, requiring the analysis to engage assumptions about the inherent political nature of human life. While inherent political nature is an intriguing argument, it is not compelling to me, and thus I would prefer to understand and present the analysis of this section of the chapter in broader forms.[20] Public philosophies regarding the access to and distribution of rights and goods play a substantial role in the development of government policy and thus higher education policy. The Enlightenment, with its philosophical emphasis on the rights of individuals rather than the birthrights of rulers, is an important example in the early years of the United States and United States higher education, as the Enlightenment philosophies—especially those analyses developed by utilitarian philosophers such as John Locke and John Stuart Mill—had a substantial and sustained impact on United States colleges and universities. What I want to do with this analysis is examine the shifting sands of time as forming the unstable foundation of political acts, to use intellectual history to examine the sustained meanings and changes of ideas relative to political acts.

One dominant idea of the 1947 Commission report—that is, policy as text—was access, across economic, racial, religious, and gender lines, in opposition to the steady exclusionary admission policies of many colleges and universities, including elite private northeastern colleges and universities.[21] The eventual approval of undergraduate financial aid in the 1965 Higher Education Act was directly linked to the 1964 Civil Rights Act and President Johnson's War on Poverty, and that link directly reflected the political ideas about the capacity of higher education to address inequality.[22] The 1947 President's Commission intended remarkably broad meaning for access, estimating that by 1960 nearly 50 percent of the nation's youth would enter higher education, and colleges and universities would through their curriculum and extracurriculum educate those youth for a pluralistic democracy. Such access would take two decades to develop, and it would require the liberal, somewhat populist, Democratic leadership of President Lyndon Baines Johnson. It would also mean that such groups as the Roman Catholics, both politically powerful and hesitant about federal involvement in education, would have to recognize a different way for them to participate in the nation *qua* democracy for all.[23] Finally, it would require that the public would have a broader interpretation of the meaning of higher education, affirming the idea that more children—and the nation as a whole—would benefit than if only the privileged (as defined by social class or race and ethnicity) were able to attend.

The discussion of access in the report by the President's Commission did not occur in a vacuum. At the same time the Committee on Civil Rights, also appointed by President Truman, was developing its report on the highly discriminatory nature of United States society. The impact of the Committee on Civil Rights on the President's Commission on Higher Education is not well documented, but the arguments of the latter were not simply coincidental.[24] Lost in discussions of the United States Supreme Court *Brown* decisions of 1954 and 1955 are prior federal efforts within the executive branch to increase the visibility of civil rights ideas, an element that becomes visible not only in the documentary analysis but also in the elevation of intellectual history, the analysis of how we develop and argue about texts. How we understood ourselves began to shift in the 1940s, as we slowly developed explicit and more broadly accepted ideas about who belonged in this nation.[25]

Civil rights was one important idea; so too was national defense. An analysis of the 1947 President's Commission on Higher Education based on intellectual history cannot ignore how the American Council on Education (ACE), a group instrumental in the development and report of the 1947 Commission, spoke about itself and higher education in the nation's defense. The Council, in the words of its president in 1940, "was born out of the exigencies of the last World War." President Zook also recalled words from the Association's constitution, stating it had been " 'organized to meet national needs in time of war.' "[26] After President Roosevelt declared a state of emergency in September 1939, well before the United States entered World War II, the ACE issued a statement entitled, "Education and the National Defense." The statement took as its basis the idea that "education is of fundamental importance in the development and perpetuation of a democratic form of government and has earnestly sought to foster cooperation as a basic principle of democratic life," while arguing that education was a natural place for contributions to the defense of the nation.[27]

Small wonder, then, in view of the specific context of the American Council on Education and the general context of victory in World War II, that the Commission report repeatedly argued that higher education, for American democracy, as the report's title stated, was a key place for the defense of the nation. In the first chapter of the first of six volumes, the Commission stated:

> Atomic scientists are doing their utmost to make us realize how easily and quickly a world catastrophe may come. They know the fearful power for destruction possessed by the weapons their knowledge and skill have fashioned. They know that the scientific principles on which these weapons are based are no secret to the scientists of other nations, and that America's monopoly of the engineering processes involved in the manufacture of atom bombs is not likely to last many years. And to the horror of atomic weapons, biological and chemical instruments of destruction are now being added.[28]

Fortunately for the Commission, in simple terms, there was a solution to such problems:

> Education for peace is the condition of our survival, and it must have priority in all our programs of education. In the words of the constitution of the United Nations Educational, Scientific, and Cultural Organization, war begins in the minds of men, and it is in the minds of men that the defenses of peace must be constructed.[29]

National defense, then, was not simply better weapons; the idea of peace, in people's "minds," was paramount. All the political acts of the world's nations would not forestall nuclear holocaust, but planting ideas into minds would. Furthermore, the nation had a responsibility to aid the world in adopting democracy, a political form far preferable to totalitarianism:

> If we cannot reconcile conflicts of opinion and interest among the diverse groups that make up our own Nation, we are not likely to succeed in compromising the differences that divide nations. . . . If we cannot achieve a fuller realization of democracy in the United States, we are not likely to secure its adoption willingly outside the United States.[30]

Education for democracy meant a better nation, a better world, for all the diverse groups.

National defense, however, is an even more complicated idea today, symbolized both by the publication and the language of A Nation at Risk. That report argued repeatedly that the nation was in danger of losing its international economic competitive position, that in essence a war for international dominance was underway, a claim reiterated in the Spellings Commission report.[31] A useful higher education to serve the nation, in its moral code and through citizens and leaders, is now decidedly an economic education. As many scholars now observe, and I most certainly agree, the contemporary economic arguments highlight and obfuscate the meaning of policy texts. They highlight, often within but not always, the issue of national defense, such as *A Nation at Risk*. Yet they also obfuscate access (other than economic access in terms of jobs, and all the possible sorting that attends contemporary arguments about access and jobs), that educating more means we are that much closer to showing the world the value of democracy and that much closer to winning whatever war we think we are fighting. The patterns and disruptions of the policy process, as we value one or another set of ideas about the meaning and purpose of higher education, are important and need to be explicit. The pattern of education policy and reform now is apparently more an issue of winning the war—particularly the economic war—while increasing the disruption of access and civil rights.

Neither the element of national defense nor the element of civil rights should be surprises to informed readers of federal higher education policy. Placing those two stories in juxtaposition, however, as elements of intellectual history, raises an intriguing theme: understanding federal higher education policy as intellectual history reveals an underlying philosophy of justice. These arguments lead me to what will be the central point of my book on the 1947 President's Commission on Higher Education. Underlying these events and arguments about higher education is a remarkably powerful philosophical conception of the role of higher education as a means of distributing justice in the form of rights (access to higher education) and goods (the private and social rates of return). Such a form of justice certainly reflects now traditional arguments about justice as argued by such scholars as John Rawls.[32] Yet as Marion Young argues, in the United States the polity and the public have focused on a philosophy of justice based on distribution.[33] The 1947 President's Commission on Higher Education speaks directly to such distribution, arguing that access to higher education offers opportunities in political, economic, and social terms that are the right of all people in the nation, that distributing access creates a better society and economy. In contrast, Young argues that we need a contemporary meaning of justice, that the justice of distribution ignores fundamental relationships among individuals and groups. She suggests that a justice of differences that incorporates processes is a more appropriate form of justice than a system of distribution. I think that inherent ideas about higher education reflect arguments about justice, justice within the nation—civil rights—and justice as we want to be observed by other nations and cultures—national defense. Young's analysis may well lead us in the present to a more (dare I say it) judicious appraisal of what we mean by education, to understand how our ideas about education are remiss. Writing through the past, mindful of the present, I conclude that the process of just treatment is more valuable than the distribution of access and goods. Affirmative action focuses us on the workforce, or more accurately, the diverse workforce, even though historically we know that meanings of race, ethnicity, and gender are problematic. The ideas of the 1947 President's Commission as well as past federal acts represent texts that are both complementary and contrary as we struggle today to identify what we mean by justice, whether higher education means social understanding or global competition. The history of federal higher education policy, as I write through the past, asks me to focus less on economic outcomes of higher education and more on the troubling meanings of higher education as a form of Americanization. Indeed, what is the process of becoming a citizen or leader of this nation? Rather than assuming that global competition is how we ought to define higher education, history affords us the opportunity to see the complexities of humans and the events of their time and also to recognize that a mere listing of names, dates, and places is only an outline. It is incumbent upon the historian to tell the story of the past through the past, to appreciate the context of the time while measured within what we know about the present.

QUESTIONS FOR DISCUSSION

1. Has the historian used documents and oral histories (depending, of course, on the era under examination) that establish a clear and convincing argument about what happened in the past?
2. Has the historian explained what differences exist between the past and the present, particularly in regard to those terms or ideas which could easily be imposed from the present onto the past?
3. Has the historian articulated whether the key issues focus on political actors and events, or the development of ideas, or the ebb and flow of social movements, or other forms of social and individual action? If not, is the reader able to easily discern the focus of the key issues?
4. Finally, is it clear from the historical narrative what people meant by a term or phrase or idea at that time?

NOTES

1. Jack Greenberg, *Crusaders in the Court: How a Dedicated Band of Lawyers Fought for the Civil Rights Revolution* (New York: BasicBooks, 1994). Here too lies an issue of presentism. It is fascinating in my history of education courses to highlight the sustained and effective coalition of Blacks and Jews in the fight for civil rights, such as the highly talented Black and Jewish lawyers in the Legal Defense Fund, a coalition now not only virtually moribund but also shattered by anger on both sides. Students rarely know this aspect of the civil rights movement.
2. See Shannon Butler Mokoro, "Racial Uplift and Self-Determination: The African Methodist Episcopal Church and the Pursuit of Higher Education" (Ph.D. dissertation, Georgia State University, 2009). I once tried to search for the origin of the concept, if not the term, "military-industrial complex," apparently coined by President Dwight Eisenhower in his 1960 farewell address. Within minutes of searching a journal database I was reading articles on the military-industrial complex in the Civil War, and I halted my search, fearing I would end up in ancient Sparta. As it turns out, given the exhibit of the Chinese terra cotta warriors at an Atlanta museum and seeing the assembly line to create those warriors, I would end up at least in ancient China.
3. In this discussion I draw heavily from a paper I presented at the annual meeting of the Association for the Study of Higher Education in 2003; see Philo A. Hutcheson, "Federal Higher Education Policy as Intellectual History," Association for the Study of Higher Education, Portland, Oregon, November 2003. On political history and sociologists and political scientists using historical narrative, see, for example, Laurence E. Gladieux and Thomas R. Wolanin, *Congress and the Colleges: The National Politics of Higher Education* (Lexington, MA: D.C. Heath and Company, 1972); David W. Breneman and Chester E. Finn, Jr., *Public Policy and Private Higher Education* (Washington, DC: The Brookings Institution, 1978); Sheila Slaughter, *The Higher Learning and High Technology: Dynamics of Higher Education Policy Formation* (Albany: State University of New York Press, 1990); Michael Parsons, *Power and Politics: Federal Higher Education Policy-making in the 1990s* (Albany, NY: State University of New York Press, 1997). None of these works claims historical analysis as such, although each employs historical examination as part of the overall investigation, suggesting recognition that policy history is important. I will freely claim, however, that historical analysis, typically wary of theory as a defining, perhaps even confining interpretive framework, is comfortable with nuances and thus a potentially powerful analytical tool for education policy scholars. As an example, while David Truman argues about the nature of interest groups and their relation to political parties, and specifically notes "the peculiar character of our party system, which has strengthened parochial relationships," historian Richard Hofstadter offers a contrasting point of view about the characteristics of political parties in the United States, illustrating their uncertain beginnings in the early years of the Republic. See

David Truman, "Interest Groups and the Nature of the State," in *The Governmental Process: Political Interests and Public Opinion* (New York: Knopf, 1951/1971), 505–515 and Richard Hofstadter, *The Idea of a Party System: The Rise of Legitimate Opposition in American Politics and Other Essays, 1780–1840* (Berkeley: University of California Press, 1969). Hofstadter concludes that the party system "protected unity at the cost of true political issues, behaviors, and conflicts." While Hofstadter escapes easy definition as an intellectual historian, he was obviously comfortable with the nature of ideas and history. See Philo A. Hutcheson, "Richard Hofstadter," in *Dictionary of Literary Biography: Twentieth Century American Cultural Theorists* (Detroit, MI: Bruccoli Clark Layman, 2001), 207–218. On protection of unity, see 216.

4. Mark H. Leff, "Revisioning U.S. Political History," *American Historical Review* (June 1995), 829. I am not arguing that political history ignores other conditions, such as social and economic ones; as Peter Clarke argues, "Politics, seen as part of real history, is inevitably intertwined with social and economic conditions." See Peter Clarke, "Political History in the 1980s," *Journal of Interdisciplinary History* 12 (Summer 1981), 45. Nevertheless, there is a decided tendency in examinations of education policy to reify the actors and acts. For example, as an unabashed representation of objective analysis of political history, see J. Morgan Kousser, "Toward 'Total Political History': A Rational-Choice Research Program," *Journal of Interdisciplinary History* 20 (Spring 1990), 521–560. Kousser argues for the application of quantitative models of rational choice theories to the study of political history. There are also, of course, other divisions within history, including social history and economic history. For a valuable example of an analysis of education policy employing both social and economic history, see Harvey Kantor and Robert Lowe, "Class, Race, and the Emergence of Federal Education Policy: From the New Deal to the Great Society," *Educational Researcher* 24 (April 1995), 4–11, 21. As documented in this paper, the Truman administration was a key factor in the development of the arguments for federal support of higher education (as well as elementary and secondary education), and Kantor and Lowe do not mention those efforts. Their analysis is in partial response to Paula Fass's arguments that the link between race (particularly for African Americans) and education became increasingly important during the New Deal and thus led to the important federal education legislation of the 1960s. See Paula Fass, *Outside In: Minorities and the Transformation of American Education* (New York: Oxford University Press, 1989), Chapter 4, "New Day Coming: The Federal Government and Black Education in the 1930s and '40s." For a historical examination that uses both social and (to a limited degree) intellectual perspectives, see Maxine Greene, "The Demands of Diversity: Implications for Public Policy," in *The Uneasy Public Policy Triangle in Higher Education: Quality, Diversity, and Budgetary Efficiency*, ed. David H. Finifter, Roger G. Baldwin, and John R. Thelin (New York: American Council on Education/Macmillan, 1991), 26–32.

5. Hugh Davis Graham, *An Uncertain Triumph: Federal Education Policy in the Kennedy and Johnson Years* (Chapel Hill: University of North Carolina Press, 1984). Curiously, while Graham addresses preceding federal activity in regard to education policy, it is a brief recounting of Congressional acts, reaffirming political history as an examination of political institutions and influences. See xvii–xviii. A variety of contributions within books and monographs also offer brief political histories. See, for example, Frances Keppel, "The Role of Public Policy in Higher Education in the United States: Land Grants to Pell Grants and Beyond," in *The Uneasy Public Policy Triangle in Higher Education* (New York: American Council on Education/Macmillan, 1991), 9–17.

6. Hugh Davis Graham and Nancy Diamond, *The Rise of American Research Universities: Elites and Challengers in the Postwar Era* (Baltimore, MD: Johns Hopkins University, 1997). The 1960s were, of course, also the time when the federal government began to provide unprecedented amounts of money for college student grants, certainly albeit slowly increasing requirements for accountability. See Rupert Wilkinson, *Aiding Students, Buying Students: Financial Aid in America* (Nashville, TN: Vanderbilt University Press, 2005). This work is particularly instructive because Wilkinson is English, and the English system of funding students is very different from the U.S. system.

7. R.H. E[ckelberry], "Editorial Comments: Federal Support," *Journal of Higher Education* 21 (October 1950): 393–394. Eckelberry, a long-standing editor of the *Journal of Higher Education*, often spoke to this point, as did some of the other contributors to the *Journal*. This reference, not incidentally, is another indicator of presentism. Today, and since the early 1970s, the *Journal of Higher Education* publishes almost exclusively articles presenting research and scholarly findings. Until the early 1970s, with the appointment of Robert Silverman as editor, the *Journal* typically published essays as well as some research and scholarly articles.

8. Jonathan Rosenberg, *How Far the Promised Land? World Affairs and the American Civil Rights Movement from the First World War to Vietnam* (Princeton, NJ: Princeton University Press, 2006), 142–143.

9. The fundamental work on the national university was published in the 1960s, and it remains important. See David Madsen, *The National University, Enduring Dream of the USA* (Detroit, MI: Wayne State University Press, 1966).

10. Preston Cloud, "The Improbable Bureaucracy: The United States Geological Survey, 1879–1979," *Proceedings of the American Philosophical Society*, 124 No. 3 (Jun. 30, 1980): 155–167. Cloud addresses the Lewis and Clark expedition as well the development of the USGS.

11. John R. Thelin, *A History of American Higher Education* (Baltimore, MD: Johns Hopkins University, 2004), 78 on military instruction. Thelin also notes the inclusion of the liberal arts as a course of study, with some states choosing to focus their new land-grant colleges on the liberal arts. On the Act itself, see http://www.higher-ed.org/resources/morrill1.htm (retrieved January 31, 2009).

12. Eldon L. Johnson, "Misconceptions About the Early Land-Grant Colleges," *Journal of Higher Education* 52 (July–August 1981): 333–351.

13. John Seiler Brubacher and Willis Rudy, *Higher Education in Transition: A History of American Colleges and Universities, 1636–1976* (New York City, NY: Harper & Row, 1976).

14. Steven Brint and Jerome Karabel, *The Diverted Dream: Community Colleges and the Promise of Educational Opportunity in America, 1900–1985* (New York: Oxford University Press, 1991, paperback edition); Laurence E. Gladieux and Thomas R. Wolanin, *Congress and the Colleges: The National Politics of Higher Education* (Lexington, MA: D.C. Heath and Company, 1972). For examinations of the 1947 President's Commission and its impact on states, see Oliver C. Carmichael, *New York Establishes a State University; A Case Study in the Process of Policy Formation* (Nashville, TN: Vanderbilt University Press, 1955); Richard Freeland, *Academia's Golden Age: Universities in Massachusetts, 1945–1970* (New York: Oxford University Press, 1992), 70–119, John Aubrey Douglass, "Californians and Public Higher Education: Political Culture, Educational Opportunity and State Policymaking," *History of Higher Education Annual 1996*, 89–90, and Sidney Gelber, *Politics and Public Higher Education in New York State: Stony Brook—a Case History* (New York: P. Lang, 2001).

15. Peter Novick, *That Noble Dream: The "Objectivity Question" and the American Historical Profession* (New York: Cambridge University Press, 1988), 7.

16. Laurence Veysey, *The Emergence of the American University* (Chicago, IL: University of Chicago Press, 1965).

17. Dominick LaCapra, "Intellectual History and Its Ways," *American Historical Review* 97 (April 1992), 430–431.

18. Ibid., 430.

19. In this sense I am relying on Enlightenment conceptions of the meaning of education. See, for example, John Locke, "Of the State of Nature," *Two Treatises of Government*, intr. By Peter Laslett (New York: Cambridge University Press, 1963 rev. edition) and John Locke, *Some Thoughts Concerning Education; And, of the Conduct of the Understanding*, ed. Ruth W. Grant and Nathan Tarcov (Indianapolis, IN: Hackett Publishing Company, 1996).

20. In a very real sense, the claim that everything is political—thus suggesting that all ideas are in one way or another ideologies—leaves attempts at analysis bereft of distinctions or evaluations. The argument is indeed beguiling, inviting readers of such a text to see that all relations are political, that in the words of one scholar, power is a process embedded in all human interactions. See Peter Digeser, "The Fourth Face of Power," *The Journal of Politics* 54 (November 1992), 977–1007. Digeser offers an adroit examination of Foucauldian notions of power, but leaves the reader with the bewildering proposition that power is everywhere all the time historically and socially situated.

21. The Commission dedicated a substantial amount of its final report to the issues of discrimination and access. See *Higher Education for American Democracy*, "Equalizing and Expanding Individual Opportunity," Vol. II, 1–69. On exclusionary practices, see David O. Levine, *The American College and the Culture of Aspiration 1915–1940* (Ithaca, NY: Cornell University Press, 1986); Harold S. Wechsler, *The Qualified Student: A History of Selective College Admission in America* (New York: Wiley,1979); Marcia Synnott, *The Half-Opened Door: Discrimination and Admissions at Harvard, Yale and Princeton, 1900–1970* (Westport, CT: Greenwood Press, 1979).

22. Gladieux and Wolanin, *Congress and the Colleges*, (Heath and Company, 1972), 16–18.

23. James L. Sundquist, *Politics and Policy: The Eisenhower, Kennedy, and Johnson Years* (Washington, DC: The Brookings Institution, 1968), 205–220.

24. Philo A. Hutcheson, "Exploring the Roots of Federal Language on Discrimination: The 1947 President's Commission on Higher Education," Association for the Study of Higher Education, Richmond, Virginia, November 2001. Paper available from author upon request.

25. An interesting representation of this development is Gunnar Myrdal's work, an explicit view of race in the United States and its meaning. See Gunnar Myrdal, *An American Dilemma; The Negro Problem and Modern Democracy* (New York: Harper & Brothers, 1944). As noted in Paula Fass, *Outside In: Minorities and the Transformation of American Education* (New York: Oxford University Press, 1989), Chapter 4, "New Day Coming: The Federal Government and Black Education in the 1930s and '40s," the nation's recognition of minorities began to change in the 1930s and 1940s.

26. George F. Zook, "The President's Annual Report." *Educational Record* 21 (July 1940), 327.
27. Ibid.; Zook, "Education and the National Defense" (Washington, DC: American Council on Education, June 1940), 7.
28. *Higher Education for American Democracy*, Vol. 1, 7.
29. Ibid., 15.
30. Ibid., 8–9.
31. National Commission on Excellence in Education, *A Nation at Risk: The Imperative for Educational Reform: A Report to the Nation and the Secretary of Education, United States Department of Education* (Washington, DC: National Commission on Excellence in Education, 1983) and U.S. Department of Education, *A Test of Leadership: Charting the Future of U.S. Higher Education* (Washington, DC, 2006).
32. John Rawls, *A Theory of Justice* (Cambridge, MA: Belknap Press of Harvard University Press, 1971).
33. I. Marion Young, *Justice and the Politics of Difference* (Princeton, NJ: Princeton University Press, 1990). Ironically, this analysis begins to take the defining discipline back to political history, for justice is inextricably linked to power, as Young notes in her discussion of power. As William Leuchtenburg argues, power is a key component of political history and too often a missing component of such historical fields as social history. See William E. Leuchtenburg, "The Pertinence of Political History: Reflections on the Significance of the State in America," *Journal of American History*, 73 (December 1986): 588.

14

THE CHALLENGE OF WRITING THE SOUTH

Amy E. Wells-Dolan

For historians of southern higher education, understanding and interpreting regional history stands out as a full-time endeavor. In terms of regional history writ large, few bodies of American scholarship have emerged as long, large, and storied in the willingness to confront the raw themes of race, class, and gender, as well as explore the contours of power and privilege that fall along a marked color line. Yet a reckoning with the vastness of the literature is prerequisite, if not discouraging. In fact, so many significant books existed about the South by 1939 that someone observed that "any one who fired a gun was likely to kill an author."[1] Today, the 649-page thesis of Joshua Isaac Newman entitled, "Dixie's Last Stand: Ole Miss, The Body, and The Spectacle of Dixie South Whiteness" gives additional testament to the weight of the task.[2]

While the organization of southern colleges and universities into ostensibly separate institutions for Blacks and Whites has tested educational scholars writing the South, I contend that academic segregation, i.e. the separate camps within the academy *and* within the historical enterprise, poses a greater threat to emerging scholars seeking to understand the South.[3] The upshot for the educational historian: the intellectual challenge of integrating oft separate "White" and "Black" narratives of experience from scholars in different academic sub-groups and fields including but not limited to southern history, American Studies, African American history, and African American Studies. Pummeled now by the interdisciplinary conceptions of the Global South,[4] the educational historian faces new trials to make his or her maybe her work about the region relevant in an era when territories are shifting, boundaries are permeable, and (southern) nationalism is ostensibly passé.

This chapter draws upon my personal experience living and writing the South. Discussion of a campus traditions project undertaken by students enrolled in my History of Higher Education course serves as a starting place for my narrative. First, I explore the insider/outsider dichotomy that has marked southern spaces and experience but also stretched and transformed these spaces. Then I turn to the historical development of southern identity and the problematical origins of southern history. I take this turn not only to exorcise the liberal conscience but also to acknowledge the personal and professional limitations that, left unrecognized, may impede historical interpretation and analysis. Though I may warn more of potential pitfalls than offer practical advice in this chapter, I hope to raise questions and provide a few insights for scholars who seek to produce meaningful work about the South. Move now, to Oxford, Mississippi.

THE PAST IN THE PRESENT

Many students enrolled in our higher education program come with the aspiration to advance in administration at a college or university—to be a dean of students or chancellor someday. A good portion come to us as "outsiders," fresh from undergraduate study on other college campuses (nationally and internationally). Others come to our program as "insiders," alumni who view fondly their "Ole Miss" days. In my teaching of higher education history to these emerging professionals, I use the exploration of the University's history and campus traditions as a lens for understanding the development of postsecondary education in America, historical scholarship in particular, and archival research methods on an introductory level. Within the framework of the course, a primary assignment involves working independently or in groups to uncover the roots of campus traditions and to trace their evolution while they read about higher education history generally[5] and the historic integration of the University by James Meredith in 1962 specifically.[6] The challenge for them becomes linking the "particular" or local with the "universal" or larger narrative about American higher education history without navel gazing or dismissing the University as simply distinct.[7]

A very real puzzlement to observers, me included, has been the veracity with which White southerners, in this case, students and alumni at Ole Miss, have cherished the obvious symbols of the late Confederacy, defending their use. Just to give a taste: among the traditions most noted here is a unique near formal-dress ritual of football tailgating in the Grove[8] and the playing of "Dixie" by the University band at athletic events. Though the display of ostensibly "Confederate" symbols has markedly decreased in the last decade, the perhaps naïve "outsider" in me believed that reason and evidence in the form of infidelity in tradition over time (i.e. the fact that the Confederate symbols only emerged in the 1930s—when southern identity captured the popular imagination)[9] might offer pause for consideration of new imagery and promote change.[10]

While students researched, read, and presented, my thinking on the South has been stretched and contorted as I have worked to make sense of my role as a scholar in this place, Oxford, Mississippi. This work mirrored the common observation that teaching enhances learning: I learned first from my own research, reading, and prior experience; then I learned again from what my students found. For me, this work has concerned me anew with practical questions about the stewardship of history, how to evaluate and integrate contested meaning and interpretations, and how to make sense of scholarship when partly motivated by the desire to transform a locale and those who abide there. Knowing that the activist impulse is something with which historians have struggled for good and bad consequence, I have wanted to know more about how two key institutional players, namely Frank Moak and Michael Harrington, approached reform of University of Mississippi students in the past.

In working with sorority women at Transylvania University (Lexington, Kentucky) as an alumni advisor, I became indignant when members used the claim of "tradition" to legitimize activities just a couple of years old. No doubt former University of Mississippi

Dean of Students Frank Moak felt this skepticism when he proclaimed that something only had to "happen once" to become a college tradition. Historian David Sansing used Moak's quote in discussion of a short-lived "organized" Shrimp and Beer festival held in the late 1970s and early 1980s on Sardis Lake some twenty plus miles from campus. A "spring rite" that capped the University's long-standing Dixie Week celebration, the festival's popularity contributed to its demise in 1983 at the hands of administrators cognizant of new national trends in "risk management" and fearful the University could no longer "control" the event. Students "reacted angrily" to the event's end and appealed to then incoming Chancellor Gerald Turner (1983–1994) to save the less than a decade-old "tradition." Turner did not yield to student demands—the Shrimp and Beer Festival ended; Dixie Week ended not long after, and the rite morphed into the more politically palatable "Red-Blue Week," named for the school colors.[11]

Like a portion of our master's students enrolled in higher education, Frank Moak graduated from the University of Mississippi—an "insider." A native of Ruth, Mississippi and winner of the American Legion State Oratorical Contest, Moak gained the endorsement of University of Mississippi Dean of Men Malcolm Guess and received a work scholarship as student custodian for Fulton Chapel to attend the University beginning in the fall of 1944. A high school student heavily involved in church activities, choir, 4-H Club, and the like, Moak became extensively involved in campus life in his first year at the University, pledging a fraternity (Delta Psi), participating in the Baptist Student Union, as well as a literary and debate society among other activities. His involvement and responsibilities grew over time so that in later years, in addition to participating in Varsity debate, choir, band, and such, Moak edited the yearbook, chaired Vesper services, and became a YMCA cabinet member and student government executive. In the process, he established himself as a "peacemaker" between students and the administration as well as becoming mentee of Dean Guess, according to Thomas Reardon, the current Dean of Students who also worked with Moak in his early days.[12]

When Moak reflected on his college years with Reardon, he associated his learning experiences with interstate travel as a student representative of the YMCA,[13] with how to work for common goals across different viewpoints and perspectives[14]—though this skill did not always earn him the recognition of his peers in his estimation. On the heels of his travel during his senior year (1947), Moak and fraternity brother, Joe Gillespie, crafted a proposal for an Institute of Southern Studies, a plan they submitted to Peter Kyle McCarter, Dean of the University. Moak and Gillespie proposed the Institute as a summer school offering to bring "mature and thoughtful people from other sections of the country particularly from the North and East" for a Mississippi intercultural exchange to promote "discussion and interchange of ideas of various cultural, political, and social peculiarities of the South." The "effect", they noted, would be "the reverse of such institutes as are put on in many of the Northern schools for the indoctrination of Southern students" with this caveat: "underlying the idea is of course, the assumption that it is important for people of different views to understand one another's thinking." Though a "Special Faculty Committee to Study the Organization of an Institute on Southern Studies" convened with Moak as a student representative, and gained the endorsement of the Summer School director, the Institute proposal stalled for lack of funding and then an administrative turnover occurred.[15]

In the meantime, Moak graduated from the University in 1948 commissioned as a Second Lieutenant and member of the U.S. Army Reserve, having participated in the

University's Reserve Officer Training Corps as an undergraduate. After service, Moak made his way with his family to Teachers College at Columbia University in 1953 where he studied educational administration with Esther Lloyd-Jones, a primary author and articulator of the student personnel movement and a key player in the development of the documents now considered foundational to the field of student affairs, *The Student Personnel Point of View* (1937, 1949). Though admitted on conditional status, Moak quickly established himself in his graduate career, Reardon conveyed, and became a student leader too: president of the Teachers College Student Council. Over time, he earned various fellowships to support his study and worked in different roles in Student Life. He earned a master of arts degree in June 1954, and doctorate of Education degree two years later, writing his thesis about his work for the Teachers College International Teaching Service Bureau, a collaborative project to enhance classroom support for teachers in metropolitan public schools by Teachers College students from other countries.[16]

Upon graduation, Moak, "a trusted insider," made his way back to Mississippi as the Director of Placement and Financial Aids in 1960 with a faculty appointment in Higher Education soon to follow. In 1962, when James Meredith finally enrolled successfully at the University despite the open resistance of Governor Ross Barnett and the ensuing battle on campus, Moak worked with seven others to assist federal marshals and identify students under arrest, earning accolades from Robert F. Kennedy in the *Washington Post*. While history of the integration of the University has principally revolved around Barnett and the campus skirmish, the story of those who worked locally to make progress and move students along in their thinking and reaction to integration exists in Reardon's dissertation but is yet to be published.[17]

Moak became Dean of the Division of Student Personnel in 1964. He served the division of student personnel for seventeen years whereby he shepherded the student body through the arduous and oft painful process of integration—with so many "firsts" related to African American students, faculty, and staff integration. He responded to student protests, football riots, and panty raids, as well as the day-to-day of student life including student discipline and campus programming, to name a few. Moak, credited with beginning the higher education program I teach in today, became a professor emeritus of higher education and Southern studies upon his retirement and wrote an unpublished history of the University's alumni association.[18]

The essence of the idea found in Moak's proposed Institute of Southern Studies came to fruition later in the form of the University's Center for the Study of Southern Culture (CSSC), which opened in 1977 supported by a consultant grant from the National Endowment for the Humanities. Today the CSSC thrives as a well-reputed interdisciplinary bachelor's and master's degree-granting academic center within the College of Liberal Arts. The Center's activities draw participants nationally and internationally, and the Center's signature publication, the *Encyclopedia of Southern Culture*, has received multiple awards.[19]

It took an "outsider," a transplanted southerner originally from Portland, Oregon, Michael Harrington, working with History Department Professor and Chair Robert Haws to craft the proposal that led to the establishment of the CSSC. Harrington, a graduate of Davidson College in North Carolina, who later earned his graduate degrees in philosophy at Emory, joined the University's department of philosophy and religion in 1970 and worked as a professor and administrator until his retirement in 2007, which he took shortly before his death. Harrington stood out on campus as a popular teacher and worked across the state in support of the humanities. No doubt Harrington knew something of southern history too, likening the start of the football season to a "reincarnation of Pickett's Charge"—a point made in eulogy by a former colleague who once co-taught with Harrington a course on the philosophy of war.[20]

Like others working on one campus for over thirty years, Professor Harrington knew a good bit about campus history and could give testament to the challenge of overcoming the University's past, particularly its history related to race. Regarding the University's heightened sensitivity to negative public relations, for example, Harrington speculated that the devastation of Hurricane Hugo in 1989 had spared the University the prolonged scrutiny of the national media in the wake of a particularly ugly hazing incident—a "prank" that left two members of Beta Theta Pi fraternity naked with inflammatory racial epithets emblazoned on their chests on the campus of nearby historically Black Rust College in Holly Springs.[21] In response to that malevolent incident, Chancellor Gerald Turner created a campus task force that advocated, among other suggestions, the creation of a required new student orientation course, University Studies (US) 101. Turner called upon Harrington to provide the blueprint for the course through an original text, *Traditions and Changes: The University in Principle and Practice.*[22]

A reading of his text shows that Harrington approached his task with a philosopher's zeal, and some may call it a White liberal zeal, as Harrington labored to "re-construct" Ole Miss students by instructing them about the University's Western origins, Mississippi and the University's objectionable past, our history of slavery and misguided notions of White supremacy, the problems of racism, sexism, social elitism and unearned privilege, diversity, and common threats to learning stemming from excessive drinking, drug use, date rape and sexual assault. Harrington's text led students through a number of thought-provoking activities. Consider, for example, a scenario for slavery reparations as described in the instructions for exercise 5-2:

> Suppose that in 2000, federal authority has been destroyed and the United States has disintegrated into a series of warring regions. The powerful city-state of Memphis reintroduces slavery to work its Delta farmlands in order to become self-sufficient. You, your spouse and children are seized by slave traders guided by their Mississippi allies. You are separated and never see each other again; you become a field hand in the Arkansas Delta. Forty years later in 2040, your health and strength destroyed by hard labor and poor living conditions, you are freed and the slave-state of Memphis destroyed by the armies of Little Rock. "You are entitled to justice from Memphis," says Little Rock: "Say what Memphis should do and why, for enslaving you and your family." But before you can speak, a couple of students from Memphis answer: "Hey, we didn't do anything to you, it was our parents, so why should we have to pay?" You answer those questions. Then return to this chapter.[23]

US 101 met opposition. Harrington gave a taste of this within his text when he included a student's comment from a US 101 course evaluation: "But Professor, you don't under-stand: Ole Miss is a place where you CAN BE a racist" (Emphasis original source).[24] Harrington's text constituted the primary reading for US 101 for a few years. However, during an administrative transition, course responsibilities were re-assigned and the text revised by a new appointee.[25] Though this change gave extended life for US 101, the course finally folded from the weight of student and faculty complaints.

The history of school desegregation revealed that because individuals experienced discrimination on the local level, ameliorating conditions for persons of color involved changing localities—a long reach for federal policy initiatives.[26] Within the added context of a state government bent upon maintaining segregation that the University of Mississippi depended on for support, the politics of segregation played out quite brutally at Ole Miss. However, in the post-Meredith years internal conflict has shifted from attention to the question of whither integration to political questions about how to move forward while maintaining aspects of campus culture and community that make it distinctive and precious. Over time, key institutional players, various insiders and outsiders, have vied for leadership and approach. Moak, "a Mississippi insider," later described his attitude as an "understanding and sympathetic" attempt to meet students where they were.[27] Harrington "an outsider to Mississippi," apparently invited discussion of that which is largely kept silent—slavery and the state's traumatic past.

A text for teaching emerging student services professionals emphasizes that as a group, students have the lowest capacity for transforming campus over time.[28] The author's point is to empower emerging practitioners to advance multiculturalism in higher education; to understand the capacity to use advocacy, policy, and services among other tools to create change, and to acknowledge the fact that administrators do play a key role in changing campus environments over time. As testament in this locale, the combined efforts of Moak, Harrington, and many others helped change the University of Mississippi. A marked increase in African American enrollment at "Ole Miss" in 2005 demonstrated an increased receptivity for Blacks to partake in the post-Meredith "Ole Miss" experience.[29]

What is striking to me in my locale is how well the University structure has accommodated contested ideologies, worldviews, and contrasting class-based experiences. This has played out on the local level where at the University of Mississippi elite-style "Old South" pre-game tailgating in the Grove occurs simultaneously with the hard-hitting community-based work of the William Winter Institute for Racial Reconciliation; where Confederate War memorials stand yards away from a memorial that commemorates James Meredith's historic integration into the university; where a renowned Center for the Study of Southern Culture has advanced critical scholarship on the region and the Global South even while activities of the Center celebrate elements of southern distinctiveness that may be considered lowbrow to some; where the nation's first Black president, Barack Obama, debated in contest for the presidency with Senator John S. McCain III, the great-great grandson of a Carroll County, Mississippi plantation owner. Are these marked contrasts and accommodations distinctly southern, distinctly "Ole Miss," or do they give insight into a larger phenomenon?

THE PERSONAL AS SOCIAL

Collective memory studies[30] gave me additional perspective into how people remembered what they did not directly experience, such as a perception of political vengeance during the Reconstruction—or even how students have brought to campus a certain "memory" of how college life was to be and how school traditions were performed and used "to guide the conduct of members in the present."[31] While these studies offered some satisfaction as to why and how students and alumni at "Ole Miss" have clung to Old South traditions with tenacity, forcing a "continual presence of the past,"[32] the probability existed that this was just a part of a larger story. In my experience living and writing the South, I have come to understand that how southern history itself was constructed, taught, and learned by generations of White and Black southerners has mattered too.

Relevant to my own memory and emotion of the South and Civil War, I grew up in Kentucky on Battle Grove Avenue, near a cemetery. I periodically begged my mother to excavate the back yard for battle relics as I had learned that many battles had taken place in and around my hometown, where I played with friends and camped with the local Girl Scouts.

Later, I attended Transylvania University in Lexington, Kentucky which commemorated alumni Senator Henry Clay and Confederate President Jefferson Davis as the longstanding names for the men's residence halls (Clay-Davis), where in each lobby hung a life-size portrait of each man. On Saturdays, I gave tours at the girlhood home of Mary Todd Lincoln, and dutifully read the museum director's sanctioned biography,[33] explaining to visitors that (1) Mrs. Lincoln was not crazy and (2) Mrs. Lincoln's hometown, Lexington, remained a Confederate stronghold though most of the state supported the Union and the state declared itself as neutral.

As a student I didn't think too much about those portraits or the larger body of southern history though I expressed at least a surface commitment to "diversity" within the campus community and its particular political milieu. My awareness and contemplation of Lexington as a southern space came later when I returned to Lexington and the University of Kentucky for doctoral study. I recall now an interesting side note: in 2001 an alleged incident of harassment against an African American student stirred controversy about the Davis portrait. At the time, Transylvania President Charles Shearer admitted the administration's concern, saying "we've been sensitive to what that portrait may mean to Black students and other students." They resolved the controversy by re-hanging the portrait in another campus space. Though the Kentucky Confederate veterans group and the Daughters of the Confederacy offered appreciation for the University's working with them and their response which gave the portrait increased "prominence," the College effectively denied such cooperation with the associations.[34]

The fact was that my identity as a southerner evolved in the period between undergraduate study and doctoral student when I moved to Ohio to attend Kent State University. This happened because folks told me I was southern. In this way, my identity was co-constructed, much like the larger regional identity of the American South. James Cobb explained that northerners and southerners co-constructed the South in contrast to the "other," and argued that northerners took the lead in crafting a regional identity. Though sectional "divergence" could be identified by the mid-1600s in patterns of agriculture and industry, a "'we'/'they' dichotomy" of northern superiority had emerged in the northern press, school texts, and by lexicographers like Noah Webster by the late 1700s.[35] By the 1850s, magazines used "'the North' and the 'United States' interchangeably" and described the South disparagingly—one account likening South Carolina to Algiers and other woeful places, as a destination where, "We must go there in disguise with pistols in our pockets, leaving our pocketbooks at home, making our wills before we go."[36] Though characterizations grew to effectively separate "Yankees" of New England and the middle colonies from the "Cavaliers" of Virginia, the Carolinas, and Georgia, cohesiveness around southern identity and politics lagged or emerged unevenly as the Civil War approached.

Cobb reiterated that architects of southern nationalism constructed it "on the fly" and without a government. Seeing themselves as the "true Americans," according to Reid Mitchell, Confederates borrowed their ideals, governing structures, and symbols from the United States and the War for American Independence.[37] Thus, the South "parodied" the U.S. Constitution, used George Washington's image on its first seal (calling Jefferson Davis, "our second Washington"), sang freely of American patriotic tunes, and even designed a first flag so close in design to the American flag that it had to be changed to prevent the firing on Confederate troops. Take, for example, the words of a young man from South Carolina who demonstrated this overriding loyalty to country, even if a boyish allegiance, as if representing the home team in a sporting match: "I go first for Greenville, then the Greenville District, then for the up-country, then for South Carolina, then for the South, and then for the United States, and after that, I don't go for anything."[38]

Thus, Cobb explained that an intense southern nationalism grew mostly out of defeat after the Civil War fueled by the New South doctrine which involved using industrial development to boost the region's economy while holding tight to the "race, political, and class hierarchies of the Old South."[39] During this era, historians and newly formed organizations such as the Southern Historical Society and the United Daughters of the Confederacy (UDC) played an essential part in the new order by washing clean the past and teaching about Northern aggression, arguing that a certain harmony existed in the old order; that masters were genteel and that Blacks had been happy and obedient under slavery, for example. Concerned particularly about the history being taught to children and college students, Mary Singleton Slack of the UDC reminded other members that "thought is power" and declared that the greatest monument the UDC could erect would be a "thought monument" in the "pulsing hearts and active brains" of the South's White youth.[40] This extended to collegiate education where, by the 1920s, 30 or 40 colleges and universities offered courses in southern history—up from just 6 in 1920.[41]

Characteristically this early twentieth-century southern history was sealed by a hypersensitivity to dissent and distaste for open disagreement as unseemly and unflattering. Thus, the region's intellectual modernization became stalled as southern historians dutifully reinterpreted the region's past and gave a more flattering portrait of slavery and the Civil War. In the wake grew a White historical memory strong enough to give Confederate membership to my home state, Kentucky, for example, a state that had not left the Union, and to erase the class and social cleavages between planters and the region's plethora of economically exploited and educationally deprived Whites. The forced resignation of University of Florida Professor Enoch Banks, who had taught the idea that the war had been fought over slavery and not states' rights, that the "North had been relatively right and the South relatively wrong," exemplified this deviation from the core principle of the sanctioned historical interpretation which was considered heretical and an actionable concern at the university level.[42]

Among the adherents to the Lost Cause or "Confederate Celebration," the work and long-term influence of the United Daughters of the Confederacy (UDC), a women's voluntary association centered upon Confederate heritage and commemoration, begs consideration as a formidable power in the creation of southern nationalism.[43] This organization—whose membership numbered 100,000 women by the end of World War I (1918)—attracted southern members far in excess of the General Federation of Women's

Clubs and the Women's Christian Temperance Union.[44] To give a sense of scope to the organization, in the state of Mississippi, which has 82 counties, 185 chapters of the UDC were founded between 1896 and 1996. In addition to the millions of dollars the UDC raised to erect monuments across the region, the Mississippi landscape was marked by 104 known Confederate monuments and 82 known Civil War Confederate cemeteries, plots and burial sites which marked the graves of thousands of Confederate dead.[45]

The UDC, with its five objectives defined as "memorial, historical, benevolent, educational, and social,"[46] became a central force in the "Confederate Celebration," and in addition to its efforts to memorialize, the UDC arguably began and propagated the field of southern history, built and funded convalescent homes for Confederate veterans and women of the 1860s (widows), and funded scholarships to colleges and universities across the nation for southern White youth. For example, in the year 1940, the UDC made available various packages of scholarships, loan funds, and tuition allowances to college students reaching a grand total of $147,846.[47] I estimated this figure to be $2.14 million in 2006 dollars and incidentally, an amount that compares to the sum given by the Rockefeller Foundation to the social sciences at the University of Virginia in the 1920s and 1930s.[48]

In addition to their role in memorializing and educating individuals through scholarships, the UDC spread its influence in a number of ways and demanded member accountability for efforts that would rival contemporary accreditation activities. Funding women to attend the South's teachers colleges stood as a central plank of UDC indoctrination efforts. Members reasoned that a cadre of southern women teachers could teach a "correct" history to the future generations of southern youth. In addition, UDC membership required individual and group activity in the writing, revision, and authorization of southern history. This included the writing and dissemination of papers and essays on local and regional Confederate and American history, UDC-sponsored essay contests (with lists of approved sources),[49] the writing and sales of children's books, and writing and lobbying the state legislature for the historical texts adopted by southern schools.[50] Though the UDC alone is not wholly responsible, the net effect involved a school textbook industry which quite pragmatically marketed two versions of school history texts for many years: a national text, and the southern version which omitted any thoughtful discussion of slavery.[51]

Arguing that history was both a "weapon of war and peace," John Hope Franklin reminded scholars in 1944 that the study of history "demanded fairness and impartiality" and cautious judgment.[52] He chastised Americans for using history more often as a weapon for waging war rather than maintaining peace.[53] While Franklin used his assertion to contrast America's liberal tradition and authoritarian strains, Franklin's observation applied to southerners and the UDC who also used history to wage a continued assault on human rights and liberties in the Jim Crow era. Undoing the violence of this history required new critical and scientifically objective approaches to history offered by C. Vann Woodward, who critically analyzed the New South doctrine,[54] for example, and by the sociologists led by Howard Odum working for the Institute for Research in the Social Sciences at Chapel Hill in the 1920s and 1930s, who painstakingly described the region through use of statistical comparisons.[55]

Despite the best efforts of these academics, however, southern historical memory and White supremacist identity loomed large enough in the hearts and minds of real and imagined southerners to foster the renewed call to war during the violent period of school integration and the Civil Rights movement.

COMING TO THE STUDY OF THE SOUTH

As Frank Moak and Michael Harrington pondered questions like how far and how fast to move a University that seemingly would not be moved, my life in the South focused upon capturing the complexity of its educational history has taught me that movement *is* possible when rooted in place. The rich landscape of marked contrasts and modifications such as those that have comprised the University of Mississippi's post-Meredith culture stand out to me as a primary benefit of living and writing the South. While non-southerners may visit and dismissively observe that "they are still fighting the Civil War down here,"[56] the South's "continual presence of the past" has invited the exploration of the history around me and the history in me in ways that other spaces and places did not. As the segregated, racialized, and gendered spaces that mark the globe were kept close in the South even as they were transformed, my authority was ever-challenged, pressing me to not be too sure in my thinking or too secure in my privilege.

In reading the South, Cobb's history of southern identity has reminded me that it requires an exceptional non-southern scholar to fully understand the South and by extension, southerners, and the experience of "otherness" that often accompanies the identity and the essence of the "lived experience" of being southern. However, in living and writing the South I have learned too that it takes an exceptional southerner to see the North in southern spaces; to move beyond the intoxicating lure of moonlight and magnolias—the preoccupation with the surface differences found in the early stages of southern identity development—to capture the South with enough depth, nuance, and complexity so as to be truly contributive to the field.

QUESTIONS FOR DISCUSSION

1. What have I learned about southern history and culture and how did I learn it?
2. How was regional history covered in my school textbooks and by my teachers or taught to me by family?
3. How has genealogical inquiry and family storytelling shaped my perspective on southern history?
4. How have media and public displays or celebrations shaped my perspectives on southern history?
5. How do public images affirm or challenge what I have been taught about appropriate gender and racial roles and interracial relationships?
6. What is my *real* comfort level in discussing slavery, racial and sexual violence, privilege and power with people of color and how does that comfort level influence my choices in reading (scholarly literature review) and writing? What is the source of my comfort or discomfort?
7. What does it mean to be Black or White in different regional contexts or in different institutions of higher education across the country?
8. What segregated, racialized, and gendered spaces exist among seemingly open and public spaces in academia?
9. What do "northern" spaces look like and how do they feel? What elements of

southern spaces occur in other places, what elements of northern spaces occur in the South?

10. How do I make intellectual connections to the Global South without relegating local, southern spaces to the peculiar or quaint?

NOTES

1. James C. Cobb, *Away Down South: A History of Southern Identity* (New York: Oxford University Press, 2005), 181.
2. Joshua Isaac Newman, "Dixie's Last Stand: Ole Miss, The Body, and the Spectacle of Dixie South Whiteness" (Ph.D. diss., the University of Maryland, 2005).
3. Peter Novick, *That Noble Dream: The "Objectivity Question" and the American Historical Profession* (Cambridge, MA: Cambridge University Press, 1988), 469–521.
4. Examples of this historical trend include James L. Peacock, Harry L. Watson, and Carrie R. Matthews, eds., *The American South in a Global World* (Chapel Hill: The University of North Carolina Press); Jon Smith and Deborah Cohn, eds., *Look Away!: The U.S. South in New World Studies* (Durham, NC: Duke University Press, 2004); and *Southern Cultures* 13 (Winter 2007) dedicated to the Global South.
5. John R. Thelin, *A History of American Higher Education* (Baltimore, MD: The Johns Hopkins University Press, 2004); Helen L. Horowitz, *Campus Life: Undergraduate Cultures from the End of the Eighteenth Century to the Present* (Chicago: The University of Chicago Press, 1987); and Frederick Rudolph, *The American College and University: A History* (New York: Knopf, 1962).
6. Nadine Cohodas, *The Band Played Dixie: Race and Liberal Conscience at Ole Miss* (New York: Free Press, 1997). Cohodas' sources included numerous individual interviews, the *Mississippian* (Student newspaper), and David G. Sansing, *The University of Mississippi: A Sesquicentennial History* (Jackson: The University Press of Mississippi, 1999).
7. David E. Kyvig and Myron A. Marty, *Nearby History: Exploring the Past Around You* (Walnut Creek, CA: AltaMira Press, 1996), 217–240.
8. See William L. Hamilton. "At Ole Miss, the Tailgaters Never Lose." *New York Times*, September 29, 2006. http://travel2.nytimes.com/2006/09/29/travel/escapes/29grove.html (accessed September 29, 2006) for one example of how the Grove is reported in the national press.
9. The establishment of the Southern Historical Society (1934) and the Southern Sociological Association (1935) exemplified this trend in the academic realm. The security or Ku Klux movement exemplified this phenomenon in the public sphere. See Guy B. Johnson, "A Sociological Interpretation of the New Ku Klux Movement" *Journal of Social Forces*, 1 (May, 1923): 440–445.
10. In addition to the activities named, students have explored Beauty Pageants and Beauty Queens; an unofficial/banned mascot but licensed Colonel Reb; historically Black Greek Letter Organizations; Women's Athletics after Title IX; the college Dixiecrats; and the history of co-education which began at the University of Mississippi in 1882, to name a few. A program for the University Greys Musical in 1954, a University fundraising brochure from 1961 that openly evoked the Confederate legacy, and a couple of newspaper photographs and articles about male students participating in Civil War reenacts at the time of the American Bicentennial (1976) were some of the interesting documents discovered.
11. Sansing, 335.
12. Thomas J. Reardon, "Frank Moak's Legacy Dean of the Division of Student Personnel University of Mississippi, 1964–1981" (Ph.D. diss., University of Mississippi, 2000).
13. Ibid., 82. These activities enhanced Moak's identity as a southerner as he represented the University, the State, and the region to his YMCA peers.
14. Reardon described Moak's first trip as occurring in the summer of 1946 when he attended the YMCA President's School in New York, took classes at the Union Theological seminary, and stayed at the Delta Psi house at Columbia. In the summer of 1947, he traveled to Lake Geneva, WI as a delegate to the National Intercollegiate Council (NICC) of the YMCA.
15. Reardon, 84.
16. Reardon, 89–103. For more on Ester Lloyd-Jones see Ester Lloyd-Jones and Margaret Ruth Smith, *Student Personnel Work as Deeper Teaching* (New York: Harper and Brothers, 1954); Margaret Ruth Smith, "The Voyage of Ester Lloyd-Jones: Travels with a Pioneer" *Personnel and Guidance Journal* (May 1976): 480. American Council on Education (1937). The *Student Personnel Point of View* documents published by the American Council on Education can be retrieved from the National Association of Student Personnel Administrators Web site: http://www.naspa.org/pubs/his.cfm.

17. Reardon, 128; "Oxford Is Shattered Town in Wake of Rioting," *Washington Post*, 2 October 1962. For an account of the battle on campus see William Doyle, *An American Insurrection* (New York: Anchor Books, 2003).

18. Reardon, 335; see Franklin E. Moak, *A History of the Alumni Association of the University of Mississippi, 1852–1986* (University: The Alumni Association of the University of Mississippi, 1986).

19. Charles Reagan Wilson and William Ferris, eds., *Encyclopedia of Southern Culture* (Chapel Hill: University of North Carolina Press, 1989).

20. Michael Harrington died in early October, 2007; Elaine Pugh, "Retired Professor Harrington Dies, Arrangements Announced," University of Mississippi News desk, October 6, 2007.

21. Cohodas described this incident and the University's response, 240–251. Harrington speculated on the media's distraction in group conversation with the author, August 18, 2007.

22. Michael Harrington, *Traditions and Changes: The University of Mississippi in Principle and in Practice* (New York: McGraw-Hill, Inc., 1995).

23. Harrington, 122.

24. Harrington, 142.

25. Timothy L. Hall, *Entering the University: A Revised Printing* (Boston: Pearson Custom Publishing, 2000).

26. Gary Orfield, *The Reconstruction of Southern Education: The Schools and the 1964 Civil Rights Act* (New York: John Wiley & Sons, 1969).

27. Reardon, 82.

28. Susan R. Komives, Dudley B. Woodard, Jr., and Associates. *Student Services: A Handbook for the Profession*, 4th ed. (San Francisco, CA: John Wiley & Sons, 2003), 431.

29. Victoria Hiles, "Minority Enrollment at Ole Miss Sets Record," *The Daily Mississippian*, 29 September 2005, 1, 6.

30. Susan A. Crane, "Writing the Individual Back into Collective Memory," *The American Historical Review*, 102 (December 1997): 1372–1385; Daniel James, "Meatpackers, Peronists, and Collective Memory: A View from the South," *The American Historical Review*, 102 (December 1997):1404–1412; Wulf Kansteiner, "Finding Meaning in Memory: A Methodological Critique of Collective Memory Studies" *History and Theory*, 41 (May 2002):179–197; David Thelan, "Memory and American History," *The Journal of American History*, 75 (March 1989):1117–1129.

31. Thelan, 1117.

32. Crane, 1373.

33. Ruth Painter Randall, *Mary Lincoln: Biography of a Marriage* (Boston: Little, Brown and Company, 1953).

34. "Transy Rehangs Confederate Portrait." *Lexington Herald-Leader*, August 19, 2001, B1. "Transylvania U. Removes Portrait of Confederate Leader in Wake of Racial Slur." *Chronicle of Higher Education*, April 13, 2001, A50.

35. Cobb, 14–17.

36. Ibid., 35.

37. Ibid., 54.

38. Ibid., 57.

39. Ibid., 99.

40. Ibid., 100–101.

41. Ibid., 103.

42. Ibid., 102.

43. Karen Cox, *Dixie's Daughters: The United Daughters of the Confederacy and the Preservation of Southern Culture* (Gainesville: The University Press of Florida, 2003); Sally Leigh McWhite, "Echoes of the Lost Cause: Civil War Reverberations in Mississippi from 1865 to 2001" (Ph.D. diss., University of Mississippi, 2003).

44. Cox, 29.

45. McWhite, 423–457.

46. Cox, 19.

47. United Daughters of the Confederacy. "Program and Prize List for 1943." University of Mississippi Archives and Special Collections, UDC/SCV Collection.

48. For inflation conversions see Robert Sahr, "Inflation Conversation Factors for Dollars 1774 to Estimated 2019." Available online: http://oregonstate.edu/cla/polisci/faculty-research/sahr/sahr.htm (accessed 15 June 2009). For information on Rockefeller Foundation gifts for social sciences research at southern universities see Amy E. Wells, "Considering Her Influence: Sydnor H. Walker and Rockefeller Support for Social Work, Social Scientists, and Universities in the South," in *Women and Philanthropy in Education*, ed. A. Walton (Bloomington: Indiana University Press, 2005).

49. See Bruce E. Baker, "How W.E.B. Du Bois Won the United Daughters of the Confederacy Essay Contest," *Southern Cultures* (Spring 2009): 69–81, for an account of how University of South Carolina student Colin W. Covington plagiarized Du Bois' 1901 *Atlantic Monthly* article on the Freedmen's Bureau (and a monograph by historian Paul Skeels Pierce) to win a UDC contest.
50. Cox, 124.
51. McWhite, 123.
52. John Hope Franklin, "History—Weapon of War and Peace," *Phylon* 49 (Autumn–Winter, 2001): 267–276, 273.
53. Franklin, 268.
54. C. Vann Woodward, *Origins of the New South 1877–1913*. A History of the South, edited by Wendell Holmes Stephenson and E. Merton Coulter, 9 (Baton Rouge: Louisiana State University Press/The Littlefield Fund for Southern History of the University of Texas, 1951).
55. Howard W. Odum, *Southern Regions of the United States* (Chapel Hill: The University of North Carolina Press, 1936).
56. This comment came from the dear spouse of a dear colleague at an Association of the Study of Higher Education (ASHE) annual meeting in Richmond, VA in 2004. At the time, the comment surprised me as a "Northeastern" perspective on the South and I have learned that it is often shared among non-southerners visiting the South.

Epilogue

Epilogue

A NOTE ON FOOTNOTES

Jane Robbins

Some people loathe footnotes. They find them tedious, or, in the case of one of my dissertation advisors who was from a business school, downright infuriating. I confess—although do not apologize—that I had 146 footnotes in the theory chapter of my dissertation. This proved to be a provocation so great that my chair had to use all his considerable political skills to smooth things enough so that I passed. Footnotes, it seemed, almost did me in.

It is fair to say that footnotes have lost cachet among the general public. They have come to be viewed with suspicion and even derision; trade book publishers, arguing that footnotes are disruptive or pretentious, two threats to broad sales appeal, have banned or severely limit their use.[1] Footnote excesses, in form and function, have rendered the footnote an easy target of satire, and even Gibbon might grant that a footnote that tops 150 pages and constitutes more than one-quarter of a book is probably too long.[2] Notwithstanding, historians love footnotes. Want them. Need them. Relish them. Indeed, we are just as likely to turn to the footnotes almost before reading anything else. Why?

There are, it turns out, good reasons, and also prurient ones, which make footnotes all the more interesting, and—to use an adjective rarely juxtaposed with anything historians do—fun. In this short note, I will review the reasons we historians use footnotes, and also briefly review what a footnote should or should not contain, when to use one, and how to write one. A few examples, keyed to the text, are presented at the end of this note. But first, the big question.

WHY FOOTNOTE?

Your Footnotes Are Your Evidence   They are the basis on which your reader establishes the credibility of what you say and the claims you make.

That is the overarching reason to footnote, and on some level, that is all you need to know, or at least the principle to keep in mind. But within this reason, we can look at a few sub-purposes:

    1. Footnotes direct your reader to the precise source of your evidence in case she or he wants to verify it or use it (or, possibly, challenge it). This is comparable to directing the reader to your raw data, or providing your database. It is the dull, but serviceable, side of footnotes, and in large part what has given them a bad name—as in my 146 source notes.

    2. Footnotes provide additional evidentiary details, including argument, that exceed the appropriate level of detail or subject of the text, but nevertheless add value to informing, persuading, or directing the reader. Fulfillment of this sub-purpose includes, for example, providing details on the esoteric organization of a given archive; referring the reader to related work of interest not directly used to construct the text; or explaining the manner in which you have chosen to apply certain concepts or theories. The latter is particularly called for if you are one of those people who, like me, use things differently from their original application, such as transferring something from one discipline to another. Sometimes you have to explain yourself.

    3. Footnotes offer a place to critique cited material that, for reasons of convention or prominence, must be cited to show you are aware of it (that credibility thing), but that you find lacking or insufficient to your work. Here is where a footnote can get rather nasty and strangely personal, although I do not recommend that. They can be subtly skewering to those in the know—a simple "cf." can be a "dagger" in a scholarly duel.[3] Scholarly critiques are helpful and often justified, and can admirably serve the overarching purpose of bolstering your credibility. But this recommendation comes with a caveat: the somewhat detached character of the footnote, hidden as it were at the bottom of the page or end of the chapter or even banished to the back of the book, can seem to give license to rants and skewering—much like anonymous email postings. So beware. And remember: footnotes are evidence and argument for what you say, not weapons.

    4. Footnotes offer a place to offer inside stories and anecdotes that are related, but not necessary, to the text. So why include them? Simply put, to share. History is a conversation, and footnotes offer a place to confide odd details, discovered secrets, considered opinions.

Items 2, 3, and 4 can be thought of as the historian's version of the theatrical aside—the author stopping the action of the narrative to converse directly and almost secretively with the reader. In this sense, footnotes can be quite intimate and even revelatory: I have learned a great deal of interesting detail from footnotes. Beyond their educational value, such asides also offer, as do their theatrical counterparts, "amusement, charm, a chance to rest" from the demands of following the narrative.[4] At the highest level, such footnotes are a rewarding and seamless extension of the text: "a superlative footnote presupposes a superlative text," the point at which they become "a work of art and an instrument of power."[5]

WHEN TO USE A FOOTNOTE

The determination of when to footnote is in part a moral question, one that I would argue falls under a general ethics of footnotes that also dictates their tone, and in part a creative one. In admonishing students on proper citation, Nancy Shields states unequivocally that a "footnote must be used for:

1. a direct quote
2. a paraphrase of an idea
3. a comment giving additional information
4. an explanatory statement or definitions
5. a reference to another part of your paper."[6]

This workmanlike list takes the purposes of footnotes outlined in the last section and makes their circumstances clear. To elaborate on the first four from the historian's perspective:

1. Footnote whenever you make a statement of fact or relate events or circumstances that you have learned from reading a source. The footnote contains the source information. This source may be a book, article, or other document; graphic material; recordings; and so on. For historians, this material is often drawn from an archive.

2. Footnote whenever you draw a conclusion or base an interpretation on one or more documents or records, without necessarily citing a particular fact or circumstance as in 1 above. For example, if you are synthesizing many documents to draw aggregate conclusions on some topic, you would footnote all documents or records to which you referred in drawing those conclusions, even if no single conclusion can be attached to any single document. In this sense, the footnote serves almost as a reference list, and also indicates relationships or connections among them.

3. Footnote when you have something to say that would interrupt the flow of your argument or narrative in the text. Think of this as a rule of coherent writing or storytelling. You want to maintain the energy or logic of what you are saying, yet provide information you deem as supplementary but that may be interesting, even important, to the reader: put it in a footnote. It is in this instance that we see that, rather than being disruptive as footnote critics claim, the footnote is actually a courtesy: it is offered for the precise reason *not* to disrupt, but to make available useful information that the reader can choose to read then, later, or not at all.

HOW TO WRITE A FOOTNOTE

The most basic footnotes, those that provide source data only, consist of a citation to the work in question. The exact format of the footnote, or its "citation style," will depend on the publication for which you are writing. For example, this book uses Chicago style, from the *Chicago Manual of Style*, widely used in trade book publishing and considered to be modern and user-friendly.[7]

Generally, journals and scholarly book publishers have their own styles, some of which have evolved over a period of years and combine elements of common styles in persnickety ways. You can find a journal's or publisher's style preferences on their web pages, usually under the section that provides guidelines for contributors or instructions for submission. The large range of slightly different, specialized styles used to make preparing or modifying a manuscript for submission a time-consuming task— one could spend many hours changing the placement of the date, for example, from the end of the citation, preceded by a comma, to after the author name, enclosed in parentheses, every time a manuscript went to a different publisher.

Thankfully, modern citation software has made this task a snap; you simply select the citation style required, push a button, and everything is converted in proper, precise form—capitalization, punctuation, special fonts, placement, everything, including the numbering and placement of your notes in the manuscript. Of course, you must enter your sources the first time—i.e., create a database from which the software can format your citations. It is a good habit to enter complete publication data every time you find an article, book, or other source that you may want to use in your writing, and to develop a coding system of keywords for your database so that you can readily find what you need. My own database contains nearly 3,000 records (so far . . .), and it is an invaluable research resource as well as an enormous timesaver when preparing footnotes and reference lists.

Although styles vary from publication to publication and software can do most of the work, there are a few common, guiding precepts for which you must take initial responsibility:

Completeness

This sounds simple, but you would be amazed how many citations contain only partial information. At a minimum, a complete citation for an article includes author, date, full title, journal title, volume, number, and page range; for a book, include author, date, full title, location of publisher, and publisher name. Edited volumes require additional information (editors, volume title in addition to chapter titles), as do technical or government reports, papers presented at conferences, websites, translations, archival resources, and so on. Check a good style guide such as *Chicago* for the conventions for each source type.

To avoid extra work and even crisis later on, be sure to record every bit of source information as you locate or are using the source. This is particularly true if you work in archives, to which you may not be able to return to get the information you need. For books and other printed material, making a photocopy of the complete title page and publishing information is useful. For records, mark the complete location information—e.g., archive, collection name/number, folder or box numbers, dates, etc.—at the top of anything you copy, or type as a header if you are entering notes into a computer. It is well worth the few minutes extra time this takes or few cents additional copying cost. For all typed notes, whether from books or records, be especially religious about recording page numbers of quoted material; that is the one thing that cannot be readily obtained without another trip to the library or archive.

Always ensure you record the complete author names of books and articles. While some citation styles may abbreviate the first names of authors or shorten the reference to say "et al." for multiple authors, others may not. The same is true for titles. Record subtitles, series names, and all other information that would constitute a complete citation.

Accuracy

Accuracy is another element that seems to go without saying, but inaccurate citations are common. Carelessness is one reason, but another culprit is citation borrowing—when a writer lifts a citation directly from an article or book for use in his or her own. This is not good professional practice, and can lead to error, or the replication of error, including incomplete source information. Always confirm citations, and if you discover you have failed to record some portion of source data, look it up. Once again, technology comes to the rescue. In addition to the electronic databases available through academic libraries that allow you to quickly locate journal articles and their complete bibliographic information, you can also now search the internet with special software tools that will pull the data off the web and insert it directly into your citation software.

Continuity

In a document with many sources, properly constructed footnotes help simplify the reader's task of following the path of the evidence, in part by simplifying the footnotes themselves. This can be done through use of accepted, and also custom-constructed, abbreviations and shortened forms that minimize the reader's cognitive load while also providing full, accurate information. Accepted abbreviations include such common usages as "ibid." to indicate that material comes from the same source as fully listed in the prior footnote, and "cf." to indicate that the reader could compare what has just been said to the source listed after "cf." *Chicago* and other good style guides provide definitions of and guidelines for using the most common abbreviations; it is worth your time to learn the distinctions among them and to ensure that your usage is consistent with good practice.

When you are using sources that will be frequently repeated, it is a good idea to develop an efficient, abbreviated title or citation form that can be used each time you refer to that source. In fact, shortened titles are now preferred to the repeated used of "ibid." for the same work, which forces the reader to trace back to the source, a frustrating experience that contributes to giving footnotes a bad name. A shortened title can be a few words that recognizably capture its longer counterpart. For archival sources, shortened citations can even be a single letter or two; just provide a "key" upfront that gives the full source information and the abbreviation that will be used, and then use that abbreviation consistently throughout. For example, if you were writing about President Conant from his papers in the Harvard University archive, you could shorten the recommended citation form "Harvard University. Records of President James Bryant Conant." to "H: JBC"; this kind of shortening can be done with any subsequent aspect of collection sources as well, such as series or folder titles and dates.

In the table below are some examples of footnotes from my own work that reflect the four sub-purposes, including the three permutations on the *scholarly aside*, outlined under the "Why Footnote?" section; all provide a form of evidentiary support.[8] They were created with a software program from my database, and are all in Chicago style.

FOUR TYPES OF EVIDENCE

Direction to the source of your evidence or claim	1. Jane Robbins. "Toward a theory of the university: Mapping the American research university in space and time," *American Journal of Education* 114 (February 2008): 243–272 plus online supplement.

Provision of additional, value-added detail, including argument, that is secondary to the text—the *scholarly aside*	2. Competitive, isomorphic pressure and the commonality of massive public funding of both publics and privates are at the bottom of a false distinction between them. It is often assumed that publics have emulated privates, but the mimicry has been two-way, and it is perhaps publics that have had the greater influence. For discussion of the "myth" of the private university, see Johnson 1966.
Critique or qualification of cited references—the *scholarly aside*	3. I use the terms "old" and "new" according to the distinction made by "new institutionalists" (DiMaggio and Powell 1991). Like Selznick, I see new institutionalism as splitting off an integral part of earlier institutional theory (Selznick 1996).
Inside story or anecdote—the *scholarly aside*	4. Seashore continued his interest in the gifted, however, and developed a series of tests for assessing musical skills such as pitch that became widely known as the "Seashore Measures of Musical Talent."

NOTES

1. Bruce Anderson. "The Decline and Fall of Footnotes," *Stanford Magazine*, January–February 1997, http://www.stanfordalumni.org/news/magazine/1997/janfeb/araticles/footnotes.html. Retrieved 4/24/09.
2. Peter Riess. *Towards a Theory of the Footnote* (Berlin and New York: Walter de Gruyter, 1983).
3. Anthony Grafton. *The Footnote: A Curious History* (Boston: Harvard University Press, 1997), 8.
4. Chuck Zerby. *The Devil's Details: A History of Footnotes* (NY: Touchstone, 2003), 7.
5. G. W. Bowersock. "The Art of the Footnote," *The American Scholar* 53, no.1 (1983–Winter 1983): 54–62, 54–55.
6. Nancy E. Shields with Mary E. Uhle. *Where Credit is Due: A Guide to Proper Citing of Sources—Print and Nonprint*, 2nd Ed. (London: The Scarecrow Press, 1997), 9.
7. *The Chicago Manual of Style: The Essential Guide for Writers, Editors, and Publishers*, 15th Ed. (Chicago and London: The University of Chicago Press, 2003).
8. Jane Robbins. "Toward a Theory of the University: Mapping the American Research University in Space and Time." *American Journal of Education* 114 (February 2008), 243–272 plus online supplement; Jane Robbins. "'The Problem of the Gifted Student': National Research Council Efforts to Identify and Cultivate Undergraduate Talent in a New Era of Mass Education, 1919–1929." *Perspectives on the History of Higher Education* 24 (2005): 91–24.

LIST OF CONTRIBUTORS

Michael Bieze has a B.F.A. in studio art, and M.A. in art history, and a Ph.D. in educational policy studies. He has been the chair of the fine arts department at Marist School in Atlanta for over twenty years, teaching art history and studio art. For many years he has served as a consultant for the College Board with the Advanced Placement Art History program. His research on Booker T. Washington and the visual arts has appeared in several publications. His most recent work is *Booker T. Washington and the Art of Self-Representation* (Peter Lang, 2008). Forthcoming next year will be *Reading Booker T. Washington* (Johns Hopkins), co-authored with Marybeth Gasman.

Katherine Chaddock is a professor of higher education administration and chair of the department of educational leadership and policies at the University of South Carolina. She is the 2009 recipient of that University's "Michael Mungo Graduate Teaching Award" and the 2009 recipient of the "Annual Research Award" for the University's College of Education. Dr. Chaddock's research and teaching is in higher education history, policy and administration. She is the author or co-author of five scholarly books pertaining to 19th and early 20th century higher education leaders and institutions, as well as numerous articles and chapters. Her biographical work includes: *Visions and Vanities: John Andrew Rice of Black Mt. College* (Louisiana State University Press, 1998) and (with Susan Schramm) *A Separate Sisterhood: Women Who Shaped Southern Education in the Progressive Era* (Peter Lang, 2002). She is co-editor (with Roger Geiger) of the book series "Higher Education and Society" for Palgrave Macmillan.

Linda Eisenmann is provost of Wheaton College, a liberal arts institution in Norton, Massachusetts, as well as professor of education and professor of history. Earlier, she served as dean of the College of Arts and Sciences at John Carroll University in Cleveland, Ohio, and director of the doctoral program in higher education administration at the University of Massachusetts, Boston. A historian interested in the social context of higher education, Eisenmann focuses on three areas of educational history: women's experiences, professionalizaton, and historiography. Her recent book, *Higher*

Education for Women in Postwar America, 1945–1965 (Johns Hopkins University Press, 2006), explores the impact of cultural expectations on women's postwar collegiate experience and development. Eisenmann is past president of both the History of Education Society and the Association for the Study of Higher Education. She holds her doctorate in history of education from Harvard University's Graduate School of Education.

Marybeth Gasman is an associate professor of higher education in the Graduate School of Education at the University of Pennsylvania. Her work explores historical aspects of philanthropy and historically Black colleges, Black leadership, and African-American giving. Dr. Gasman has authored or co-authored several historical books, including *Reading Booker T. Washington* (Johns Hopkins, 2010); *Envisioning Black Colleges* (Johns Hopkins, 2007); *Charles S. Johnson: Leadership beyond the Veil in the Age of Jim Crow* (SUNY, 2003). In addition, she has edited *"Doing" the History of Higher Education* (Routledge, 2010), *Uplifting a People* (Peter Lang, 2003), and *Understanding Minority Serving Institutions* (SUNY, 2008). Dr. Gasman has published articles in the *History of Education Quarterly*, the *American Education Research Journal*, *Educational Researcher*, *Teachers College Record*, and the *Journal of Higher Education*. Her research on Black colleges has been cited in *The Washington Post*, the *Wall Street Journal*, the *Chronicle of Higher Education*, *Diverse Issues in Higher Education*, National Public Radio, *U.S. News and World Report*, and CNN. In 2006, Dr. Gasman received the Association for the Study of Higher Education's Early Career Award. She is also the recipient of a University of Pennsylvania Excellence in Teaching Award. She was recently named a Penn Fellow by the president and provost of the University of Pennsylvania.

Jordan R. Humphrey is a fourth year Ph.D. candidate in the higher education program at The Pennsylvania State University. She currently holds the Higher Education Program Alumni Council (HEPAC) Fellowship with the Penn State Alumni Association. Jordan earned her M.S.Ed. in higher education management from the University of Pennsylvania and her B.A. in political science and Spanish from Franklin & Marshall College. Her research interests focus on the history of higher education, with particular emphases on liberal arts colleges in the twentieth century; mission change during periods of crisis; the emergence of land-grant institutions; institutional change and adaptation; the influence of extracurricular activities on student and university life; and Quaker higher education. Jordan's dissertation is entitled, "Liberal Art Colleges in the Tumultuous 1940s: Institutional Identity and the Challenges of War and Peace."

Philo Hutcheson is associate professor of educational policy studies at Georgia State University. He received his Ph.D. (1991) in higher education from the University of Chicago. His publications include "The Truman Commission's Vision of the Future," *Thought and Action* 23 (Fall 2007): 107–115, "Setting the Nation's Agenda for Higher Education: A Review of Selected National Commission Reports, 1947–2006," *History of Education Quarterly* 47 (August 2007): 359–367, a co-authored article, "National Higher Education Policy Commissions in the Post-World War II Era: Issues of Representation," *The Sophist's Bane* (Fall 2003), and *A Professional Professoriate: Unionization, Bureaucratization, and the AAUP* (Vanderbilt University Press, 2000). He is nearing completion of a book on the 1947 President's Commission on Higher Education.

Sharon S. Lee (M.A., history, University of Wisconsin-Madison) is a Ph.D. candidate in the department of educational policy studies at the University of Illinois at Urbana-Champaign. Her professional experience includes eight years of administrative work for the Asian American Studies Programs at the University of Wisconsin-Madison and the University of Illinois at Urbana-Champaign. Her research interests include Asian Americans in higher education; higher education policy analysis; issues of access and diversity; history of education; and campus climate.

Jana Nidiffer, associate professor and chair, department of educational leadership at Oakland University, teaches courses on current, historical, gender-related, and method-ological issues higher education. Her primary research interests include: access and opportunity in higher education, largely from an historical perspective; women's entrance and participation in higher education; the history of university administra-tion; and the declining access of poor students in the late nineteenth and early twentieth centuries. Her first book, *Beating the Odds: How the Poor Get to College*, is co-authored with Arthur Levine. She has also completed two books that examine the development and contributions of women as administrators in higher education: *Pioneering Deans of Women: More Than Wise and Pious Matrons* (Teachers College Press, 2000) and *Women Administrators in Higher Education: Historical and Contemporary Perspectives* (SUNY Press, 2001). She has published in *History of Education Quarterly, American Educational Research Journal, About Campus,* and *Education Policy,* as well as contributing several book chapters and other miscellaneous publications.

Darryl L. Peterkin, Assistant Dean for Student Services in the College of Liberal Arts at Morgan State University, received his M.A. and Ph.D. in History from Princeton University; and his B.A. in American Studies from Yale University. Prior to coming to Morgan State University, Dr. Peterkin was Senior Program Officer and Director of the Center to Serve Historically Black Colleges and Universities at the Southern Education Foundation in Atlanta, Georgia. He has held positions as Director of Studies for Butler College at Princeton University; Dean of the Honors Program at Dillard University; Director of Faculty Recruitment and Development for the National Faculty in New Orleans, Louisiana; and Assistant Professor of History at Xavier University of Louisiana. He has also been a consultant for the United Negro College Fund's Institute for Capacity Building. A specialist in the Colonial, Revolutionary, and Early National periods of American history, Dr. Peterkin conducts research on the history of higher education in Early America and has presented papers at annual meetings of the History of Education Society. He is currently at work on a biography of Joseph Caldwell, the first president of the University of North Carolina at Chapel Hill. Dr. Peterkin is an active volunteer for the Association of Princeton Graduate Alumni, the Yale Alumni Fund, and the Alumni Association of the North Carolina School of Science and Mathematics. He has partici-pated in the American Historical Association, the Southern Historical Association, the North Carolina Historical Association, the History of Education Society, and the Society for Historians of the Early American Republic.

Jane Robbins is Senior Lecturer in Organizational Leadership in the Department of Leadership, Policy, and Organizations at Vanderbilt University/Peabody College, and a consultant in organizational strategy and change. She teaches courses in leadership, innovation, organizational theory, and ethics, and received a Peabody Roundtable Donor Educator Honoree awarded in 2009. A historian and institutional analyst of research universities, her research interests include conflict of interest in university-industry relations and its effects on institutional integrity and trust; university patenting and technology transfer; leadership decision making; and the theory of the university and its role in society. Robbins has published articles in *American Journal of Education and Perspectives on the History of Higher Education*, and is working on a book on conflict of interest in higher education. She received her Ph.D. in Higher Education Management from the University of Pennsylvania and her M.A. in Critical and Creative Thinking from UMass/Boston.

John R. Thelin is university research professor and a member of the educational policy studies department at the University of Kentucky. He likes to write works that help connect past and present in understanding American higher education. An alumnus of Brown University, he concentrated in history and was elected to Phi Beta Kappa. John earned his M.A. and Ph.D. at the University of California, Berkeley. He is author of *A History of American Higher Education* (2004) and *Games Colleges Play: Scandal and Reform in College Sports* (1994)—both published by the Johns Hopkins University Press. Before joining the faculty at UK he was Chancellor Professor at The College of William & Mary in Virginia and Professor at Indiana University. John has served as President of the Association for the Study of Higher Education and received the American Educational Research Association's award for outstanding research in higher education.

William G. Tierney is university professor, Wilbur-Kieffer professor of higher education and director of the Center for Higher Education Policy Analysis at the University of Southern California (USC). His research focuses on increasing access to higher education, improving the performance of postsecondary institutions, and analyzing the quality of for-profit institutions. His center is currently involved with USC's Electronic Arts Game Lab in creating an interactive web-enhanced game for teenagers that will enable them to develop successful strategies for applying to college. His most recent books are *Urban High School Students and the Challenge of Access* and *The Impact of Culture on Organizational Decision-Making*. He recently chaired a panel for the U.S. Department of Education and the What Works Clearinghouse that resulted in the monograph: *Helping Students Navigate the Path to College: What Schools Can Do*. He is currently involved in a life history project of low-income first-generation high school students en route to college.

Christopher Tudico is a Ph.D. candidate at the University of Pennsylvania's Graduate School of Education. Christopher broadly studies the history of the Latino experience in American higher education. He holds a B.S. from Georgetown University and an M.S.Ed. from the University of Pennsylvania. Christopher edited *Historically Black Colleges and Universities: Triumphs, Troubles, and Taboos*, along with Marybeth Gasman. He is currently writing a history of the Josiah Macy, Jr. Foundation with George E. Thibault. Christopher will complete his dissertation, "Before *We* Were Chicanas/os: The Mexican American Experience in Californian Higher Education, 1848–1945," in 2010.

Wayne Urban is professor and coordinator of the higher education administration program and associate director of the Education Policy Center at the University of Alabama. He has been chosen as the Paul W. Bryant Professor in the College of Education at Alabama for 2009–2010. Before coming to Alabama in January of 2006, he taught at Georgia State University and the University of South Florida. Additionally he has taught at several other American campuses and at universities in Poland, England, Canada, and Australia. He has held two Fulbright fellowships and received research support from the Spencer Foundation and the National Endowment for the Humanities. Recently he has served as chair/president of the International Standing Conference for the History of Education. He is author or co-author of seven books and numerous articles, chapters, and reviews, including *Gender Race and the National Education Association: Exceptionalism and Its Limitations* (2000) and *More than the Facts: The Research Division of the National Education Association, 1922–1997* (1998). In 2010 his book, *More than Science and Sputnik: The National Defense Education Act*, will be published by the University of Alabama Press.

Amy E. Wells-Dolan is an associate professor of higher education in the department of leadership and counselor education at the University of Mississippi. Her research interests include the history of higher education in the South, philanthropy, and her historical work about education in the South has appeared in the *New Encyclopedia of Southern Culture, History of Higher Education Annual, Urban Education,* and edited volumes including *Historically Black Colleges and Universities: Triumphs, Troubles, and Taboos* (2008), and *Women and Philanthropy in Education* (2005). At the University of Mississippi, she is a founding member of an interdisciplinary liberal arts working group on the Global South, a member of the Advisory Board for the Center for Excellence in Teaching and Learning, and served the University as a primary project facilitator and author of the University's Quality Enhancement Plan (QEP) for Improving Student Writing, an comprehensive community-based initiative in support of the University re-affirmation or accreditation by the Southern Association of Colleges and Schools (SACS).

INDEX

Valentine, Edward 16
Vanity Fair 19
Vermont 16
"Vertical" institutions 74, 76
Veysey, Laurence 164
Vietnam War 22
Virginia Military Institute 16

Wabash College 79
Wage premium 106–7, table 8.2
Wall Street 81
Walter Prevenier 164
Walterboro, South Carolina 28
War on Poverty 180
Washington and Lee University 15–16
Washington, Booker T. 4, 11, 84–101, 209, 210;
  figures 7.1, 7.2, 7.3, 7.5, 7.6, 7.7
Washington, D.C. 45, 78–9, 175
Washington, George 176, 194
Webster, Noah 148, 193
Wertenbaker, Thomas Jefferson 12
Wheaton College 209
Whitman, Walt 122, 124
Wichita, Kansas 98
Wiebe, Robert 77
Wilkinson, Rupert 75
Willard, Emma 61
William Winter Institute for Racial Reconciliation
  192

Willis, Deborah 88, 97
Wilson, North Carolina 98
Women: educational history of 58–61; in higher
  education 4, 10, 12, 14, 44, 56–67, 137–9, 147,
  154, 161, 188, 195, 209–11, 213; women's
  colleges 9, 10, 45, 58, 164; women's rights 12,
  92; women's studies 151, 160; *see also*
  suffrage
Women's Christian Temperance Union
  195
Woodward, C. Vann 195
Woody, Thomas 56
WordStat/Simstat 111
Working Woman 19
World War I 39, 92, 194
World War II 21–2, 25, 27, 34, 37, 39–40, 50, 54;
  internment of Japanese Americans during
  153–5
Wright, Bobby 165

Xavier University 211

Yale University 13, 43, 75
YMCA 189, 197
Young, I. Marion 182, 186

Zimmerman, Jonathan 155, 157
Zook, George F 180